THE DOUBLE LIFE OF
LAURENCE OLIPHANT

VICTORIAN PILGRIM
AND PROPHET

Being the incredible history of Laurence Oliphant:
his early success; his occult life with
Thomas Lake Harris;
his marriage to Alice le Strange;
their sexual mysticisms and Zionist communities;
truthfully told and amply documented
to confound the skeptic.

BY

BART CASEY

Laurence Oliphant at 25 years old.

A POST HILL PRESS BOOK
ISBN (hardcover): 978-1-61868-796-8
ISBN (eBook): 978-1-61868-795-1

THE DOUBLE LIFE OF LAURENCE OLIPHANT
Victorian Prophet and Pilgrim
© 2015 by Bart Casey
All Rights Reserved

Cover Design by Christian Bentulan

Post Hill Press
275 Madison Avenue, 14th Floor
New York, NY 10016
http://posthillpress.com

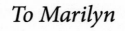

To Marilyn

"Most people are, I suppose, more or less conscious of leading a sort of double life—an outside one and an inside one. The more I raced about the world, and took as active part as I could in its dramatic performances, the more profoundly did the conviction force itself on me, that if it was indeed a stage, and all the men and women merely players, there must be a real life somewhere. And I was always groping after it in a blind dumb sort of way..."

Laurence Oliphant, 1887
Episodes in a Life of Adventure

TABLE OF CONTENTS

INTRODUCTION

This is the story of a man who seemed to live two lives. In his normal "outside" one he was a successful author, journalist, Member of Parliament and friend to diplomats and royalty. In the other "inside" one—just as real to him—he was a frequent visitor to heaven, where he spent time with angels. He could accept all this—even with a wry, self-deprecating smile—partially because he'd always been encouraged to make up his own mind and be confident in his conclusions, two of which were that traditional religions were empty charades and that a world full of wars was a virtual lunatic asylum. Why shouldn't there be a reality beyond the everyday where a just God was planning to set things right? Isn't that what had been prophesized and held sacred for thousands of years? Shouldn't we be trying to reconnect with that reality and move everyone along to some happier conclusion than the one the modern world was offering?

*

Most of us, I suppose, leave such thoughts behind at school and just get in line with everyone else trying to carve out a life, career and legacy to fill our conscious time. It can be impossibly hard to hold out for anything more. But that was not the path taken by Laurence, who was born into a privileged yet hard-working Scottish family in 1829. From his earliest days, he lived by two priorities: first, to be a loyal son of the British Empire helping to spread its power and influence, and, second, to develop his Christian faith to guide his own behavior and aid his fellow man. And as he made more and more progress on his "career development" side, he never lost track of the other, nagging twinges of conscience that competed for his spiritual attentions. Finally he felt that nothing less than full commitment to those more mysterious underdeveloped yearnings could restore balance to his own life.

Consequently, at age 38, he abandoned his efforts to "get ahead" in the dissipated world of Victorian Britain and turned to a life of cleansing labor and subservience under the guidance of a passionate prophet named Thomas Lake Harris. Harris claimed to be in touch with the celestial realm where great things were underway to restore mankind to its rightful place united with the Deity. By joining the Brotherhood of the New Life, Laurence hoped to take on a leadership role in the sacred task to restore man to his original place in the Divine Plan.

For fourteen years, Laurence labored doing the bidding of his prophet on this sacred task, until he became convinced Harris had lost track of his original mission and become too enamored of his own manufactured importance and life of luxury and license.

Breaking with Harris allowed Laurence and his lovely wife, Alice le Strange, to spend their remaining years trying to make a practical difference for at least one suffering group on Earth: the persecuted Jewish peoples fleeing the pogroms and atrocities of Eastern Europe. That work was probably their most important legacy.

*

The world has changed forever since Laurence lived from 1829 to 1888. Then beliefs were simpler, information was scarce, and the pace of life was slower. Yet, in the everyday world, it seemed breakthroughs were occurring daily, including steam power, railroads and telegraphs. Perhaps that's why it was easier then to expect imminent breakthroughs between man and God?

Seen from today, I suppose the most likely reaction to Laurence's strange story might be interest in his early successes and achievements, followed by uneasy or even disapproving curiosity about his supposed celestial explorations. Next might be a feeling of relief when the principal characters came back onto comfortable ground in Haifa to do something sensible, spending their final days comforting Jewish refugees.

Laurence himself, however, was unapologetic about his singular wanderings. He had always been encouraged to make up his own mind having escaped the strictures of classroom education. He never took advantage of his professional credentials although he was a lawyer admitted to the bar in Ceylon, Edinburgh and London, nor did he try to scale the levels of any other normal career, instead making a living from his pen. In addition, the celestial world was real to him. In fact, it became even more real after his wife Alice died and stayed present with him, visiting from the other side. And while he balanced his lively and amusing essays about his travels with his encounters from the spirit world, he never hid behind the spiritualist's veil of manufactured mystery and high seriousness. Indeed, he understood his viewpoints often provoked deep skepticism and so he was always quick to see the humor and comedy behind the unusual assortment of beliefs that became his cannon.

That's why no matter how far he strayed, he was always welcomed warmly back to join his more tradition-bound colleagues at his club, or companions like Queen Victoria for dinner, and lead a very 'normal' conversation about politics or social issues. Nor would he be self-conscious if his friends simply asked "what have you been doing?" because he knew the strange ground he covered was also secretly very interesting to them as well. Certainly none of his acquaintances planning a visit to the Holy Land in the 1880's missed the opportunity to visit with the refreshingly odd Oliphants at Haifa or at their mountain retreat at Dalieh.

Sadly the oddness of Laurence and Alice Oliphant after their deaths was judged to be dangerous territory by family solicitors, and most of their story was swept under a false rug of propriety – which was perhaps a prudent but nonetheless very sad finale for two such attractive individualists.

Was Laurence crazy to believe there was an actual Deity and celestial spirits somewhere in a parallel world waiting to save him?

Did that make him any crazier than the generations who built churches, cathedrals, temples and mosques all over the planet so they could pray to their own chosen spirits?

Or are we the odd ones, who no longer make any spiritual quests, and see the sacred beliefs of centuries as quaint fairytales to fall back on occasionally as we glide through this digital world?

Perhaps this book will let readers form their own opinions about Laurence and Alice Oliphant and help them appreciate the richness that came from two remarkable Victorians who lived with such complete independence. It is quite a story.

PART ONE:

MAKING HIS MARK

CHAPTER 1

SON OF EMPIRE

In 1829, a baby named Laurence was born[1] into the ancient Scottish clan Oliphant at the British Cape Colony in southern Africa. His parents, Anthony and Maria, were both prominent and popular members of society. While such good fortune did not bring instant wealth to the lad, it did provide entry into a world of connections and opportunity for anyone with gumption.

Laurence's father Anthony was the third youngest son in a family where the title and estate north of Edinburgh went only to the oldest—but all the Oliphant brothers had the pedigrees they needed to launch successful careers in the military, business, arts, law, government and, most importantly, in the British Empire. It is perhaps hard for us today to appreciate Britain's place in the world immediately after Napoleon's final defeat at Waterloo in 1815. Finally, it seemed, the jostling with France, Holland, Spain and Portugal for empire-building was settled, and London was beginning a century of expansion and world domination. Although the American colonies had broken free, Asia was opening up to British influence and the vast riches of India were its crown jewels.

Two of Anthony's older brothers joined the East India Company. One became a Captain in the Madras Engineers before age thirty, and the other— James— finished his career as East India Company Chairman— a position, at the time, roughly equivalent to Roman Proconsul for its most prestigious province. James was also married three times, producing eighteen first cousins for Laurence. Another older brother became a noted composer, artist and Member of the Royal Academy.

Early on, Laurence's father Anthony was very attentive to his studies, pursuing law and winning admittance to the bar both in Edinburgh and London. In the sea of family connections, he then won a position as Personal Secretary to Thomas Bruce, the 7th Earl of Elgin, who years before had saved the friezes of the Parthenon at his own great expense (and later almost went bankrupt by selling them for half his costs to a grateful nation). Having served Elgin well as secretary, Anthony was able to leverage his legal training to insert himself into the fast-moving arena of empire-building focused on South Africa in the early 1820s[2].

After Napoleon occupied Holland in 1806, the British had sent a fleet of 61 ships to secure the Cape Colony from the Dutch. Its Table Bay Harbor was the exact midway point on the shipping route from Europe to India and had to be guarded at all costs from French control. Once Napoleon was finally defeated in 1815, the British garrison remained firmly in place to help establish long-term British control.

In 1820, to strengthen the British position against the Dutch and the native Xhosa tribesmen, Parliament made a substantial bet on colonization by paying to relocate thousands of its citizens to the Cape. Unemployment rates in Britain were high after the Napoleonic Wars, with many officers reduced to half pay. More than 90,000 applications were received for this once-in-a-lifetime opportunity for subsidized emigration to the Cape. Acceptance meant a new start in a brave new world— with free transport, free land and a stipend for each family selected. More than 4,000 souls won new lives. After a journey of 6,000 nautical miles, these colonists arrived at the Cape in

60 separate ship landings between April and June 1820. Farms for each were laid out in belts of adjoining properties at the eastern edge of the colony, bordering the "Neutral Zone" agreed with the Xhosa leaders. The policy created a new populated buffer between older British occupied lands and those where the Xhosa were forced to live under British "administration." Although initially the original Dutch settlers remained, living as fellow Europeans among the British, many became more distressed as churches and schools were Anglicized, and soon they migrated north to establish the Orange Free State. Later, tensions with the both the Xhosas and the Dutch would boil over into trouble, but in these early days the colony remained tense but calm— closely watched by the British government a world away in London.

Around 1826, Anthony Oliphant became involved in planning for the justice system in the new colony to transition from a Dutch to a British model. For his diligence working on the design and implementation of this new regime, he was given the position of Attorney General at the Cape of Good Hope, a post he would hold for eleven years. Eyes at the highest levels of government would watch young Anthony as he represented the interests of the Crown— making his appointment a very special opportunity.

In 1828, now well established at the Cape and aged 37, Anthony married the "pretty and vivacious" Maria Catherine Campbell. Maria was the seventeen-year-old daughter of Lieutenant Colonel Campbell of the garrison's 72nd Scottish Highland Regiment. Maria's mother descended from the Cloetes, a prominent Dutch family who had come to the Cape in 1654 and founded the first permanent European settlement there. Laurence was the couple's first and only child, born one year later in 1829, and was welcomed to the inner circle of the elite at the Cape. The new governor of the colony, Sir Galbraith Lowry Cole, was the closest friend of the Oliphants and graciously agreed to be Laurence's godfather. In honor of that connection, Laurence was given the family nickname "Lowry."

Age differences in the household were unusual, with Anthony twenty years older than his wife, and she only eighteen years older than their child. Family life for them was loving, close and easy. Louis Liesching, a boyhood friend of Laurence who spent some of his own youth living in the Oliphant home, said sometimes "it was difficult for strangers to divine the relationship between these three." According to Liesching[3], the household was rather relaxed for its time. For example, Anthony would begin his day reading the newspaper in his dressing gown with his feet in a tub of warm water, often receiving early visitors that way. After breakfast some other time, Laurence and Louis wanted to try a new boat, and as they left to do so, Laurence's mother followed in her dressing gown and slippers. She jumped right in and the three set off. In their excitement, they had forgotten the paddles, and soon they drifted alongside a busy public highway. Only by ripping a board from the side of the boat and using it as a paddle were they all able to row home and avoid the scandal of being seen in public in their pajamas.

Any social or political aspirations of the Oliphants were balanced with the priorities of a real and pervasive spiritual life. Externally, Anthony and Maria played their parts as leaders in government and society, but at home they were also soul mates— both conservative "evangelical"[4] believers in the gospels of Jesus Christ and the certainty of his Second Coming and judgment. In addition, Anthony was a follower of the Scottish divine, Edward Irving[5], who not only preached an imminent Second Coming, but also emphasized the importance of returning the Jews to Palestine as a prerequisite for completing the Divine Plan before the end of the world. The Oliphants took pains to cultivate a restrained and reflective code of behavior for themselves, and, as parents, they saw the development of Laurence as a devout Christian as one of their most serious responsibilities. This meant family time set aside every day for self-examination, discussion and the "scrupulous record" of every backsliding into bad behavior.

Prayers, study of the gospels and new promises to avoid temptations and transgressions were important parts of family life.

Thus, from the start, Laurence had these multiple priorities set for him: to uphold a strict and moral code of behavior; to become a positive force for improving other people's lives on earth; and to succeed at a career serving Queen and country in the British Empire. Given who and where they were, actual day-to-day life at the Cape for the Oliphants was a lively blend of piety and celebration as a continuous influx of relieved, wide-eyed and important visitors came ashore for rejuvenation and entertainment. As a result, Laurence grew up living a split life— on the one hand, very thoughtful about his spiritual and moral condition; and, on the other, very active and comfortable as the junior host in a happy, bustling household full of guests, in which he was "a boy with a pony and lots of cousins."

Sadly Maria was troubled by poor health during Laurence's early childhood and spent much of the time on her sofa. Finally in 1837 or 1838, when Laurence was eight or nine years old, Maria felt poorly enough to go to Britain to see medical specialists for her health, taking Laurence along for company. Indeed, he was growing up "something of a hothouse plant, brought up at his mother's feet." Mother and son divided their time between the "musty hallways" of the family seat at Condie, Scotland, and Uncle James's lively cousin-filled house at Wimbledon in southwest London.

One story from Condie about this time shows Laurence's growing social savvy and sense of humor. Local Scottish ladies came one day to see the young Mrs. Anthony, their exotic visitor from the Cape. And while they waited in the drawing room, their conversation turned to how pretty a lady she was, and how sad it was that her young son should be so plain. At that point they were startled by a comment from the corner of the room where Laurence had been playing unnoticed with his blocks, from which he now dryly observed, "Ah… but I have very expressive eyes."[6]

Laurence was sent off to a small school, for five or six boys, operated by Parson J. O. Parr at Durnford Manor, near Salisbury. This produced some of Laurence's first writing in the form of letters sent back home to his mother, often in reply to her direct questions about how he was progressing on the spiritual side:

> You asked me to speak to you as I used to... I should tell you some of my besetting sins. One of them is not saying my prayers as I ought, hurrying over them to get up in the morning because I am late, and at night because it is cold; another is my hiding what I do naughty and keeping it from Mr. Parr's eyes, not thinking the eye of God is upon me, a greater eye than man's.[7]

Condie, the Oliphant ancestral home outside Edinburgh.

School reports showed that Laurence wasn't perhaps the smartest of students, although his writing was remarkable by today's standards for ten-year-olds. He was, however, within the family "already a favourite everywhere, the brightest, restless child," virtually fearless, and with an inquiring mind.

With Laurence away at school, Maria put her energies into lobbying for more recognition and advancement for her husband,

Anthony, who was still laboring as Attorney General at the Cape. She succeeded in this in 1840 when, through her efforts, he was offered the much more prestigious office of Chief Justice of Ceylon, second in rank only to the Governor of that larger colony. This was followed quickly in 1841 by a knighthood as a Companion of the Order of the Bath, the chivalric order often used to recognize civil servants performing duties with distinction.

Newly honored and promoted, Sir Anthony now had to move the household to Colombo himself. It was essentially an eastward step to the next major gateway along the Europe-to-India route, because many ships also called at Ceylon when arriving and departing from India. Soon after he arrived, he received word that both Maria (now Lady Oliphant) and Laurence were seriously ill— but thankfully the danger soon passed. Missing them dearly, he sent a most thoughtful, spiritual letter to young Laurence. In it, despite his lofty office, he confides a startlingly frank appraisal of his own shortcomings. Indeed from about Laurence's age of ten, both parents always spoke with him as an equal, no doubt imparting a good deal of added confidence to their already precocious son. Sir Anthony wrote:

Colombo, 31 May, 1839

After mamma and you went away from the Cape for mamma's health, mamma asked the great people in England to remove me from being Attorney General at the Cape, and to make me Chief Justice at Ceylon, and they consented and I went to Ceylon after mamma had been a year away; and when I arrived at Ceylon I heard my son had been almost dead and that mamma was so ill that it was not likely that she would ever come out to me, and I became very sorry: and I did not see anybody that I have ever known before… I had been so long living by myself without having prayers every morning at breakfast-time and on Sunday evenings, that I had fallen away a great deal from the love and fear of God, because I had neglected His Word... so I had become careless in my speech, and used bad words thoughtlessly... and I spoke foolish things for want of something to say...[8]

He goes on to tell how he invited an officer who was a new acquaintance in Ceylon to go on a drive in the country and then vented his feelings to him in an uncontrolled outpouring. Apparently, whatever he said went beyond the normal bounds of polite language, for a short while later the officer declined a follow-up dinner, saying that he feared by accepting, he would be putting himself in dangerous company for his spiritual balance. Sir Anthony, shocked, responded immediately with hurried apologies, he explained to his son. Perhaps he had offended the officer with loose speech? If so, Anthony asked him not to avoid him, promising he would mend his tongue and praying that the two might yet enjoy each other's company on evening rides and that, in fact, he was hoping to introduce him to Lady Oliphant and Laurence once they joined him in Ceylon. Happily, reported Sir Anthony, the devout soldier relented and became a close friend. Sir Anthony had wanted to pass on to his young son this cautionary tale about the importance of maintaining personal discipline.

Lady Oliphant's health improved to the point where she traveled out to Ceylon[9] to rejoin Sir Anthony in 1841. Laurence remained at school in Scotland. Later that year there were reports of him, now about 12, having a particularly good time at the second wedding of his uncle, the Laird at Condie, where he was dancing and "kissing the lassies." At any rate, he was sorely missed by his parents, who soon sent for him. A neighbor in Columbo had two boys the same age, so Uncle James was asked to find a suitable tutor for all the boys to share. He located a Mr. Gepp, just graduated from Oxford, whose first assignment was to escort Laurence on the journey from England to Ceylon in the winter of 1841. The journey was "a great frolic and delight" for both student and tutor. Laurence reports they traveled by "the overland route" that winter, and "so imperfect were the arrangements in those days that it took us two months to reach Ceylon."

The two started their adventure boarding a steamer at London Bridge for Calais. They then bounced across France in the covered bench seat for passengers on the top of a "diligence" stagecoach, moving incessantly for eight days and five nights, and having to be dug out of the snow one night in Chalons. From Marseilles, they boarded a man-o-war for Malta, since there were no passenger steamers at that time. Laurence's only recollection of this leg of the trip was pitching headfirst over the quarterdeck onto the main deck during a sack race and being knocked "insensible" for twenty-four hours, but otherwise "none the worse." From Malta they changed ships for Alexandria, where the arrival was particularly memorable:

> The East burst for the first time upon my surprised senses... carriages had not been introduced; the streets were narrow, ill-paved and crowded with camels, donkeys, veiled women, and the traffic characteristic of an Eastern city, but all was life and bustle: the place was just beginning to quiver under the impulse of the movement which the invention of steam was imparting to the world...

They continued by small boat, towed by horses, down the Mahamoudieh Canal as far as Atfeh, where floodgates ended the journey, and then by steamer on to Cairo. Since there was "no civilized hotel" at that time, they were quartered in a native "khan" or stable, where bare cells opened onto a corridor "filled at all hours of the day and night with a mob of grunting, munching camels and their screaming, quarreling drivers." And since the Suez Canal was not to open until 1869, they next crossed the desert in "vans," pulled by four horses each, arriving at Suez to board the brand new steamer *India* for its maiden voyage down the length of the Red Sea. At one point in their journey, their ship suddenly ran aground:

> … the scene of panic usual on such occasions occurred. All the passengers, male and female, were on deck in the lightest of attire in a moment, and were somewhat reassured by the fact that the sea was as calm as a mill pond, and the ship as motionless as a statue—so much so, indeed, that one weak-minded cadet, who had been the butt of the younger members of the party all the way, thought the opportunity a good one to write his will, which he proceeded with great earnestness and good faith to do in the saloon…

They soon floated off the reef and continued, running out of coal along the way, landing at the harbor in Mocha, the functional capital of Yemen. There the Sultan received them and, after being presented a musket from the ship and nearly killing several of his subjects testing it, assisted them in re-fueling so they could continue on to Aden, where repairs were made on the ship bottom. This gave Laurence and his tutor a chance to explore and savor the quaint and flimsy surroundings, whose "character possessed all the charm of novelty; and the conditions of existence generally were… strange and unlike anything to which I had been accustomed." Repairs complete, the remainder of the voyage proceeded at slow speed on to Colombo, where they arrived sixty days after leaving London Bridge.

*

Colombo in 1842 was not, perhaps, The Garden of Eden, which many Ceylon natives believed to have been on their island. The famous African explorer, hunter and author, Sir Samuel White Baker, opens his classic work *Eight Years' Wanderings in Ceylon* with this description of the city in 1845:

I never experienced greater disappointment in an expectation than on my first view of Colombo… There was a peculiar dullness throughout the town… a want of spirit in everything. The ill-conditioned guns upon the fort looked as though not intended to defend it; the sentinels looked parboiled; the very natives sauntered rather than walked; the very bullocks crawled along in the midday sun, listlessly dragging the native carts. Everything and everybody seemed enervated…[10]

In spite of Baker's first impressions, one can only imagine the joy of Laurence's parents when he and his tutor, Mr. Gepp, finally showed up to enliven family life in what was already a busy household. Visitors were continuously coming and going to the house of the Chief Justice, located in the center of the residential government enclave in town. Lady Oliphant "always placed 'Darling' in a position of influence and equality" among their guests at the dinner table, so Laurence became very comfortable in the company of older influential adults, willing both to listen and to speak his mind. He loved his new life in Ceylon, and was never again subjected to "school discipline" after he arrived there.

Besides the sea-level residence in Colombo, Sir Anthony also had an impressive "cottage" up in the hill country for maintaining his wife's well being. About a dozen years earlier, Governor Edward Barnes had built a road 40 miles long from Peradeniya, elevation 1,000 feet, up to the village of Nuwara Elyia at approximately 6,000 feet. Today you can travel there via a historic and scenic train direct from Colombo, but in the 1830s it would have meant a full day's journey. Here is Laurence's description of the transformation from sea-level port to mountain retreat:

One left Colombo with a thermometer ranging perhaps from 90° to 95°, and in twenty-four hours was enjoying the blaze of a crackling wood-fire, glad to turn into bed under a thick blanket, and in the early morning to turn out again and find the edges of puddles on the road fringed with a thin coating of ice. The reaction from the enervating heats that had been escaped produced a delightful feeling of exhilaration...[11]

Even Sir Samuel Baker, who had been so disappointed by Colombo, had the highest possible compliments for this mountain village where he was sent to recover from a nasty bout of jungle fever:

> I was only a fortnight at Nuwara Eliya. The rest-house or inn was the perfection of everything that was dirty and uncomfortable... But the climate! What can I say to describe the wonderful effects of such a pure and unpolluted air? Simply, that at the expiration of a fortnight, in spite of the tough beef, and the black bread and potatoes, I was as well and as strong as I ever had been; and in proof of this I started instanter [sic] for another shooting excursion in the interior.[12]

In fact, Baker brought in his brothers and their assorted family members and servants and used that retreat as a base for eight years of wandering through Ceylon. For a time he imported European farm animals and carried on a somewhat successful experiment with large-scale farming. He also provided the West with eyewitness descriptions of the incredible array of fungus, flora and fauna, including elephants, leopards, spiders, snakes, oysters and shark in his 1853 classic *The Rifle and the Hound in Ceylon*. Baker often hunted with young Laurence at his side, who wrote that the footprints of elephants could often be found mornings in the kitchen garden, and cheetahs occasionally had to be shot at from the house for attacking the livestock.

Nuwara Eliya became the charming colonial enclave where Maria and her fellow ex-patriate wives retired in the hot high season of January through May "for health." The first thirty tea plants grown in Ceylon[13] were said to have been planted by Sir Anthony in his garden at Nuwara Eliya in order to provide healthful refreshment for his seemingly fragile wife. When Maria was resting at Nuwara Eliya, she would receive daily letters from Laurence in Colombo, relating the gossip of the town, his observations and stories of his escapades below. In fact, daily letter writing became the exercise book for his highly engaging writing style. Here he learned to use his cleverness and wit to spin a yarn that enthralled and amused readers like Lady Maria.

Meanwhile, Laurence and his boyhood friends made it their mission to explore the entire territory. They sailed around Ceylon's 830-mile coastland and hiked and hunted throughout the interior. Laurence tells one memorable story of a visit he made to climb the 7,500-foot high Adam's Peak, or Mount Sri Pada, Ceylon's holy mountain. On top of this elevation is a four-by-three-foot impression considered by Muslim legend to be the first man's footprint, supposedly made while Adam was standing on one foot for a thousand years' penance after being expelled from the nearby Garden of Eden. Laurence's problems began on the second day of that climbing trip on a trail where tree roots were wet from the morning mists and crossed the trail:

> The path at the spot was scarped on the precipitous hillside; at least three hundred feet below roared a torrent of boiling water – when my foot slipped on a root, and I pitched over the sheer cliff. I heard the cry of my companion as I disappeared, and had quite time to realize that all was over, when I was brought up suddenly by the spreading branches of a bush which was growing upon a projecting rock.[14]

As Laurence hung suspended over the white water rapids, the native bearers took all the rope from their waist bands and the tied packages they were carrying, and lowered the hastily connected length of string down to Laurence, who fastened it under his armpits. Then he was hauled up safely to the path again, where he quickly recovered. He cheerfully shrugged off this escape from near death, showing the great good humor and habitual resilience he would later display as a war correspondent.

This Eden for an adolescent was Laurence's playground until 1846, when at the age of 17 he was sent back to England to be tutored for Cambridge. But just as the noose of formal education was about to slip around his neck, his mother and father arrived in London to announce that Sir Anthony had been granted a two-year sabbatical as his first vacation since taking on colonial postings. They planned a European tour. At once, Laurence, son of an attorney, launched into an impassioned oral argument in favor of joining them for two years of travel around Europe. His mother agreed, and in short order he was free of the tutor and the prospects of university in favor of a unique itinerant college education. This only stimulated his love of adventure, and probably put an end to any chance he would ever be happy pursuing any traditional career. Of his new circumstances, he wrote: "I found myself, to my great delight, transferred from the quiet of a Warwickshire vicarage to the Champs Elyssés in Paris."[15]

Laurence later remembered that while they were in the French capital he made an educational visit with his father to a private collection of lifelike colored paper-maché figures portraying the horrible symptoms of venereal diseases on human flesh. Perhaps Sir Anthony suggested going to this exhibit because he noticed young Laurence's nascent enthusiasm for paid sex, free of any romantic entanglement. Laurence wrote:

> I deeply regret that the lesson did not bear the fruits it ought to have done in my youth; nevertheless, it made a strong impression on me, and had a restraining influence. I have felt it my duty, therefore to do what lay in my power to cleanse this filthy sewer which pollutes the whole world with its stench.[16]

The family continued beyond Paris and spent an entire year on the well-worn trail of the traditional Grand Tour, still then considered an ideal curriculum for completing any well-to-do young person's education about the world and its peoples. They explored Germany,

Switzerland and the Tyrol by rail and carriage, often stopping for extended periods of fishing. Then the caravan rolled into Italy, in the late 1840s a patchwork of disparate kingdoms largely under the thumb of the Austro-Hungarian Empire. Indeed, local sentiment for war with Austria was strong and growing.

Sir Anthony seems to have inherited the penchant of other Englishmen who, far from avoiding areas of unrest, steered into the middle of civil chaos— such as those who reported firsthand on the horrors of the French Revolution's Reign of Terror in the 1790s. Sir Anthony arrived with his family right into an unquiet Italian landscape. In Rome, Laurence reported "joining a roaring mob one evening, bent I knew not upon what errand" and pulling on ropes to tear down the arms fixed to the front of the Austrian Legation. Another time he was "roused from my sleep about one or two in the morning" and joined another crowd headed with battering rams to the doors of the Church of Propaganda Fide, where they rioted against Austrian oppression, and crashed in to find that the clerical occupants had fled. The excitement of these experiences may have stimulated Laurence's later enthusiasm for all sorts of dangerous situations.

Moving away from the Vatican Kingdom, the Oliphants had a startling encounter in Livorno, on the northwest coast of Italy, which had fallen totally into the hands of "the scum of the population." On arriving in the town, a group of six porters fell upon the family's luggage and demanded an outlandish sum for carrying it all to the hotel. The Oliphants refused and were hauled in front of the local magistrate. Though threatened with jail, the Oliphants refused to pay the outrageous sum demanded by the porters, and were so adamant that the judge asked the porters to lower their fees, without success. Finally, to the astonishment of Sir Anthony, the judge reached into his own pocket and paid the fees himself. The owner of the hotel later explained that if the judge had not produced the required fees, he probably would have been stabbed to death that night on the way home. Having had a good lesson in the realities of the Tuscan justice system, the Oliphants immediately sent money to reimburse the hapless judge.

The next day, from the hotel, Laurence and family watched the arrival of two new English visitors with luggage, who were also descended upon by the same group of porters. But Laurence writes they appeared to be "university men in the prime of 'biceps'" and "must have been pupils of some great master in the noble art of self-defense" because in a matter of seconds the six porters were strewn about the quay unconscious, unable even to draw their knives while the Englishmen retrieved their luggage and marched in triumph on to the hotel.

From Italy, the Oliphants followed a southern course towards home in Ceylon, with adventures in Greece and a month on the Nile before crossing the desert to Suez and returning by ship to Colombo. Back home in the capital, Laurence and his parents abandoned all thought that he would go back to university and he began three years' work as his father's Private Secretary and an apprentice attorney. For this he was given the "exceedingly liberal" salary of £400 per year, allowing him to put aside considerable savings. During this period, he was also officially "called to the bar" in Ceylon – in those days before any written exams were required to actually become a lawyer. Laurence completed his unconventional "education" by handling twenty-three murder cases in the courts of Ceylon before the age of twenty-two. He also had the chance to watch his father's experience and integrity in action. Soon after the family returned to Ceylon, there was a minor revolt among the local population, who were chafing against rumored new laws and taxation. The inexperienced new governor of the colony, Lord Torrington, and several junior officers over-reacted, instituting harsh martial law and executing natives to whom Sir Anthony had recommended showing mercy. In 1850, Parliament held an inquiry, which led to Torrington's dismissal and the vindication that, during the troubles, Sir Anthony had performed as perhaps the sanest and steadiest of all the colony's leaders.

*

It was a dinnertime conversation about hunting with guests in Colombo that launched Laurence on the lifelong career of travel writer. In 1850, London had been enthralled and somewhat scandalized by the visit of the Nepalese Prime Minister and de facto Ambassador, Prince Jung Bahadoor. This envoy from another world dazzled the town with his turbans, exotic garments and jewels. He also seemed to enjoy liaisons with some of the town's better-known courtesans. Now the saucy prince was returning to his native land, bearing a letter to his Rajah from Queen Victoria, and was getting off the ship in Ceylon along with his fellow London passenger Sir Anthony. At dinner in Colombo with the Oliphants, Jung Bahadoor invited Laurence to join him on the last stages of his journey home to Katmandu— and to experience the Nepalese custom of elephant hunting.

Laurence captured the story of this adventure in his daily letters home to his parents, as well as in his journals. He was then able to edit these narratives into his first book, dedicated to his father Sir Anthony, and entitled *A Journey to Katmandu (the Capital of Napaul), with the Camp of Jung Bahadoor; Including a Sketch of the Nepaulese Ambassador at Home*. In the preface, Laurence shrewdly notes that the most recent book in English about Nepal dated from 1819, more than 30 years earlier. And with a reporter's instincts, Laurence rightly judged that the public would be willing to pay for more gossip about the dashing Jung Bahadoor.

Once Laurence joined the prince and his party aboard ship, there was hardly a dull moment. Noting "time never seemed to hang heavy on the hands of the Minister Sahib," Laurence detailed the shipboard routine for the ten-day passage to Calcutta: first, two hours of rifle practice blasting bottles, then more with the pistol. Next, training the hunting dogs on deck, followed by backgammon or gymnastics. Then pipes in the evening and tales of travels. Laurence became especially friendly with the prince's younger brother, Colonel Dhere Shum Shere, whom he found brave, jovial and light-hearted.

Arriving on land in Calcutta, they lingered and discovered Laurence's role as Jung Bahadoor's shooting companion was his "passport" to notoriety everywhere. Old acquaintances of his father and Uncle James presented themselves, sending their regards home to Sir Anthony and Lady Maria in Laurence's daily post. Young ladies came up to him constantly at social occasions, and he became expert at one-evening romances before his itinerary moved him along to new engagements the following day. He reported that he seemed to have a acquired a talent for making himself instantly comfortable and well liked by everyone he met— something he pointed out that he must have learned from his mother's behavior as consummate hostess at home. The text about the journey after leaving Calcutta reads like a travel guide, with descriptions and recommendations for must-see markets and temples. Laurence and his British companion, Colonel Cavannah—who was also Jung's interpreter—bounced northward together, dragged by coolies through the night on a paved road known as The Great Trunk Road of Bengal. Seven days after leaving Calcutta they reached "the Holy City" of Benares where they attended the marriage ceremony of Jung Bahadoor to the thirteen-year-old second daughter of the ex-Rajah of Coorg. Laurence wrote that the new child bride

> was seated in a howdah. Jung introduced her to me as "his beautiful Missus"—a description she fully deserved. She was very handsome, and reflected much credit on the taste of the happy bridegroom, who seemed pleased when we expressed our approval of his choice.

Yet even as Laurence was gallivanting around on this adventure, he received letters from his mother at home asking about his spiritual state, a topic that must have been a daily family exercise for monitoring spiritual progress. In his replies, Laurence took care to address these inquiries, although on this particular trip he wrote "it is difficult to practice habits of self-examination riding upon an elephant with a companion who is always talking or singing within a few feet."

Besides the book's detailed descriptions of Nepal, its customs and inhabitants, the most exciting part of the adventure was the Nepalese wild elephant hunt during which tame elephants and handlers attacked a wild elephant herd and attempted to capture new animals for their elephant army. Despite Laurence's background as a hunter and sportsman, host Jung Bahadoor at the last moment forbade him from joining: the hunt was simply too dangerous, he declared. Laurence insisted, however, and agreed to undergo special training to get ready. First, he took off his shoes, wrapped a towel around his head, and mounted an elephant while holding onto a rope wrapped completely around the animal's mid-section. Then, imagining a tree branch coming toward him at speed, Laurence repeatedly had to hurl himself to the right or the left, clinging against the side of the beast as if the elephant were scrambling on a wild chase through the forest. Then he had to pull himself back up into the mounted position, only to hurl himself back against the sides again and again. Although he lost a lot of skin, Laurence finally performed all these tests to the prince's satisfaction, and was finally allowed to join the hunt.

Each hunting elephant had two passengers: an experienced mahout as driver, and a second rider at the back holding a board with a spike which was to be pounded into the base of the poor animal's tail when it was time to charge. Laurence was to perform this secondary task, but things became more challenging than the practice when the chase actually began:

Away we went… and I looked upon it as a miracle that every bone in my body was not broken. Sometimes I was jerked into a sitting posture, and, not being able to get my heels from under me in time, they received a violent blow. A moment after I was thrown forward on my face, only righting myself in time to see a huge impending branch, which I had to escape by slipping rapidly down the crupper, taking all the skin off my toes in so doing, and what would have been more serious, the branch nearly taking my head off if I did not stoop low enough. When I could look about me, the scene was most extraordinary and indescribable; a hundred elephants were tearing through the jungle as rapidly as their unwieldy forms would let them, crushing down the jungle in their headlong career, while their riders were gesticulating violently.

Elephants were successfully captured and added to the elephant army already tamed by the mahouts and their helpers. After his intense hunting experiences, Laurence lingered in Nepal and India, rounding out his sketches of exotic surroundings for his armchair travel readership at home. Laurence hoped his letters home had the makings of a commercially viable book and afterwards set to work putting them into shape for sharing with prospective publishers once he returned to London.

While Laurence worked on his first book, a major change took place in the Oliphant household. In October 1851, at age sixty, Sir Anthony began his retirement. He had led a distinguished career, completing service as Attorney General in South Africa with a knighthood; then prospering as Chief Justice in Ceylon; and even being recognized by the Parliamentary inquiry board for his cool head during the colony's troubles. Britain's reward to him was to be a life of luxury back home. Sir Anthony, Lady Maria and Laurence all returned to London that fall for one endless round of dinner parties during "the constant dissipation of a London season."

Given Laurence's experience as a barrister in Ceylon, the family decided he should train for acceptance to the bar in both London and Edinburgh to further strengthen his professional credentials, with the thought of perhaps following in the colonial legal steps of Sir Anthony. Laurence was no longer a plain child, but a confident, fit and red-cheeked youth of the world. He quickly fit in everywhere and was a particular hit with the ladies. His cousin and biographer Margaret Oliphant says:

> Laurence was by no means unqualified 'to please a damsel's eye'[17] in his own person, and was almost certain to be, under any circumstances, the most entertaining and attractive person in his neighbourhood wherever he was…

His close friend at the time, Oswald Smith, later remembered how twenty-three- year-old Laurence burst onto the social scene at one weekend house party at the time when ice skating had become the rage. Laurence had never skated before, but he threw himself into it with "reckless audacity" and at the end of two days was the best skater at the party. Oswald wrote "I can recall his figure vividly now as he dashed rapidly 'on the outside edge backward' with peal after peal of his delightful laughter, the gayest of the gay."[18]

Laurence also knew how to make people take notice of him while doing legal studies in London, as he described in this November 1851 passage from a letter to his father:

> I have eaten some stringy boiled beef at Lincoln's Inn Hall in company with three hundred others, not one soul of whom I had ever seen before; but I unhesitatingly talked to my next neighbor, and soon, by dropping in an unconcerned manner remarks upon a tiger I knocked over here, and a man I defended for murder there, talking learnedly about Ceylon affairs, etc., etc., incited the curiosity of those whose reserve would not otherwise have allowed them to notice me, too much to let them remain silent.[19]

As part of his grooming for a promising future, Laurence was formally introduced to the Queen at court. He said, "everybody was in uniform; the few who were in civil costume looked like servants of the royal household." As he went, in order, to kiss the Queen's hand, he wrote:

> The Queen looked me in the face much harder than I expected, and I returned the gaze with such a will that I forgot to kneel, ultimately nearly going down on both knees, after which, finding the backing-out process rather irksome, I fairly turned tail and bolted.[20]

At the same time, with an introduction through his composer uncle Thomas, Laurence was able to place his new book, *A Journey to Katmandu*, with the London publishing house of John Murray (Lord Byron's publisher a few decades before). He then worked through the final editing and proofing of the book, which was released to great success in 1852 to a public eager to hear more of the exotic Nepalese Prime Minister and his faraway land. The popular response went to Laurence's head, and despite the ease with which he met the qualifications for admission to the bars in London and Edinburgh in these days before examinations, a career in law now paled for him in comparison to the attractions of traveling to remote places and writing about them. The only problem was where to go that was not already covered in the shelves of travel guides and adventure tales already written.

CHAPTER 2

THE WRITING TRADE

Laurence's answer to his search for the next exotic location to write about came quickly. In the summer of 1852, he and Oswald Smith, his friend from the skating party, set off on a sporting expedition to the Russian Lapland, where they had heard that "region swarmed with guileless salmon who had never been offered a fly, and (where) it would be easy… to get a shot at some white bears."[1] Unfortunately their plans for sport were thwarted at St. Petersburg where customs officials tried to assess an outrageous fee on their equipment, which they promptly sent back to England. Oswald remembered Laurence "had been bitten by the literary success he had had"[2] and would be happy to go in any direction as long as it gave him good material for his next book. So, with hurried planning, they re-directed themselves without equipment and embarked on an adventure of more than one thousand miles across the interior of Russia by boat and horse-drawn carriage. They tried without success to hire a guide who could speak both English and Russian, but ultimately set off alone into the unknown. Oswald remembered Laurence had "unwavering high spirits" and was never discouraged by tedious delays, but instead was "continually bursting forth into snatches of song." At one point, however, relations with their carriage driver became strained, and

Laurence didn't hesitate to hold a revolver to the man's head to get him to move on. When they finally arrived at the next city and were meeting with the British Consul there, the official told them they "were lucky to have arrived at all."

The two ended their summer adventure far south at the Crimea, "then an unknown and unexplored peninsula, and the mysterious city of Sebastopol, of which many legends, but no definite and clear information, had reached the world." Sebastopol was a closed military enclave of 40,000 and off-limits to visitors, especially since Russia was threatening Turkey at that point, and the Czar was expected any day for an inspection and review of the Russian fleet there. Laurence and Oswald arrived in pretty rough shape at the end of their trans-Russian journey. They hardly looked like traveling Englishmen or spies as they rode into town on the back of a peasant cart, driven by the German farmer they had just hired as an interpreter and guide. Laurence wrote:

> A thick coating of grey dust rendered all minor differences of costume imperceptible; and as we leant back, half hidden amongst bundles of hay, with our hats slouched over our eyes, as if to keep the sun off, we flattered ourselves that we looked extremely like phlegmatic German peasants from some neighbouring colony.[3]

Once in the town, their cart driver arranged lodgings for them at a friendly German house in the middle of town. From that base, Laurence spied all over, taking in the sights as "the suspicious eye of each officer I passed chilled the blood in my veins." The account of this lightly-planned journey became Laurence's second best-seller, *The Russian Shores of the Black Sea in the Autumn of 1852 with a Voyage Down the Volga and a Tour Through the Country of the Don Cossacks*, published in 1853 by the firm that would become his lifelong publisher, William Blackwood & Sons of Edinburgh. Laurence must have had a premonition about the importance of the Crimea to his country's future, because the tensions between Russia and England were escalating into what would shortly become the Crimean War. A second edition of his book was printed late in 1853, and Laurence added another chapter airing his views on the coming conflict. By March 1854, the book was in such demand that it went into its fourth edition. So it must not have been a complete surprise back in London when Laurence and Oswald were summoned to army headquarters at the Horse Guards Parade at Whitehall.

The travelers gave the senior British generals, Lord de Ros and Sir John Burgoyne, a complete description of the fortifications of the Sebastopol harbor—and asserted the lack of any fortifications on the southern approach to the town from Balaclava. As Laurence said "there was no more impediment to an army, which should effect a landing at Balaclava, from marching into Sebastopol than there would be for an army to march into Brighton from the downs behind it." He even suggested a strategy for a successful attack to Sir John, although he knew he was out of his element, and only did so "with the greatest diffidence."

Now all of Laurence's energies and aspirations were focused on taking part, in some way, in his country's actions in the Crimean campaign, although he certainly avoided any thought of joining the army. He worked his considerable family connections hard to find an opening, and was actively considering an offer from *The Times* to serve as their war correspondent, when another remarkable opportunity came his way from an entirely new direction.

*

James Bruce, 8th Earl of Elgin, was one of the Scottish elite intertwined with the Oliphants. Bruce was an enlightened career diplomat, first appointed Governor of Jamaica in 1842, and then promoted to the top British North American job as Governor-General of Canada in 1847. He was a supporter of "responsible government," believing that an elected body should be primarily responsible to its people for effective government rather than merely enforcing the edicts of a remote monarch. This parliamentary approach allowed a British colony to govern its own affairs without much interference from London, and eventually led Canada both to attain peaceful independence and keep its formal British ties. Later Elgin would finish his career as Viceroy of India.

Now, in 1854 near the end of his Canadian posting, and at the suggestion of some of Lady Oliphant's lady friends, Elgin inquired whether young Laurence would be available to become his personal secretary for a specific mission to negotiate an improved trade agreement between Canada and the United States. There would be social engagements to plan, important correspondence to handle, as well as a treaty to write, and since Laurence's father had worked in a similar capacity as secretary for the 7th Earl, the precocious young author seemed a particularly good fit for the job.

When the offer came from Lord Elgin, Laurence was still hoping to get involved in the Crimea, but he convinced himself to hope for both: a short-term assignment with Lord Elgin, and then a speedy return to Europe in time to go to the war zone. After Laurence departed, Sir Anthony and Lady Oliphant took quarters in Edinburgh, surrounded by relatives and friends. Their hope was that Laurence would eventually embark on a proper diplomatic career; at that point Sir Anthony, retired, could relocate himself and his wife in whatever corner of the Empire their son landed. Sir Anthony wrote to a friend: "The wife is buttoned to Lowry's coattails and I am tied to her apron strings. I am just like the last carriage of a train, waggling after them just where they please to lead."

Laurence was "all eyes" on his first visit to America, traveling with the esteemed British delegation in May 1854 and recording his impressions in a series of letters home to his parents. He particularly liked the American train cars during the day since they "were always full of pretty girls, and if the scenery is not pretty you can look at them— they are always sure to be looking at you."[4] When the British party arrived in Washington, talks on trade with British Canada had been bogged down in wrangling for the previous seven or eight years. In an interview with the United States President, Franklin Pierce, and his Secretary of State, William L. Marcy, Lord Elgin was told there would be no hesitation for a freer trade agreement from the government, but that no new law could be put through the American Congress without the support of the Democratic senators, who were, at the time, in the majority and in violent opposition to any wishes of the government.

It happened that Lord Elgin and Laurence arrived in Washington on the day when the Kansas-Nebraska Bill passed, after months of acrimonious debate. The new legislation was a significant milestone, defining the two new large territories, and establishing that any decision about slavery would be up to each territory's residents. This set the stage for a fierce contest on the ground between pro-slavery forces and abolitionists. Laurence later wrote that this bill "was to open an extensive territory to slavery, and intensify the burning question which was to find its final solution seven years later in a bloody civil war."[5] The British visitors were a welcome novelty after the heated slavery debates, and they were immediately included in a non-stop marathon of lunches, dinners, dances and other social engagements celebrating the bill. Reviewing his journal from the time, Laurence re-called this entry from his first week in Washington when he was sandwiched between an abolitionist senator and his pro-slavery opponent during lunch. He wrote:

I am getting perfectly stunned with harangues upon political questions
I don't understand with the nomenclature appropriate to each. Besides

Whigs and Democrats, there are Hard Shells and Soft Shells, and Free Soilers, and Disunionists, and Federals, to say nothing of filibusters, pollywogs and a host of other nicknames.[6]

After that lunch, well irrigated with champagne, Laurence went to an afternoon of dancing hosted by the French minister. Most likely this was followed by a formal dinner somewhere else in the city, as the British were totally immersed in the process of making new allies. At first, Laurence didn't see the sense in the nonstop festivities. Once he realized, however, that all the new friends he and Lord Elgin had made were Democratic senators, he began to comprehend his boss's strategy.

After about ten days of making allies in Washington, capped off by a ball in honor of the Queen's birthday, Lord Elgin told Secretary of State William Marcy that he believed an updated trade agreement could now be concluded without the objections of key Democrats in Congress. After three days of drafting and proofing documents, with Laurence actually doing most of the writing, the Canadian-American Reciprocity Treaty was ready to be signed. Laurence wrote the following melodramatic description of Marcy at the midnight signing:

> His hand does not shake, though he is very old, and knows the abuse that is in store for him and members of Congress and an enlightened press. That hand, it is said, is not unused to a revolver... He is now the secretary of state; before that, a general in the army; before that, governor of a state; before that secretary of war; before that, minister in Mexico; before that, a member of the House of Representatives; before that a politician; before that, a cabinet-maker...[7]

Despite the impression the agreement "had been floated through on champagne," Laurence judged the treaty a great achievement for Lord Elgin and "of enormous commercial advantage to the two countries," and especially for Canada. He noted that in the year before the mission, trade between Canada with the United States totaled $20 million. The year after the agreement, it increased to $33 million, and then continued an ever upward climb.

Finally, the British delegation left Washington for Canada, travelling north through New York, Boston, Maine and Montreal, back to Spencer Wood, Lord Elgin's residence as the Governor-General outside Quebec. Although Laurence had been expecting to return to England and the Crimea, he agreed to continue on as secretary to Lord Elgin, who was losing many of his staff as they were re-called for action in the Crimea and needed help making several changes before he wound up his Canadian administration.

Astonishingly, the twenty-five year old Laurence was asked to step in as Superintendent-General of Indian Affairs when Lord Elgin's brother, Colonel Bruce, was ordered back to join his regiment. The Indian Affairs appointment came "with two colonels, two captains and some Englishmen long in the service and was not popular"— and not permanent. Treasuring his flighty independence, and expressing what would become a description of his eventual life-long career path, Laurence wrote: "nothing can be a greater curse to a young man wishing to get on than a permanent appointment."[8] However, Laurence was very happy with this opportunity to explore the West while on the government payroll:

> bark-canoeing on distant and silent lakes or down foaming rivers, where the fishing was splendid, the scenery most romantic, and camp-life at this season of the year – for it was now the height of summer – most enjoyable.[9]

It is very telling that Laurence did not "slack off" and turn his travels into a mere holiday. He had schools to inspect, councils with the Indians to hold, and tribal disputes to settle. He also managed to sign a treaty giving Canada 500,000 new acres on an island in

Lake Huron, purchased by Laurence from the Indians at a very low price. He also knew all of these very improbable activities would be excellent material for a new book, which he would indeed write about as *Minnesota and the Far West*, his third book, published in 1855. After several months on the Indian trail, Laurence returned to the seat of government in Quebec, where the change of governorship was finally underway.

Elgin and Laurence took a farewell tour of Upper Canada and then concluded a final few months at Spencer Wood in "a whirl of gayety" to mark the end of the Elgin era and the beginning of a new one. Balls, dinners, garden parties, and picnics were the order of the day," and making these entertainments succeed was all very much in the job description of the young secretary. Just before one ball hosted at Spencer Wood, Lord Elgin reminded him that "the success of the ball depends upon me." Laurence noted in a letter home, "I have introduced four new dances into Quebec. What an enviable reputation to have, and how astonished my Edinburgh friends would be!" In managing all of these important social events, Laurence was much engaged with the ladies, in a society where, as he wrote, every young gentleman faced with the social season has his special girl – in the Canadian slang of the day called his "muffin." However, to reassure his mother he was not about to be ensnared in any serious relationship, he confided he was "utterly heartless" as he interacted with the ladies:

> There is a class of sins which are very difficult to resist, because you cannot put your finger on the exact point where they become sins. Now, for instance, a certain degree of intimacy with young ladies is no harm; and it is difficult to define where flirting begins, or what amount of even joking or laughing, though perfectly innocent, is not expedient, and one gets led imperceptibly on without feeling the harm that is being done to both parties until it is too late.[10]

He was happy to play the role of the gracious host, and dance with girl after girl at each ball, but he kept himself detached behind a veil of propriety, as his diplomatic staff post required. That was the heartlessness he mentioned cultivating. On the less guarded and more personal side, he still carried on a spiritual dialogue in his correspondence with his mother, but now his words included hints of doubt. One wet Sunday morning when bad weather kept him from going to church, Laurence wrote of his frustration with the remoteness of the savior who was supposed to be the go-between mankind and the Deity:

> Everything around me testifies to the existence of a Being who is all pervading; but the Son is nowhere visible and does not, so to speak, force Himself upon the senses. It is a totally different act of the mind which is required to accept Him as a positive fact.[11]

The young man, thrust out all day in the busy affairs of personal diplomacy, was in private longing for a more direct and intimate experience from his religion. In fact, Laurence had begun moving away from simply reporting on his evangelical probity to his mother in his letters. He was starting to question her traditional set of beliefs and to look for a faith he could embrace on his own. He also took time to evaluate the religious choices of the acquaintances he met along the way. He thought one man weak by becoming a Roman Catholic—because he wanted to be told what to believe, rather than think things out himself. He judged another person happy as a good Episcopalian only because he enjoyed the show of religion without any concern for its basic foundation. Laurence decided that, above all else, he was going to be independent in his own religious views until he himself became convinced of the truth. He possessed a reporter's mindset, and if he didn't actually see something, he didn't believe it. So far no creed had won him over. Yet he was longing to discover a connection with God that would be direct and real— one that did not simply rely on blind faith that the Deity did, in fact, exist.

Meanwhile Lord Elgin was pleased with Laurence's performance, yet a bit mystified with the moods of his young secretary, who seemed to vacillate between manic gaiety and soul-searching guilt. When he was not front and center choreographing entertainments or handling correspondence, Laurence was spending hours in his room reading obscure religious books and mulling over his spiritual state:

> Lord E. says he never knows what I am at, at one moment going to the extreme of gaiety, at another to disgust and despondency. All he wishes is in a good-natured way to amuse people; and he therefore can hardly sympathize with my reactions every now and then.... He sees my twinges of conscience, and asked me the other day whether I was going to lay all the sins I seemed so oppressed with at his door... and (he said) if you have got anything to repent of, I wish you'd wait and do it on board ship...[12]

Finally, after a last month transitioning Lord Elgin and his successor, Sir Edmund Head, Laurence and Lord Elgin set sail home for England in below-zero temperatures at the end of December 1854. Laurence had expected the mission to be an eight-week trip. Instead, it had lasted eight months.

*

Back in London at the start of 1855, Laurence joined up with Lady Oliphant and Sir Anthony, who had felt a bit lost without him. They had not yet committed themselves to buying a new home in Britain because they wanted to be able to move near Laurence, if he was lucky enough to get a good diplomatic posting. Now temporarily together again, the three moved into "not very comfortable" but happily shared accommodation. Meanwhile, disturbing reports from the Crimean conflict supercharged the atmosphere of the city. For the first time, blow-by-blow war news was arriving instantly over the new-fangled telegraph, and the news was not good. Perhaps most worrying was the incident immortalized by England's poet laureate, Alfred Tennyson, as "The Charge of the Light Brigade," in which the poor communication of a somewhat vague order along the chain of command resulted in a lightly armed British cavalry force charging an entrenched Russian artillery battery who knew they were coming. The British high commander's intention was for that cavalry unit to follow and harry another retreating enemy artillery force nearby, but that subtlety was not understood by the commanders on the field. As a result, the cavalry unit heroically charged and suffered terrible losses. In fact, in the aftermath of that tragedy, Parliament ordered an investigation into the overall conduct of the war.

Laurence was determined to see the action himself, and with his knowledge of the region from his 1852 Russian excursion, he knew enough to concoct a potential role he might fill. He lobbied hard to be made an envoy to convince Chechnya's leader, Imam Shamil, to join with the British and the Turks against the Russians. He argued this idea forcefully with Lord Clarendon, the Foreign Secretary, who finally gave him permission to travel to the war zone in August 1855, first to make his case to Lord Stratford de Redcliffe, the British ambassador there, and then to proceed with his mission, if the ambassador agreed. Meanwhile, Sir Anthony was fed up with his own inactivity in retirement and, in a telling display of his closeness for his son, decided to go along with Laurence, who would also be well paid by *The Times* as an on-the-ground war correspondent.

Father and son arrived in Constantinople "in the blazing August weather" and found the ambassador had de-camped to his summer embassy overlooking the Bosporus at Therapia. Laurence left Sir Anthony to sightseeing and traveled out to interview the ambassador.

On the eve of the parliamentary war investigation, Lord Stratford was very glad to see Laurence and wanted to hear from him about the war reporting at home, where he feared he was being misrepresented. Although he did not immediately endorse Laurence's mission to Chechnya, he did invite him to stay on as personal secretary in Therapia for a few weeks, and then to join him in on a yacht trip to the battle zone to award medals. Now Laurence could finally see the Crimean action firsthand. He wrote back to *The Times*:

> Long before we saw land, we saw the vivid flashes of the guns and heard the reports when we got nearer: a heavy cannonade was kept up all night. Very curious to be rigging out in ball costume (to dine in the Admiral's ship, *The Royal Albert*) to the sounds of booming guns of the bombardment.[13]

Laurence was welcomed into the allied camp attending the siege of Sebastopol that had started almost a year before and was in its final stages. Sir Anthony also traveled up to the area with other non-combatants hoping to see the city after its fall. Indeed, after the siege ended in September, Sir Anthony returned to Britain with enough of an adventure behind him.

For the next three months, Laurence joined chief *Times* correspondent William Russell and the other field reporters to cover the fighting, adding his own dispatches to the flood of reports coming back to *The Times*. Thanks to the telegraph, no other war ever had such up to the minute reports sent back to a newspaper's readership and there was almost an unlimited demand for more stories. He wrote to his mother that the money from the newspaper was the only way he could justify his vagabond life, since there was nothing else that would pay him as much. Throughout his many reporting adventures, Laurence was never timid or shirking. He was always seeking the heart of the action, and the excitement that came from living on the edge—and he was often on the battlefields. One day he wrote his mother how he lay down under a bank to read one of her letters with "a pretty brisk shower of missiles flying about," but added he was "never better"[14] and in fact enjoyed eating her letter, which was his only food for the previous thirty-six hours. Sometimes he became directly involved in the action. For example, he wrote to Lady Oliphant about what he called "my battery," which he was ordered to build after the Turkish commander mistook him for a serving officer. Laurence had been summarily put in charge of two hundred men with artillery pieces and ordered to make the battery two hundred yards from the Russian front lines in the middle of the night— which he did. Remembering it all, he wrote, "luckily they never found us out, we worked so quietly... (and) these batteries did good service two days after." When the Turkish commander complimented the British on Laurence's performance, he was startled to learn Laurence was not a soldier at all, but only "a gentleman who is traveling with us." Privately he basked in the glow of this achievement and the approval he thought it would receive from his mother and father back at home.

Despite the lighthearted anecdotes in his letters back home to his parents, Laurence was going through a rough time by the end of 1855. The weather turned bad with never ending rain. As was his normal practice, he included updates on his spiritual state also in his letters. In one he wrote his thoughts were depressed and he was privately "gloomy and disgusted." He said:

> My conscience is never satisfied with my conduct, nor my understand-
> ing with my belief, so that altogether I live in a state of internal conflict
> and argumentation.[15]

Finally, he caught an illness in the dark and wet tents and had to travel home to recover.

Although he was intending to return to the action, those plans were upended by a sudden end to the war, negotiated by Napoleon III and the French who had many times more casualties than the British and who wanted to improve their relations with the Russians for other diplomatic agendas. They wanted a fast settlement, which Laurence thought was a disillusioning betrayal. Sick at the carnage amid such diplomatic posturing, Laurence turned down an invitation to re-join the British ambassador in Constantinople as private secretary and decided to leave town to clear his head.

About this time, there were rumors that Laurence became serious about a girl in Britain, and perhaps was even near engagement. The girl's name was not reported, but it seems very possible that it could have happened. Although Laurence had a good income from his vagabond reporting lifestyle, there would have been the question of how he would plan to support a wife—and possible family—in the upper class lifestyle of the time to which they would have been accustomed. Perhaps a wish to gather more savings attracted him to seek more reporting assignments, even though that would mean leaving the country again for more travels?

At any rate, by early summer 1856, Laurence joined John Delane, the editor of *The Times*, on a press tour back to the United States. Laurence was not officially an employee of the newspaper, but Delane recognized his reporting talent and was willing to pay for any printable reports he might turn in. On the ground in America, American luminaries such as Ralph Waldo Emerson and New York newspaper editor Horace Greeley welcomed the British. Laurence renewed former acquaintances from his North American mission with Lord Elgin and traveled through the plantations of the South to New Orleans, which he thought "in the winter of 1856-57... was socially the most delightful city in the Union." But later he also wrote: "From what I saw and heard... it was not difficult to predict the cataclysm that took place four years later."[16]

Heading even further south—perhaps in a lapse of judgment, or possibly at the suggestion of *The Times* or the Foreign Ministry—our manic young reporter accepted an invitation to join the notorious

"Walker's Army" sailing from New Orleans with 300 men to reinforce mercenaries already on the ground taking over Nicaragua. His own stated reason for the venture seems a little bland:

> My own motive for accompanying this expedition did not proceed from any sympathy I felt in its object, but from the prospect… of visiting an interesting country under novel and peculiar circumstances, and of experiencing sensations which were altogether new to me.[17]

At this time before the Panama Canal, Nicaragua was a favorite stop on the shipping route from New York to San Francisco. There, goods could travel inland from the Caribbean by river into Lake Nicaragua and then pass over a thin ribbon of land to the Pacific coast. Then they could be loaded back onto another ship and resume travel north to California. Walker was an American filibusterer, which originally meant "one of a class of piratical adventurers who pillaged the Spanish colonies in the West Indies," according to the *Oxford English Dictionary*. He had concocted a plan to found pro-slavery states in Central America to supply the Southern plantations in America at the time. He had already had some success when he briefly conquered the Baja peninsula in Mexico, christening it as the Republic of Southern California. He proposed running that territory under the laws of Louisiana, also making it a slave-friendly state. That effort had soon faltered, but now Walker was making progress in Nicaragua at the time Laurence went. The motivation was clear for Walker's mercenary army since their leader promised land and wealth for everyone who helped with the takeover. Laurence could have been very useful to Walker if he liked what he saw on the ground in Nicaragua and sent in favorable reports to the British press. Indeed Walker would go on to become President of Nicaragua, reintroducing slavery and developing more ambitious plans for colonizing more of Central and South America under his control, until he was captured and executed by the neighboring Hondurans.

Actually, Walker's image at the time Laurence sailed towards him was much worse than he thought. The British rated him a shameless opportunist and virtually a pirate, and when Laurence's ship neared its destination, it was stopped, boarded and seized by one Captain Cockburn with men from a British squadron anchored there to keep the peace. When Laurence's accent betrayed his origins, he was removed from the ship as "a British subject, being where a British subject had no right to be." He was probably headed for arrest and incarceration, until he found out the Commodore of that particular squadron was his cousin, the future British Admiral John Elphinstone Erskine. Writing about Laurence, his fellow Oliphant clan member Margaret Oliphant wrote with familial fondness about his good fortune:

> Thus our young man 'fell on his feet' wherever he went, and instead of suffering at all for his wild and unjustifiable undertaking, found himself in excellent and amusing quarters, restored to all the privileges of his rank—the admiral's cousin at sea being as good for all purposes as a king's cousin ashore.[18]

Despite all the adventure, one can sense Laurence was becoming uneasy at his lack of a clear direction and career path at age 27, and those feelings would only get worse. Ending the trip, he stayed in Central America a little longer, traveling to Panama to scout locations for a canal between the Atlantic and Pacific—and indeed reporting on the canal's possibilities might have been behind his mission there all along. Although he probably did increase his savings with reports on his observations published as an article in *Blackwood's Magazine* and later in a book called *Patriots and Filibusters* (1860), the trip didn't seem to advance his marriage prospects at home. When, back in London, he allegedly met his former girlfriend at a dance, she was rather dismissive, greeting him reportedly by saying, "Oh, how d'ye do? I thought ye were hung."[19] Of course, death had been the penalty that Walker had suffered, although at the hands of a firing squad, not a hangman. Meanwhile Laurence was very concerned about his future job prospects and he lobbied his official contacts hard for some other meaningful position, hopefully with travel and adventure included.

*

Just as twenty-seven-year-old Laurence's career (and romantic) prospects were uncertain during this period, so were his spiritual and religious beliefs. He questioned the evangelical creed of his parents and he did not see much comfort in the traditional religious options of nineteenth century Britain. The mainstream Church of England, Presbyterian, Congregationalist and Roman Catholic camps seemed focused on narrow points of dogma or clerical concerns rather than on giving followers a radically more relevant and personal religious experience. As a result, Laurence and many others at the time were seeking new spiritual foundations.

For example, it was at this time the eighteenth century teachings of Emanuel Swedenborg (1688-1772) were being exhumed, re-examined and re-published. Swedenborg was a brilliant Swedish scientist who systematically wrote with distinction about mathematics, chemistry, physics, anatomy and physiology well into his fifties. But at that point in his life, his investigations evolved beyond the limits of traditional science into an examination of the life force and "soul." He started with theology, and from there crossed over to direct interaction with the spirit world. Then, for more than twenty years more, his writings on the celestial sphere were "a revelation from God for a new age of truth and reason in religion... the second advent."[20] He wrote about visiting other planets inhabited by spirits and speaking with them in long conversations. The British Swedenborg Society began about 1810 and, over the next fifty years, translated, published and distributed his writings from bookshops and libraries across Britain.

Over in America, a less tradition-bound and more refreshing atmosphere encouraged spiritual self-discovery. A movement known as the Second Great Awakening gained power earlier in the century, led by impassioned revivalist preachers exhorting people to make more personal and emotional links to their religions. For example, in the 1820's, thirty students at Amherst College in Massachusetts were emboldened to embark on enlightened lives after attending a "revival meeting"[21] and, about the same time, young Joseph Smith wrote up the details of his meeting with the angel Moroni, when he received the golden tablets of the *Book of Mormon* to translate. Later, Transcendentalists, such as Ralph Waldo Emerson, reacted against the strictures of prevalent Western organized religions by investigating widely and reading Hindu texts such as the Bhagavad Gita and the Upanishads for inspiration. Emerson articulated the inherently American approach to self-realization:

> We will walk on our own feet; we will work with our own hands; we will speak our own minds... A nation of men will for the first time exist because each believes himself inspired by the Divine Soul which also inspires all men.[22]

Later Laurence would be well known to Emerson, who wrote of inviting the young British author to visit him at his club in Boston.

In addition to new sources of inspiration, several American experimental communities started to offer a more intensive experience, such as New Harmony (1825), Brook Farm (1841) and Oneida (1847)—although few would stand the test of time. And by the mid-nineteenth century, the show-me American mood was hoping for some obvious and overwhelmingly convincing evidence of a vibrant spiritual world finally to appear.

Like many other American revelations, that evidence began to manifest itself in the unlikely setting of far western New York State's "burnt out district," so-called because the turf was so heavily evangelized it was thought there were no more unconverted people for new preachers to burn. But more evangelical fuel did appear during the winter of 1847-1848 in the village of Hydesville, near Rochester. For some time that winter, the family of John D. Fox had been disturbed by episodes of loud knocking in their bedroom and from the cellar underneath.[23] Over time, these knocks were joined by noises like the sounds of footsteps, as well as sensations of being touched by a cold hand or large dog. The youngest daughter, Kate Fox, was particularly attuned to the strange disturbances, and finally put a personality to the force behind the sounds—one "Mr. Splitfoot," as she called it. Kate and her mother soon discovered Mr. Splitfoot could respond intelligently, rapping answers to questions such as "can you count to ten" or "how old were you when you died?" (Answer: 31 knocks.)

On the night of March 31, 1848, the Foxes could keep things private no longer, and Mr. Fox invited the nearest neighbors over. These people then also witnessed another otherworldly question and answer session, with the knocking responses as a kind of Morse code. The astonished neighbors then called in others, and so on, and word soon spread widely. People crowded into the house to experience the phenomena themselves, while others waited outside, peering in through the windows. A committee was appointed to pose questions, and the raps continued as aides to the committee searched for the source of the sounds.

As news of this commotion spread, the Fox family continued to be beset by rapping, touching and the moving of furniture around their rooms. Mrs. Fox and her daughters moved to a hotel in Rochester, but discovered to their dismay that their union with the spirits accompanied them to each new location. Public events were held. Three successive demonstrations were performed in the largest meeting place in Rochester, Corinthian Hall, where standing-room-only crowds again witnessed the phenomena, with all attempts at explanation failing. Finally, the third performance was cut short when "rowdies" in the audience threatened to come up on stage to make a very close examination of the girls' undergarments for noise-making devices. Thereafter the Fox ladies shared their skills only in more protected séances.

The Fox family were invited to New York City, and made repeated demonstrations to a select group of worthies, including author James Fennimore Cooper; poet and editor of the *New York Evening Post* William Cullen Bryant; and editor of the *New York Tribune* Horace Greeley. No one could come up with any explanation for the phenomenon, and after grilling the Foxes for weeks, Greeley published an editorial stating that after being subjected "to every reasonable test and the keen and critical scrutiny of hundreds who have chosen to visit them," no one had caught the Foxes causing the "rappings," nor had anyone invented a "plausible theory for the production of these sounds, nor the singular intelligence which has seemed to be manifested through them."

These sensational events opened the floodgates as mediums of every stripe came forward in virtually every town and village of western New York State. One traveling witness published a letter about his "six weeks tour of the West" during the summer of 1852. He saw speaking, dancing and pointing mediums. The speaking mediums became fluent in languages they had never studied. The dancing ones became entranced after wild and "eccentric" gyrations. And the pointing ones were able to move large objects through the simple efforts of making a pointing gesture, as in one story reported from Washington D.C. about a séance conducted by a certain Mrs. Miller, during which she moved three generals seated on a grand piano around a large room simply by pointing her finger.

*

Laurence was paying close attention to the news of these exciting spiritual developments as it was exported from America to Britain. Oswald Smith, his friend from the earlier Russian adventure, sometimes went along with Laurence on some of his investigations in London. Oswald wrote:

> I remember also going with him to the séances of a then fashionable American medium (I think Hayden was her name) where the ordinary rapping and spelling out replies were exhibited. The success was limited, and the details, which I could give, are not worth recording. Oliphant did not seem much impressed by them. Nor do I think he long dallied with this kind of manifestations. Indeed he said that he soon passed beyond them, and warned others against them.[24]

Oswald also reports that Laurence was experimenting with some of the fashionable unexplained practices himself. One time in 1854, Oswald saw Laurence mesmerize a young lady at an evening party, but he was "utterly unable to release her from the influence which he had obtained over her." Oswald remembers the incident was actually rather painful for Laurence, but as we will find out soon enough, it was only the start of his explorations of mysterious otherworldly phenomena.

CHAPTER 3

DIPLOMACY AND LOSS

While young Laurence was visiting séances and struggling to get his own future launched, the British wasted no time clarifying Lord Elgin's own next assignment. The star diplomat was asked to break through the stalemate stalling British expansionism in the Far East. Specifically, Lord Elgin was tasked with finally opening up the free flow of trade for Britain with China, and possibly unknown Japan. And, as soon as he accepted this new mission, Lord Elgin invited Laurence to join him again as personal secretary. Not only would the young man be useful in all his official duties, but Lord Elgin also appreciated Laurence could help publicize any success the mission achieved in another one of his popular books, potentially with Lord Elgin as hero.

At the time in 1857 when the new British mission departed for Asia, the British could not be proud of their standoff with China. In the early decades of the nineteenth century, British merchants had built a gigantic illegal business as drug dealers, selling Chinese buyers opium grown inexpensively in Turkey and India. By the 1840s, estimates claimed ninety percent of males under age forty in southern China were addicted. To put it mildly, "business activity was much reduced, the civil service ground to a halt, and the standard of living fell."[1] To crack down on British drug trade, the emperor dispatched a special emissary named Lin Tse-hsu to Canton (today's Guangzhou).[2] This official seized foreign factories, burned drugs, imprisoned merchants and closed the port city. Furious at these blows to their lucrative business, the British navy attacked the Chinese government forces to re-open their illegal trade. In this First Opium War, the Chinese were no match for the British who ended up controlling most of southern China by mid-1842. The Chinese government was made to sign harsh treaties and pay reparation to merchants whose drugs had been destroyed. They were also forced to open five "treaty ports," including Canton, where western merchants would be free of Chinese law, governed only by the laws of their native lands. China also formally ceded Hong Kong to the British, and was ordered to make even more favorable treaty terms at a future negotiation to take place in the next ten to twelve years.

It was the reluctance of the Chinese to engage in those follow-up negotiations, as well as a notorious trigger incident, that led to Lord Elgin's mission in 1857. The trigger event occurred in late October 1856, when Chinese officials seized a suspicious vessel named *Arrow*. That ship was previously registered as British at Hong Kong, but its paperwork had expired. Twelve of the crew were arrested as pirates, and the British flag was torn down and desecrated. In point of fact, without paperwork the *Arrow* was not British at the time, although the local British authorities feigned outrage, as if it had been. This led to a standoff with the shaky British position on one side, demanding apologies, and the Chinese, on the moral high ground, re-buffing them.

The downward spiral accelerated. To increase pressure, the British began a slow but continuous bombardment of the city of Canton. When no apology was forthcoming, they next occupied all forts protecting the city. Then an American ship was hit by Chinese fire, and the United States used that as an excuse to become actively engaged in the hostilities as well and took over other Chinese positions. The Chinese responded with guerrilla tactics, attacking the western fleets with fire-boats by night, taking and beheading hostages, and posting a bounty of $30 for each Western head brought in for redemption. They increased this reward to $100 per head as the situation continued to deteriorate. Describing the situation, Laurence wrote:

> The Chinese continued to kidnap, assassinate, seize steamers, and annoy us in sundry cunningly-devised methods. We continued to hunt them in creeks, burn villages where outrages had been committed, and otherwise pay them out to the best of our ability—not, it must be confessed, in a manner calculated to increase their terror for our arms, or their respect for our civilization.[3]

Attention back in London now became fixed on settling the impasse in the Far East. Laurence wrote, "Generals and officers of high rank were leaving town by each successive mail" and his new position must have seemed to Laurence a great opportunity to become part of the movement towards opening China—and even Japan—and to record the exploits of a most exciting adventure. Accompanied by a fighting force of 5,000 men, Laurence, Lord Elgin and his "special embassy" departed for the East in March of 1857. The British were also in full partnership on this expedition with the French, who had been enraged by the martyrdom of a French missionary, Father August Chapdelaine. That poor man had been arrested, beaten and locked in an iron cage at the door of his jail. He was, in fact, already dead when the Chinese beheaded him.

Laurence was one of many talented and aspiring young men swept up into the mission, although his position was not a formal one. He was not a junior diplomat, educated in the right schools and eager to climb up the ladder of his chosen profession. Instead he was the hand-picked personal secretary of Lord Elgin, the mission's leader, and a popular author, obviously in search of adventure and good material for his publishers. One of the young diplomats traveling with Laurence on the long voyage out to Asia was Henry Loch, later a distinguished colonial administrator. He remembered that while the junior staff members were making their introductions to each other aboard ship, Laurence turned their conversation to a discussion of spiritualism and "spirit-rapping," quite different from any topic such a group might be discussing normally. Laurence's lack of classroom learning also left huge gaps in his knowledge. For example, the same young fellow shipmates were very amused after Laurence borrowed a volume of Shakespeare—which was all new to him—and then appeared the next day exclaiming how good it was. But besides conversation and literature, Laurence also used his quiet times in early morning and late evening to continue his spiritual reading and letters home to his mother about his quest to find a path to lead him closer to the real Deity.

Interrupting Laurence's celestial pondering, real-world surprises met the British as their ships came into Asian waters, throwing the entire mission into question. Arriving at the southwestern tip of Ceylon, they heard the first news of mutinies among the native forces in India. At their next stop, they discovered more about the Indian atrocities and that news was grim. At the time of the revolt, the East India Company's private army combined 50,000 British and 200,000 Indians of mixed Muslim and Hindu religions. While there were several "causes" for the mutinous rebellion, new ammunition for 1853 Enfield rifles actually sparked the bloodshed. The guns used pre-greased paper cartridges. To fire them, the shooter had to bite off some of the tallow-greased paper, releasing the powder. Rumors spread that the grease was from either pork, offensive to Muslims, or beef, offensive to Hindus. Some enlightened British officials cautioned not issuing the cartridges to native troops until the rumors were investigated, but other commanders insisted on forcing the use of the cartridges, punishing resistors for disobeying orders.

In late March 1857, the first violence came when a soldier named Mangal Pandey shot at his Sergeant-Major on the Barrackpore parade ground outside Calcutta. He was restrained, court-martialed and hung on April 8. As further punishment, his entire regiment was shamed, stripped of uniforms and disbanded. Disgraced former soldiers returned home, seething from the insults.

Next, a few weeks later at the city of Meerut, Lieutenant Colonel George Carmichael-Smyth, "the unsympathetic commanding officer of the 3rd Bengal Light Cavalry," ordered 90 of his men to practice with the new ammunition. All except five refused. The 85 others were court-martialed and most were sentenced to ten years of hard labor. They were stripped of their uniforms and taken away to jail. The next day was Sunday, with British officers off-duty. There were rumors of a potential jailbreak but the British took no action. Then tensions exploded. Rebelling sepoys attacked the British housing quarters, killing men, women and children before busting the prisoners from jail. The same scene unfolded in the nearby town where Europeans were murdered as they relaxed in cafés or shopped at the bazaar. Overnight, revolting soldiers left for Delhi, only 40 miles away, and 50 more Europeans were killed. These mutineers also sought official recognition from the figurehead Mughal Emperor living there, and the rebellion continued to spread and gain strength throughout Northern India.

Lord Elgin could not have known these precise details, but he knew his fighting force of 5,000 men was already in Asian waters and could make a difference. He ordered many of the ships with his regiments diverted to India at once. Meanwhile, he and Laurence had to wait several weeks in Singapore for their new custom-built command ship *Furious*. This was a steam powered paddle wheel frigate, with full sailing rigging, over 200 feet long with 16 guns, including two on pivots on the upper deck. It sailed with 175 crew and was designed for Lord Elgin's mission because its size, technology and armaments would all make an impressive statement to the Chinese about the firepower behind the British.

While they were waiting, Laurence used the time to explore the Malay Peninsula, starting with the bustling port city of Singapore. Laurence was impressed with the industriousness of the resident "70,000 Chinamen... and not a single European who understands their language." He wrote:

> Every street swarms with long tails and loose trowsers; throughout whole sections of town are red lintels of door-posts covered with fantastic characters which betoken a Chinese owner. At early dawn the incessant hammering, stitching, and coblering commences, which lasts until nearly midnight; when huge paper lanterns, covered with strange devices, throw a subdued light over rows of half-naked yellow figures, all eagerly engaged in the legitimate process of acquiring dollars by the sweat of their brow.[4]

The son of the Malay ruler also invited Laurence to take a short excursion north into the mainland jungle to see its wonders first hand. Laurence would write his reports on this as a guidebook section for his armchair travelers reading his inevitable next book:

> It is a relief to escape from the slanting rays of the sinking sun, and dive into the dark recesses of the forest, where tall, limbless trees rise to a gigantic height, and weave their topmost branches into an impenetrable shade, while orchids five or six feet in diameter, cling like huge excrescences to the leafy roof... Occasionally troops of monkeys noisily swing themselves from branch to branch overhead, and birds of gaudy plumage glanced across our path.[5]

This forced tourist holiday ended when the *Furious* finally sailed into port ready to move them on into the action. First, Lord Elgin ordered a quick trip to China to assess the stalemate there. Laurence captured their first experience of Chinese scenery in both prose and sketchbooks as they steamed past villages destroyed by fighting—either by skirmishes between the British and Chinese—or between imperial soldiers and the many rebels active in the Taiping Rebellion which was ravaging the country at the time. In fact, Westerners did not have a monopoly on far-fetched religious revelations then since the Chinese civil war began when the rebel leader dreamed he was the lost brother of Jesus Christ. Twenty million souls would perish in that conflict—more than twenty-five times the 700,000 killed in the American Civil War a few years later.

Reaching the front lines, Lord Elgin interviewed the British forces holding the forts in the Canton River about three miles from the city. The British had held them about a year, but actual hostilities between the British and Chinese were at a standstill and the blockade had proved ineffectual at forcing any action. Nor could Lord Elgin add much impact now that most of his 5,000 troops had been directed towards the mutiny in India. As a result, Lord Elgin decided he would be more help in Calcutta supporting his friend, Governor-General Lord Canning, now even that city was at risk. He then ordered another of his larger ships, the *Shannon*, onward immediately to defend British India while he and Laurence followed close behind on the *Furious*.

Arriving in Calcutta, Lord Elgin and Laurence found an atmosphere of total panic. Lord Elgin's China forces were a godsend, coming well before other reinforcements could possibly arrive, and the fresh troops were immediately dispatched to Lucknow, where Europeans were under siege. The *Furious* was put to work bombarding, blockading and rescuing at key points of trouble. In Calcutta, Laurence wrote "almost every private house was an asylum for refugees," with more arriving daily with stories of narrow escapes. One of Laurence's housemates was a lady who had decided to leave her town at 9 p.m., fearing trouble, and "by 6 o'clock the next morning every man, woman and child in the place had been murdered." Remembering the scene in his later autobiography, Laurence wrote:

> The whole country seemed slipping from our grasp: Delhi and Agra were in the hands of the mutineers; an English garrison, with a numerous party of civilians, with ladies and children, were besieged in Lucknow, which Havelock had not yet succeeded in relieving; the solitary survivor of the Cawnpore massacre had only arrived two or three days before. He was pointed out to me one afternoon in awe-stricken tones by a friend.[6]

That survivor was Captain Mowbray Thomson who told how, in June 1857, sepoys besieged the European section of what is today the city of Kanpur. After three weeks, the Europeans were offered safe passage out of the town, but in confusion, firing broke out as they were boarding boats on the river, and most of the men were massacred. The surviving five men and about 250 women and children were then taken for confinement to a building called Bibigurh house. Conditions were dreadful. In one week, twenty-five bodies were dragged outside, dead from dysentery and cholera. On 15 July, word of an approaching relief force led to the decision to kill all the hostages. When the sepoys refused to do this, two Muslim butchers and three other men went inside and murdered everyone with knives and hatchets. "The walls were covered with bloody handprints and the floors littered with human limbs."[7] Then bodies, most dead but some living, were then crammed down a well until it was full, with others dumped into the River Ganges. Later, when the British re-took the town, they made the captured sepoys "lick the bloodstains from the walls and floor" before they were hung or strapped on the fronts of cannons and blown to pieces, the traditional Mughal punishment[8] for mutiny. These atrocities fueled the anger on both sides.

Meanwhile, in Calcutta, Lord Elgin was determined to ride out the storm. He stayed at Government House, advising and encouraging

Lord Canning, and Laurence came to dine with them there every day, passing gates guarded by native soldiers holding only ramrods since all of their actual rifles had been confiscated. Laurence wrote, "there was a universal sense of living on a volcano."

Slowly the crisis improved. After a month's stay, Lucknow was relieved by the aid of the China troops and Lord Elgin felt he could finally return to his own agenda. So he and Laurence left India, without the mission's original ships or troops, accompanied only by a small party on a commercial P&O steamer "chartered and fitted up for the accommodation of the embassy." They arrived back in Hong Kong two months after they had left China, and awaited a new reduced expeditionary force of 1,500 troops sailing from England to join them. Laurence was depressed at how the events in India diminished their own mission into insignificance. As he passed his days anchored on the ship, he wrote to his mother:

> I have one consolation, that you will be much more relieved thinking of me cooped up in a ship in harbor for the next three months, where there are neither women nor Chinese, than if I were doing anything else.[9]

His mother probably understood what he would be doing with women on shore and it is very telling that Laurence was comfortable making such a joke about it to her, but Laurence and Lady Maria seemed comfortable sharing any secrets with each other. In her letters to him, Laurence's mother chided him for his wanderings from her own set of beliefs, but it was too late by this time because he had already moved on to beliefs uniquely his own:

> I am a thorough Christian so far as my reverence for and belief in every moral principle Christ has propounded is concerned; but I am utterly opposed to the popular development of Christianity—indeed I think it quite inconsistent with His teaching. I never felt so deep an interest

in any subject, and am thankful for the leisure I have to think and read on it. (Ep I 211)[10]

When new troops from Britain finally arrived, Lord Elgin re-energized his mission. First, he delivered an ultimatum to the Chinese Commissioner at Canton that the many acts of hostility against the British, together with the refusal to fulfill treaty rights justified outright war. Without paid reparations and new adherence to the treaties, Elgin threatened the combined British, American and French forces would be forced to take Canton. Next, when the Chinese made "stubborn and unyielding" replies, the combined western forces assembled below the walls of the city and attacked. Laurence was glad of the action after many months of waiting and suffering through feelings of insignificance. With his usual total disregard for his own safety, he joined right in with the British troops storming the city walls:

> It was strange, for instance, in this nineteenth century to find one's self adopting the contrivances of a bygone age, and scaling walls by means of ladders in the face of the enemy. I do not know when I have felt a keener thrill of emotion than when we raced for the ladders at the taking of Canton, and clustered up them like bees, holding on to one another's legs, and nearly pulling each other down in the eager scramble... Then came the rush into the city, with its million of inhabitants, all crouching in terror...[11]

Despite the ferocity of the assault, the western forces did not encounter much resistance from the residents. In fact, it was becoming clear that there was a great capacity for the Chinese government to simply ignore the demands of the "Western barbarians" at the edges of their Celestial Kingdom. There was little rejoicing at their victory as Laurence and his British colleagues were not impressed by the city they now controlled:

The foulest odors assail the olfactories. The most disgusting sights meet the eye—objects of disease, more loathsome than anything to be seen in any other part of the world, jostle against you. Coolies staggering under coffins, or something worse, recklessly dash their loads against your shins; you suspect every man that touches you of an infectious disease; and the streets themselves are wet, slippery, narrow, tortuous and crowded.[12]

Early on, there was excitement when Commissioner Yeh, the local official they had been negotiating with, was caught trying to escape by climbing over his garden wall. Inside his house, the British found that none of their letters of demand or protestations had even been forwarded to the seat of government in Peking. There was also a memo of "lessons learned" from dealing with the Western barbarians at the end of the First Opium War, fourteen years before. It explained that the awkward intruders were "blindly unintelligent" and could be held at bay by deceit. In some cases, it advised, it was useful for "a direction (to) be given them without explanation of a reason why." In other cases "their restlessness can only be neutralized by demonstrations which dissolve their suspicions." Or at other time, "they have to be pleased, and moved to gratitude by concession of intercourse on a footing of equality." But all of these tactics were to be deployed simply with the express purpose of stalling and avoiding any real resolution of the issues.

Lord Elgin and his allied colleagues from America, France and Russia all agreed the only way to get attention in Peking was to move much closer to the capital. So the combined fleet sailed 760 miles northeastwards to Shanghai. Finding government officials there conveniently absent, the allies continued a further 595 miles north to attack the city of Tientsin (today's Tianjin), only 70 miles from Peking. The actual attack, Laurence remembered, was a somewhat "absurd" affair, although it provides another example of his absolute indifference to danger during hostilities, and his eagerness to experience excitement. The local residents had closed the huge gates to the city, but Laurence and two junior officers decided to sneak over a lower wall and attack the defenders from behind:

> We scrambled up unobserved, and, drawing our revolvers, suddenly dashed with loud yells upon the dense mass of people holding the gate on the inside. These, too panic-stricken to think of counting our numbers, and not knowing how many were behind us, fled in all directions, and we had quietly unbarred the gates and let in the troops before they had time to recover themselves. In this amusing operation not a shot was fired or a drop of blood spilled.[13]

At least the British had the attention of the Chinese government now, and after more months negotiating and maneuvering, accords for the freer flow of trade were tentatively reached, not only with Britain, but also between China and the United States, France and Russia, all of which signed their own versions of the so-called treaties of amity and peace of Tientsin.

After the treaty ceremony, Lord Elgin wisely decided they should remain in Asia to make sure the agreements were actually put in to action. That meant awaiting the arrival of five commissioners with whom they would hammer out implementation details and new tariffs. Since this would incur a hiatus of several weeks, it was decided that the British mission could make a brief side trip to nearby unknown Japan, especially since the Americans had recently succeeded in making brand new trade agreements there as well.

*

The distance between Shanghai and Nagasaki is only 450 miles, and they made a quick passage over a calm sea. After such a protracted period of disagreeable engagement with the deceitful Chinese, the

British were disarmed by the show of friendliness by the Japanese, who had been totally isolated from the outside world for over two hundred years. As the British sailed into the harbor at Nagasaki on the southwest tip of Japan, they moved freely past the point at which all foreign ships until recently had been required to stop. When they anchored, they were:

> boarded by a boat-load of Japanese officials, the novelty of whose appearance and costume detained us. They came crowding on the deck in the most easy, unembarrassed manner imaginable, smiling blandly, and affably talking Dutch, which, however, nobody on board understood.[14]

Soon after, the British came ashore at the factory settlement on the island in Nagasaki that had been the only piece of Japanese earth where Dutch, British and Chinese merchants were tolerated. There they met with the resident ex-patriate merchants, several of whom were Scottish, including Thomas Glover who later played an important role in this evolving story by helping Japanese students escape to study in the West. Now Lord Elgin learned all restrictions against the entry of foreigners into Japan had been recently removed. They were, quite simply, welcome to go wherever they pleased. Finally, Laurence's spirits rose as it looked like he would have a considerable "scoop" telling the story of the first unfettered British access to a virgin land. Excitedly, Laurence set out to explore the town and the contrast with Canton was dramatic:

> As we traversed its entire length, no foul odors assailed our nostrils, or hideous cutaneous objects offended our eyesight; nor did inconvenient walls or envious shutters debar us from inspecting as we passed along the internal economy of the shops and dwellings on each side. Light wooden screens, neatly papered, and running on slides, are for the most part pushed back in the daytime, and the passer looks through

the house, to where the waving shrubs of a cool-looking back garden invite him to extend his investigations. Between the observer and this retreat there are probably one or two rooms, raised about two feet from the ground; and upon the scrupulously clean and well-padded matting, which is stretched upon the wooden floor, semi-nude men and women loll and lounge, and their altogether nude progeny crawl and feast themselves luxuriously at ever-present fountains. The women seldom wear anything above their waists, the men only a scanty loincloth.[15]

They walked around all day enchanted and returned quite late to their ship for the first night. Then, true to the first information received, they were able to travel directly to the capital of Yedo (Tokyo), 600 miles away. In a matter of days, Lord Elgin was able to conclude and sign a treaty for freer trade and interaction between Britain and Japan. At its signing, Laurence wrote to his parents:

The commissioners were capital fellows, and so different from the Chinese, so full of animation and life, and very go-ahead. They are the most good-tempered people I ever met, and Japan is the only country I was ever in where there is no poverty and beggars are unknown. Much as I should hate going to China in any capacity, I would willingly go to Japan, and I am sure… you and papa would like it.[16]

Laurence was so smitten with the adventure and freshness of his Japanese experience that his book includes a long chapter on the history of Japan, including the alleged treachery of the sixteenth century Dutch in framing the missionaries as agents of evil, leading to massacres and the closing of the country two hundred and fifty years before. Next follows a travelogue of more than one hundred and forty pages, with minute observations on activities as diverse as shopping, visiting a riding school, going to a tea-house, using a bathing room and on the organization of prostitutes.

There can be no doubt Laurence's reporting on prostitutes was based on his personal research among them. The prostitutes were apparently as clean and well ordered as every other part of Japanese society and were divided into four levels, each with their own separate quarter of Yedo. Ladies in the highest rank lived in beautiful houses with servants and were expert in cooking, music and conversation. They were viewed universally as prime candidates for upper class matrimony, without any social stigma. Laurence also included a chapter speculating on the future of Japan and the West and cautioning his readers that care that must be taken to keep the relationship on a cordial footing.

As the British departed back to China in triumph, it was less clear to them that a Japanese civil war was looming over the very issue of opening up the country to the west. Two months after they left, they learned the Tycoon—who "is ostensibly the administrator of the empire"[17] in partnership with the spiritual leadership of the emperor or Mikado – had actually died while they had been in Yedo—possibly by his own hand over his welcoming policies towards the west. Perhaps the seeming friendliness they had encountered was only a façade to keep the Westerners at bay while plans for resistance could be made? Certainly, as the reader will find out, things were very different on Laurence's second visit to Japan two years later.

But meanwhile, the usual languor and delays attended implementation of the treaty with the Chinese. In fact, to test the general level of sincerity in the treaty for truly opening up the interior to trade, Lord Elgin insisted on going deep into China himself. The British traversed the Yang-tse-kiang river on a five-week journey. During that interlude, the British steamed past territories controlled by the rebel forces fighting against the government in the Taiping Rebellion, but generally found their right to passage was indeed open. Lord Elgin and Laurence even stopped to meet with the rebel leader, Hong Xiuquan, at his capital in Nanking. From approximately 1850 to 1864, he led his forces of the Taiping Heavenly Army against the unpopular ruling Manchu dynasty, in what would be the deadliest war of the nineteenth century.

However the rebellion was technically an unresolved domestic Chinese issue at the time, and Lord Elgin concluded real progress had been made in his own treaty with the established government, although he would discover its enforcement would require a second trip to China for him in 1860. So the China and Japan mission was satisfied enough to finally depart for home on March 4, 1859, more than two years after its mission had begun, yielding Laurence more than enough material for a good two-volume book.

*

His two years away had been the longest time Laurence had ever been separated from his parents, and both sides were eager for re-connection. However, one night during his long voyage home, the spirit of his father, Sir Anthony, appeared to him in a dream and told Laurence he had just died. Describing this vision to his traveling companions the next morning, Laurence was so upset that his friends took pains to belittle the dream, distract him and cheer him up. But the time had been noted, and when they came to the next port to collect mail, Laurence found his dream matched the exact evening of his father's sudden death. Sir Anthony and Lady Oliphant had gone to a London dinner party, seemingly in their usual good health, but Sir Anthony had suddenly dropped dead without warning.

The China mission arrived back in England on May 7, 1859, landing at Plymouth. Distraught with their loss, both Lady Oliphant and Laurence only became closer than ever when they reunited. While they grieved they turned in desperation to the abundant world of spiritualists and mediums around London at the time. They made several unsuccessful attempts to contact Sir Anthony on the other side, which Laurence found pathetic and fraudulent. However their real interest continued as they sought out more information and conversations about spiritualism with their friends. Laurence had heard about one new series of lectures that Spring of 1859 that was attracting attention in London. Some of Lady Oliphant's friends had also gone to hear some of them. Laurence and his mother decided to find out more, although at the time they could not know how contact with the lecturer, Thomas Lake Harris, would eventually transform their lives.

*

One of the rising stars in the American spiritualist firmament, Thomas Lake Harris had an interesting career along the way to his 1859 lectures in London. He was born at Fenny Stratford, Buckinghamshire, England, on May 15 1823 and at age five moved with his family to a lonely childhood in the "burnt out" corner of western New York State. Harris's beloved mother died when he was nine – something he never got over — and he got along poorly with his stepmother and his father. To escape these less than welcoming realities, the young Harris turned inward and grew up bookish and self-studying.

Feeling outcast, he first became attracted to the comfort of Universalism, with its worldview that God was "the loving parent of the widespread family of man." Craving a more personal connection with this all-powerful parental force, his first epiphany came in 1841, at age eighteen, when he returned from an autumn stroll and found his room "illuminated with a soft moonlight radiance, full of the sparkles of invisible gems." In the center of this light, the spirit of his dead mother, Annie Lake,[18] appeared and spoke to him. This was the first of many visions and spirit interactions that would continue throughout his life, the most powerful always involving celestial females.

Growing in confidence, Harris left his parents to study theology with a Universalist minister and his family, who were nice enough to show kindness to a callow, scholarly young man. They remembered him in these early days around 1843:

> He used to be at our house every evening – a quiet, bashful, unassuming young man, of very delicate physique, and in very delicate health— looking indeed, a half-starved young fellow. Yet, when alone in the study with [the minister] and myself, he showed a great deal of vivacity, even brilliancy, of conversational gifts.[19]

The Universalists taught Harris theology, and helped him get opportunities to earn a few dollars each Sunday preaching poetical sermons to Universalists around western New York. He also contributed verse to Universalist publications, including the annual *Rose of Sharon* and *The Ladies' Repository* magazine. He spent time in Boston and, by 1845, was married and settled in New York City, for twenty months, as pastor at the Fourth Universalist Church. He was becoming more confident of his instincts, and he began enjoying a growing reputation.

By 1848, at the time of the Foxes' rappings, Harris came under the influence of Andrew Jackson Davis, a kindred spirit a few years his junior, who claimed to be clairvoyant and able to receive communications from the spirit of the dead Swedenborg.[20]

Harris became an enthusiastic disciple, buying into the belief that spiritualism was "an enlargement of natural science and philosophy, regarding it as the basis of a new social order in which human powers and institutions would be carried to perfection." He evangelized this view as a traveling preacher for several months, but when he next saw Davis, he was shocked to find his prophet at the center of a "free love" scandal having sex with a married woman. Purity-minded Harris then broke with Davis and continued his own more pious spiritual pursuits.

Harris's beliefs were coming into sharper focus. As a first filter, Harris made an affirmation of Christianity, believing in a real heaven, and an equally real hell, with Christ as the essential advocate for mankind between good and evil. So, whatever his beliefs were to become – and they were to become very strange – he was fundamentally Christian. Next, he divided the spiritual landscape into two areas. In the first realm were earthly spirits, who were inherently mischievous, malicious and evil. Pure and benign celestial spirits lived in the second realm with the Deity. These beings, he believed, could ultimately lead man back to the position lost at the fall of Adam, and then on through to the end of this world and a new paradise where mankind would be restored to the company of angels. He was determined to rise above the interference of the pesky earthly spirits and spend more time in the celestial realm.

In 1850 he had an important spiritual episode when an angel appeared to him holding an open book from which, he was told, much would be revealed. The same vision was repeated many times, deepening his confidence that he was embarking on a special journey of continued revelation from the celestial world beyond. About this time, his wife died during the birth of his third child. He saw her spirit ascending to heaven at her death, and her spirit visited him frequently after this.

It was becoming clear that the ever-evolving Harris could not be contained within the tame tenets of any mainstream churches of the time, and he rejected the Universalism that had trained him up and given him the title "Reverend." He needed to be his own man, and in the early 1850's, he increased his travel around the Eastern and Southern United States.

With the mania around manifestations of the spirit world intensifying, Harris took an important turn away from the crowd. Not content with interacting with dime-a-dozen spirits terrorizing farm families like the Foxes of Hydesville by making noises or moving furniture around, he put himself on a much higher trajectory. He began to establish an other-worldly rapport with the beings in the topmost echelon of the spirit world. He sought out connections not with just spirits, but angels; not just with angels, but archangels; and not just archangels, but perhaps even something much, much higher. This began the "Apostolic" phase of the spiritualism movement, where a tiny few claimed to be the vehicles for revelations directly from God to mankind.

Now Harris needed to get away from the tabloid sensationalism of lowlier spiritualists, and a good opportunity soon presented itself. A New York City minister named J. L. Scott was convinced he had established a direct connection, not just with spirits, but with the Deity himself. Scott had been based most recently in "burnt-out" Auburn, New York, near Syracuse, where the fast-growing circles of rappers, dancers, speakers, pointers and other characters intent on sharpening their otherworldly skills probably did not appreciate his claim to be connected directly to the Deity. Then, in a revelation from on high, Scott announced he had received the order to re-locate to a more private haven in Mountain Cove, Fayette County, West Virginia. About one hundred people followed him there, to live in a shared community, with promises of housing, jobs, schools and salvation for all. This tribe settled in Mountain Cove, leasing property and dividing it in the fall of 1851. Unfortunately, even with Scott's daily face-to-face audiences with God, they were not able to "make rent" by February 1852. Ownership was returned to the landlord, and at the low point for the community, Scott was told, in another revelation, that he should journey up to New York City in search of new blood and new funding. There he found Thomas Lake Harris, now head of the well-heeled congregation of the Church of the Good Shepherd, and ready for something new.

Harris gathered up some of his own supporters and, in the spring of 1852, relocated to Mountain Cove as co-leader with Scott. The leases were renewed in May, and the community continued to evolve. Members "established a church, two stores, a mill and a school for their children."[21] They published a newspaper called the *Mountain Cove Journal and Spiritual Harbinger*. Unhappy and contentious members were sent away, and both Scott and Harris became the dual disciples of the Deity. They announced their minds had been blended by God to give consistent direction to all the others. Everyone else was told to cease any spiritual or medium-like activities of their own, because these could become openings for the omnipresent earthbound evil spirits and demons to interfere with the true divine plan. In addition, the house Harris and Scott lived in was to be separated into a separate lease, paid for by the other members as the "Gateway to Heaven" on earth.

The effect of these edicts, and the financial burdens placed on their few followers, were unsupportable for the settlers in Mountain Cove, many of whom also wanted to explore their own spiritual gifts in spite of the alleged evil spirits. By the beginning of 1853, the community disbanded and Harris was back in New York City. Although Mountain Cove had been a fiasco, he managed to escape the experience relatively undamaged and now was certainly more knowledgeable about how *not* to run a successful spiritual colony.

As the interest and manifestation of all things otherworldly continued to spread, respected and resourceful observers of the phenomena came together as a kind of brains trust in New York City. A newspaper was started in May 1852 called *The Spiritual Telegraph*,[22] to bring authoritative reporting to the movement. The editor was Reverend Samuel Byron Brittan, a respected minister with personal experience of trances and visions, and a dedicated spiritualist. Also active in running the paper was Charles Partridge, another respected New York businessman—the proprietor of a very large match factory—and a spiritualist.

Harris became a frequent visitor to the offices of the *Spiritual Telegraph* and Partridge and Brittan became his first publishers. A

Universalist at the time remembered Harris had "in a wonderful degree the gift of improvising" and could spontaneously compose and recite verses for hours at a time. Indeed, Harris embarked on an ambitious publishing schedule that would rival Laurence's own growing catalog. His first three books, published by Partridge and Brittan between1854 and 1856, were all collections of poetry dictated by Harris in a trance-like state.

The first of these, *Epic of a Starry Heaven*, is surrounded up front by an introduction from publisher Brittan, and at back by appendices about the strange circumstances of its composition. Apparently the book unfolded as a collection of poems recited during successive trances over fourteen consecutive days in during November and December 1853. Specifically, the dictation came in 22 separate sessions, each of which produced between 125 and 250 lines. Every word was written down by Partridge, who also timed each session. Observers described Harris as he delivered the poem:

> There was a slight involuntary action of the nerves of motion, chiefly manifested at the beginning and close of each sitting, or during brief intervals of silence, when some new scene appeared to the vision of the medium. The eyes were closed, but the expression of the face, which was highly animated and significant, varied with every change in the rhythm and was visibly influenced by the slightest modification of the theme. The voice of the speaker was deep-toned and musical, and his enunciation distinct and energetic. Occasionally he exhibited considerable vehemence, but when the nature of the subject required gentleness, his voice was modulated with great delicacy, and at times his whole manner and utterance were characterized by remarkable solemnity and irresistible pathos.

The poem's sections do not tell a story, but instead share a series of revelations made during Harris's Swedenborgian-like journey around the planet territories in the heavens accompanied, apparently, by the spirit of Dante. They visit locations such as "the Seventh Spiritual Sphere of Earth, and the Electrical Ocean of the Solar System between Earth and Mars." Here are some of the sights on Jupiter:

> I see a company of angel-men,
> And angel women 'sociate with them;
> White sheep in fields of ether star the meads
> Of chrysolite. Each flock a woman feeds
> With silver lilies, which all radiant grow
> In spiral pathways, where her bright feet glow.
>
> Pale moon-flowers, azure veined, ope crimson lips.
> Birds drink their nectar. Each one, as it sips,
> Draws rapture from sweet fragrance, and upsoars
> Buoyant and warbling to celestial shores.[23]

More of the same sort of visions and revelations were shared in his second book, *A Lyric of the Morning Land*, also published in 1854. But this was not just a celestial travelogue, as in the earlier Epic. Importantly it includes one vision in which Harris meets the female half of his own being, born at the same moment as he, but resident in the celestial realm, separated from him on earth. Her name is Lily, Queen of Lilistan. From the moment of that meeting, his life would be driven by efforts to re-join her and quite literally bind with her to become the original "two-in-one." By doing so, he would show the way for all mankind to restore themselves to union with the divine, something taken away from humanity at the fall of Adam. After this, many of Harris's poems describe further visions of Lily and reports on their exploits.

By standards of the time, Harris's poetry was actually rather good. Stylistically, some reviewers remarked on the similarities between Harris's verse and the work of the dead poet Percy Bysshe

Shelley. Unfortunately, assertions by Harris supporters that its lines were indeed given to Harris by the dead Shelley's spirit dampened enthusiasm for them as literature, but with his three new books, Harris enjoyed a popular following and growing income. In 1855, he married again, to Emily Isabella Waters, who had a lively belief in fays and faeries populating this world. She was to remain with him for the next thirty years before being committed to an insane asylum.

Publisher Brittan encouraged Harris to continue on his path of "self revelation" and the evolving spiritualist embraced that way with zeal. After meeting Lily in heaven, Harris abandoned dictating poetry in trances, as in his first three books. He began to spend significant time with Lily in the spirit world—usually at night—and to publish descriptions of activities there. His popularity as a published poet and minister dampened a bit as more and more people learned the somewhat wacky inspiration for his writing and his self-revealed eccentric beliefs—yet he was eloquent and charismatic enough to keep publishing and make several speaking tours around the United States. He was an excellent speaker and, in person, cultivated an otherworldly demeanor. In particular, his eyes could morph from quiet limpid pools to fierce daggers of intensity in an instant, to startling and hypnotic effect, showing glimpses of the fires within.

By 1857, when Laurence was setting off for Asia with Lord Elgin, the nature of Harris's beliefs and his degree of self-confidence were evolving again. In New York City, members of the Christian Spiritualist intelligentsia were breaking into two distinct camps. Both found inspiration in the works of Swedenborg, but the first group, led by Henry James Sr., saw those writings as most valuable for focusing man on the spiritual realms of thought and affection, leading to a heaven of brotherly love which could save man from the hell of materialism and pre-occupation with selfhood. The second group, however, saw the writings of Swedenborg as simply first stage revelations. They believed updated second stage ones and interactions with "the other side" were about to arrive for those chosen to receive and report them.

Harris eagerly positioned himself as the leader of the second group. He decided to break with spiritualists Brittan and Partridge who had published his poems. New revelations came to him then, but at the same time, he had been beset by a terrible physical struggle. Writing about it later, he believed he was being tested and literally tortured by the demons on the earthly spiritual plain. These evil creatures were everywhere and came at him continually from all sides. He wrote in the introduction to his poem *Song of Satan* "I knew what it was to die daily." Here is his description of the last of many attacks which occurred while he was going about mundane daily business in New York:

> While in a place of business in a lower part of the city, the most powerful
> of these Infernals, with some heavy instrument, smote me upon the
> head and gave a fiendish and exhultant shout after accomplishing his
> end.[24]

Literally staggering from the blow, Harris felt a growing sense of paralysis and oncoming death. At that moment, through sheer force of will, he managed to pray earnestly to the Lord for deliverance. Apparently, this was the culmination of his testing, and finally, by direct divine intervention, the Lord stepped in and Harris was saved. He wrote he came to his senses suddenly and "found myself in the house of a dear friend," not knowing how he got there   Reflecting later, he believed all the trials he endured fighting these evil spirits, and his divine rescue, constituted an "initiation" into a new "celestial degree of sight." That day began a new phase of easy celestial access for Harris and he found he could rise easily above the distractions of the earth-bound demons and enter into the celestial world at will to interact with the spirits there.

Warming to this topic, Harris wrote how, walking in the celestial realm, he came across a group of spirits in assembly—and was invited by the spirit of Socrates to join them. Plato was there, as well as Swedenborg himself, who also joined the conversation and spoke warmly to him. In this ongoing vision, Harris was lectured on various topics by angels, and apparently completed some sort of celestial curriculum that elevated him enough to be made a priest in the new world order. He was congratulated in this new role by the spirit of Swedenborg and then told by an angel to "go no more among spiritualists." The spiritualists, it seems, had been infiltrated by the evil earthbound spirits and were preaching and publishing untruths dangerous to the future of mankind. Swedenborg then told Harris to move on from Swedenborg's own earthly body of work to update the revealed word of God with a newer version. Indeed, the spirit told Harris his new writings should even be endorsed and published on earth under the sponsorship of the Swedenborg Society.

When he returned from his trance, Harris started to preach to the Swedenborgians, presenting himself as a self-ordained minister in their Church of the New Jerusalem. These new revelations alienated both the spiritualists and the American Swedenborgians as the first were told they were misleading believers having been tricked by demons, and the second were told Harris was simply taking over from Swedenborg with new and improved revelations from heaven, all with the specific blessing and support of the dead Swedenborg himself. This did not go down well with the conservative Swedenborgians faithful to their traditional prophet, who saw Harris as a blasphemous interloper. Since Harris was rejected by both groups, the small circle of his own ardent supporters clustered ever more tightly around him, accepting his declarations and believing him to be a divine messenger.

At this time, his supporters were centered in New York City's Greenwich Village in a congregation called the Church of the Good Shepherd, which held its services at the chapel of New York University in Washington Square. Members included Mr. and Mrs. Horace Greeley and life-long Harris followers Jane Lee Waring and James A. Requa. Harris's travels around the southern states also created pockets of followers for him at the Church of the Messiah in Griffin, Georgia, headed by Alfred Buckner, and at the Church of the Divine Humanity in New Orleans led by Reverend George W. Christy who also was making frequent visits to the celestial realm.

Then one day in early 1859, while the salvos in the American dogmatic argument continued, Harris was visited by an angel who essentially told him the celestial plan was for him for go immediately to England, for a change of scene. Coinciding with this revelation, he then received an invitation from Garth Wilkinson and the British Swedenborg Society to preach in London. Probably neither Wilkinson nor his London-based society had heard of Harris's latest pronouncements usurping Swedenborg's place of honor. At any rate, Harris sailed with his wife for England on May 5, 1859, starting the fateful trip on which he was to meet the Oliphants.

Thomas Lake Harris at 63 years old.

CHAPTER 4

UNEASY IN LONDON

During the years Laurence was with Lord Elgin's mission in Asia, Harris consolidated his dedicated following into a congregation in New York City, edited the *The Herald of Light: A Monthly Journal of the Lord's New Church*, and published several more books. Now, in Spring 1859, he was invited to lecture in England by Dr. Garth Wilkinson, a distinguished physician, homeopath and free thinker who had also translated work of Emanuel Swedenborg (1688-1772)[1] from Latin to English for the first time, making the 18th century master's thinking more accessible to interested Victorians. Besides sponsoring Harris, Wilkinson was just the sort of open-minded authority who would have been attractive to the Oliphants as a respectable seeker after truth, in contrast to the theatrical spiritualists who had already disappointed them.

In May 1859, Harris was staying with Wilkinson in Hampstead and about to begin lecturing under the sponsorship of the British Swedenborg Society, a well-endowed and respectable New Church organization with an impressive headquarters and bookstore in the West End of London.[2] Harris was also arranging British publication of several of his written works, all of which had been well received in America. His lectures were eagerly anticipated because of the decade of reporting from the United States about the miraculous activities of the American mediums such as the Fox family. Spiritualist interest in Britain was a bit more restrained, but nonetheless genuine. The lectures also coincided with Laurence and his newly widowed mother trying to re-connect with the spirit of Sir Anthony after his father's death. But none of those séances worked. Laurence was drifting uneasily after his trip to China and Japan with Lord Elgin, writing up his notes into his future book about the mission and privately becoming more and more desperate to find some worthwhile alternative to his seemingly pointless life. Since he was well acquainted with Garth Wilkinson, Laurence could have very well have gone along to hear some of Harris's earliest lectures.

Those attending got more than they bargained for in the electrifying presence of Thomas Lake Harris, a charismatic prophet who quickly became counted more a performer than a spiritualist. Years later, Laurence wrote a novel about a fictional prophet named Mr. Masollam, based on Harris. Here is what he said about the great man's face to the world:

> There was a remarkable alternation of vivacity and deliberation about the movements of Mr. Masollam. His voice seemed pitched in two different keys, the effect of which was, when he changed them, to make one seem a distant echo of the other—a species of ventriloquistic phenomenon which was calculated to impart a sudden and not altogether pleasant shock to the nerves of the listeners. When he talked with what I may term his "near" voice, he was generally rapid and vivacious; when he exchanged if for his "far off" one, he was solemn and impressive... His brow was overhanging and bushy, and his eyes were like revolving lights in two dark caverns, so fitfully did they seem to emit flashes, and then lose all expression... Those rapid contrasts were calculated to arrest the attention of the most casual observer, and to produce a sensation which was not altogether pleasant when first

one made his acquaintance... He might be the best or the worst of men.[3]

On the evening of May 23 1859, Harris was introduced to London as the second speaker of the evening at the Music Hall in Bedford Square. He "took the chair amidst the enthusiastic greetings of the audience." Apparently, he then delivered his remarks *ad lib*—as an extemporized trance speech—and the reviewer of the British *Spiritualist Telegraph* wrote "the audience was as it were electrified by his deep-soul utterance."[4] The review ended with the heartfelt wish that Harris would soon let them all hear more.

Soon Harris was speaking on a regular schedule at the Marylebone Institute off of Portman Square on Sundays from May 29, with words at the 11 a.m. morning service and again in the evening at 6 p.m. Although the experience was apparently riveting, it is very interesting that another review published on June 15 could not actually summarize what the great man had said:

We are quite unable to give an idea to our readers, who were not present, of the wondrous flow of soul which characterized both the prayers and the discourses... and when we add that the whole was actually an improvisation, and that even the texts from which he preached were only given to him spiritually a few minutes before he began the discourse, we hardly add to the marvel.[5]

Laurence had been reading and pondering the entire religious landscape alone, as a solitary student, trying to clarify his own place in the spiritual world. His only discussion of his thinking had been in his endless letters to his mother. As a result, it would have been a considerable shock for him to encounter the charismatic and almost hypnotic prophet Thomas Lake Harris, speaking on stage about his powerful vision of celestial truth, and claiming to be exploring the very real celestial world in the company of various senior spirits and archangels.

Furthermore, Harris was declaring that events in the spirit world were gathering momentum and reaching a critical point which would shortly bring the end of the world and usher in a new world order. The many miseries of the world, such as the Crimean War, the Indian Mutiny, China's Taiping Rebellion and the looming hostilities of the American Civil War were all manifestations of the chaos surrounding the end. All of this had been revealed to Harris in his visions and visits to the other side, where he had seen that humanity was being misled by the popular notions and spiritual manifestations, which were in truth the works of evil spirits and demons intent on interfering with God's divine plan.

Perhaps a less desperate and more traditionally educated mind would have dismissed such claims as fantasy. But, at this particular moment, and when delivered in person by such a confident and convincing force as Harris, it was not surprising that yearning young Laurence could be won over to believe it all—and that his distraught widowed mother Lady Oliphant might eventually also believe, with her son's encouragement, that she might find the peace she was looking for with Harris's protection, guidance and teachings as well.

Meanwhile, Laurence pressed Dr. Garth Wilkinson for a personal introduction to the private and secluded Harris. Wilkinson resisted, as the physician later said, "with the expressed opinion that the acquaintance was not for Oliphant's good," sensing it could be dangerous to match such a willing follower to an almost maniacal leader.[6] Nevertheless, not to be put off from such a deeply desired connection, Laurence went over on his own to where Harris had taken rooms on Queen's Terrace in the St. Johns Wood section of London, perhaps fittingly not far from the London Zoo. Reportedly, Laurence spent considerable time pacing back and forth in front of the great man's lodgings before finally getting enough nerve to knock on the door to make his introduction. He was indeed received by the hard-to-approach celestial explorer. Harris probably realized Laurence represented a possible entry point for reaching far deeper into the elite British society than the officers of the Swedenborg Society. No doubt, Harris heard out the effusions of his enthusiastic new fan. But the prophet probably also judged he should take his time assessing just how stable this young man was, given he was so desperate to come on board with Harris's celestial mission, as if it was just another of Lord Elgin's expeditions to remote earthbound territories. Harris knew that the Oliphants would have to be handled very carefully, so he allowed the connection with them to begin cautiously, and he went on to incubate their growing bonds with him with great care.

After his first series of lectures, Harris decided a period of John-the-Baptist-like isolation would be best for him to contemplate his next moves, and he retired into seclusion at a farmhouse near Bolton Abbey in Yorkshire for the summer of 1859. In October, he emerged for a few months to preach at the Mechanics Institute in Manchester, and then in December began a second lecture series back in London, emphasizing "personal regeneration by the Divine Breath"—an advanced state that could be achieved by very deep meditative breathing. He also announced a great change was about to take place in society, as human life was about to open to a new degree of interaction with the spiritual and celestial realms, culminating in a new age.

With the new lectures in London, it became clear to British audiences that the way-out content of Harris's lectures did not represent mainstream American beliefs, nor did it resonate with any version of reform thinking, spiritualism or Swedenborgian discussions currently underway in England. In fact, he was viewed as a curiosity, albeit a very eloquent and impassioned one. When Harris warned of the "abuses" of spiritualism involving the demonstration of "physical phenomena" such as the rapping, table tipping and finger pointing movement of furniture then popular in local séances, James Grant, the editor of the *Morning Advertiser*—a newspaper second only to *The Times* in its circulation—reported that the lecture was "an extraordinary and triumphant exposure of Spiritualism," and gloated that the charlatanism had been exposed. The February 1860 edition of the *Spiritual Magazine* then responded that Harris was only exposing "abuses," and that there continued to be truly useful and real spiritualistic activities underway as well, and a fairly acrimonious journalistic debate then ensued between the two sides. Amid the publicity, it was about this time that Laurence made the first mention of Harris in his letters to his mother, urging her to check with an acquaintance she knew well—Miss Emily Fawcett, one of the Oliphant family's oldest and closest friends—who could give her reliable reports about Mr. Harris.

While the pro-spiritualist forces tried to defend their foggy ground, the British Swedenborgians were also furious at the claim that the spirit of the dead Swedenborg himself had inaugurated Harris as their new leader—and that Harris expected their own Swedenborg Society to pay for publishing his blasphemous writings. As all these discussions filled the spring and early summer of 1860, the enraged Chairman of the British Swedenborg Society discovered his own headquarters bookshop was selling Harris's books and he had them all thrown out.[7] The proprietor of the bookshop, William White, was then served with legal papers to evict him both from the shop and from his lodgings above it. The Society even hired officers from the Society for the Suppression of Vice to forcibly take over the shop, which must have been a welcome change from their regular activities combating prostitution and pornography. Not to be outdone, the evicted bookseller Mr. White responded by hiring the well known prize fighters, Jem Mace and Jem Dillon, "together with several of their associates," to take back the shop by throwing the vice officers out into the street in a well-publicized melee, and re-establishing Mr.

White. That fracas was finally settled in December 1860 when the courts ruled Mr. White could have two months in which to gather up his possessions and leave the Swedenborg shop and rooms in an orderly manner. Besides the troubles of Mr. White, Garth Wilkinson's own brother was fired as the Secretary of the British Swedenborg Society as well.

Somewhat shaken by these reactions to his 1860 London lecture series, Harris lived in Scotland for the first part of 1861, where he converted more followers and reached some additional new conclusions, propelled by the conviction that "right breathing"—or "open breathing"—would lead him to the "Divine breath," also more familiarly known as the Holy Ghost or Holy Spirit.[8] In particular, he believed the isolation he had experienced in Yorkshire was part of the formula for future success. He decided that a community—a Brotherhood of the New Life—rather than a church with congregation, should be his preferred environment, where he could be separated from the distractions of the world, and be surrounded by supportive like-minded followers, all pursuing the divine breath.[9] So late spring 1861, he received divine direction to return to America. It had been revealed to him "the Anakim," the sorcerers of the last age[10] before the deluge, were intent on causing the breakup of civil society in Europe and America. He wrote "they seek to inaugurate a reign of blood such as the world has never seen."

At this point, as the shocks of the American Civil War began unfolding, Harris's evolved spiritual beliefs had three central elements, all revealed to him by his self-study, visions and reflection. First was the bi-sexual nature of the Deity. Although fundamentally Christian, Harris believed that even the apostles, who were Christ's closest disciples, had misunderstood the true nature of God. Scriptures came to refer to the Deity by the pronoun "He," when in fact half of that Being was the Divine Feminine. Discovering and connecting with that lost mother—and wife—was the driving force of Harris's future religious and sexual passion.

Second, he now knew mankind had been deprived of the means of connecting with the celestial realm when the gift of respiration, or divine breathing, was lost at the fall of Adam. As a result, mankind was only aware of two spheres—body and soul—when, in fact, there was a vast third "celestial" world, populated with countless faeries, spirits, angels—as well as the Male-Female Deity itself—with whom communications had been lost. Through re-discovering the correct form of respiration, Harris believed Man could reconnect with the celestial world, and experience the divine infusion of the Holy Spirit, or Holy Ghost, and resume a direct link to God. Harris himself believed that he had started on the seven-stage path[11] of regaining these powers of respiration during what he announced had been a three-year cycle over the years from 1857 to 1860.

Thirdly, on the other side in the celestial realm, every right-breathing man and woman had a spirit counterpart of the opposite sex, from whom they had been separated at birth, and with whom they must join and unify to achieve the true "two-in-one" state of fulfillment, becoming half-male and half-female again themselves, leading to ecstasy and reunion with the bi-une God. And, when the time was right, these spiritual counterparts would actually descend down to earth and live here with the chosen survivors signaling the end of the world. Then the vile and unworthy would disappear during a time of rapture, and the chosen would live in eternal bliss in a new life together with their reunited missing halves in the new world order.

But Harris also knew achieving this heavenly state would not be easy. Evil spirits and demons were everywhere, and were, in fact, the architects of every woe experienced on the nineteenth century earth. The battlefields of the American Civil War and other wars, the slums of Europe, afflictions such as syphilis, and all manner of suffering, were caused by these agents of evil. Standing up to them, regaining lost ground, and ultimately triumphing over them would be a herculean, almost impossible challenge. But over time, Harris came to believe that this very redemption was his own sacred task, and that he was "the pivotal man" who would set everything right.

Harris was preparing to embark on a great new adventure, retiring from the world into a new utopian community called Brotherhood of the New Life, which he planned to start in New York State. There would be no partner for "blended minds" as he had tried before with Reverend Scott in the ill-fated Mountain Cove community. He would be the only undisputed leader and prophet. And importantly, the Brotherhood would behave practically enough to avoid any of the money problems that dogged other utopian communities. The idea was to become self-sufficient agriculturally through healthy hard work—and even achieve prosperity in business ––while also exploring the limits of the spirit world and preparing for the imminent end of the world.

Angels told him to get on with his mission. In May 1861, on returning to New York City, Harris announced in *The Herald of Light* publication that he was essentially retiring from his public writings and ministries to let his understanding of the newly revealed cosmos continue to unfold, in what would become a second three-year cycle, from 1861 to 1864. During that time, he would reach a kind of equilibrium appropriate for ushering in the new world. He would achieve this by studying and introducing a healthy degree of physical "natural industry" to balance his mental and spiritual pursuits.[12] Essentially, he told his wealthy New York City congregation he was leaving town, and he invited several of them to go with him.

*

Meanwhile, after his first meeting with Harris, Laurence pondered his new prophet's teachings while he and his mother continued to mourn. He also kept himself busy earning money with his writing and reporting while trying hard to obtain a diplomatic post. At the end of December, 1859, he finished his new book *Narrative of the Earl of Elgin's Mission to China and Japan in the Years 1857, '58, '59*. It quickly became a best seller. Meanwhile, while he was waiting for official job opportunities, he continued taking on reporting assignments, not too far from his widowed mother at home, funded jointly by the Foreign Ministry and various publications eager for on-site coverage of European trouble spots.

On his first trip, he visited the city states being amalgamated into what was to become modern Italy so he could report back on the evolving situation to London. He met General Garibaldi for a lengthy interview and was invited to accompany him on a planned raid against the ballot places in Nice where a referendum was being held on the transfer of Nice to France from Italy as a payment to allow other areas of French influence to be formally ceded to the new Italy. That raid was eventually abandoned due to more pressing concerns for Garibaldi in Sicily, and Nice's peaceful transition to France proceeded uninterrupted. Laurence always regretted not going along with the general to the action in Sicily where Garibaldi won a great victory over the army of the entrenched Bourbon monarchy in spite of his unusual battlefield tactic of making a bayonet charge uphill.

Instead of following Garibaldi, however, Laurence continued on with a visit to tiny Montenegro and wrote up an amusing story of being given a room in a kind of lodging house for special guests in the small town of Cettinje. He was enjoying his dinner served on top of a chest in his room, when he was interrupted by "a stalwart Montenegrin, looking magnificent in his national costume."[13] After a polite speech, which Laurence could not understand, other than its gentlemanly delivery, the dishes had to be briefly removed from the top of the chest, allowing the visitor to reach in and retrieve a significant bag of gold, one of many left inside filling the chest to the brim. The table setting was then restored and Laurence's meal resumed. The next morning he learned the chest was in fact the treasury of Montenegro and his visitor had been its chancellor of the exchequer.

Highly readable and amusing articles on these visits earned him good money, widened his reading audience, and gave him some slight direction for his work. But now he was glad to win his first official diplomatic position from the government as First Secretary of Britain's new Legation in Japan. Lord John Russell, the Foreign Minister, had recommended Laurence for the post in a letter to Queen Victoria herself. And so Laurence headed back to Asia in early 1861, just two years after leaving.

He found the region much troubled. In China the Taiping Rebellion continued, while the British and French were still struggling with the government to enact the treaties of Tien-tsin which Lord Elgin had signed in 1858. In fact, it had been a new Chinese atrocity that led to Laurence's job opportunity. In October 1860, British representatives were taken prisoner while in a Chinese military camp, negotiating in good faith. Under severe pressure from the British, most were soon returned, but others were kept in the custody of a traveling troop of Tartars. Several were tortured by being neglected in cages and bound up too tightly, so their skin broke, their wounds became infected—and then infested with bugs—and they died horribly. One of these was a Mr. de Norman, on loan to the China mission from his official post in Japan, and Laurence's new position was to be his replacement.

Laurence arrived in Japan at the end of June 1861, and joined the small band of British diplomats stationed at the capital on the park-like grounds of a temple in the Shinagawa suburb of Tokyo. The welcoming attitudes of the past had totally disappeared and resentment towards the Westerners ran high throughout the city. As a result, 150 Japanese guards assigned by the government protected the compound. Even so, the delegation's housing was not particularly secure, since the open construction of the buildings created inside rooms separated only by flimsy sliding paper panels. None of the British traveled outside the grounds without a bodyguard of twenty to thirty mounted Japanese escorts. The many troops of "Lonins" around town posed special danger. Laurence describes these as:

> … an outlaw class, the retainers or clansmen of Daimos [feudal Lords] who, having committed some offence, have left the service of their prince, and banding themselves together form a society of desperadoes, who are employed often by their old chiefs, to whom they continue to owe a certain allegiance, for any daring enterprise by which, if it fails, he is not compromised, while if they succeed in it, they have a chance of regaining their position.[14]

Laurence later thought the beauty and seeming peacefulness of the temple grounds allowed a false sense of security to pervade the delegation. On the night of July 5, he stayed up late to watch a comet, turning in after midnight. A dog he had recently befriended was sleeping across his threshold, but soon began barking furiously. Laurence awoke and heard the muffled sounds of struggle very near at hand. He got up and tried to arm himself for a likely fight. Unfortunately, his servant had cleaned his pistol earlier in the day and returned it to its locked storage box without giving him back its key. The only weapon he could find was his riding crop, and with this in hand, he stepped out into the corridor. In the low light, he saw a tall, helmeted figure dressed in black body armor brandishing a two-handed sword. This person came at Laurence, swinging his sword in a massive overhead blow, while Laurence struck back with the riding crop. These moves were repeated several more times by each side, but without either assailant much injured. While Laurence tried to figure out why he had not been cut in half, the rest of the British were roused by intruders who cried out after stepping with bare feet onto pins holding newly-collected insect samples for the British Museum left drying by the window. Benefitting from the delay, Laurence was soon joined in the hall by another member of the delegation who fired a loaded pistol at Laurence's attacker, knocking him down. Sounds of robust fighting seemed to show their bodyguards had rallied and engaged with the attackers, so the members of the delegation gathered together in one of the paper-screened rooms. At this point Laurence realized that he had in fact been badly cut across his forearm and shoulder and was losing a lot of blood. The minister in charge of the British delegation, Sir Rutherford Alcock, had surgical experience and was able to stitch up parts of Laurence's wounds on the spot, some of which had been cut through to the bone. This fast action greatly helped with his healing later on, but Laurence never again would regain full usage of the fingers on his left hand. His servant unnerved him while giving him water, asking "Do you think they will torture us, sir, before they kill us?" Leaving the room, Laurence staggered next door and first bumped into a severed Japanese head lying in a pool of blood, before he had a second disconcerting experience, crushing a disconnected eyeball underfoot. Then he became quite dizzy as their guards again seemed in control of the situation, and he dropped off into an uneasy sleep.

Outrage at the british Legation at Yeddo:
Attack on Messrs. Oliphant and Morrsion.

The next day, Laurence saw the cause of his survival was a stout beam spanning the hallway where he fought. It had, unseen, taken the brunt of the sword blows directed at him in the low light. He wrote:

> Its edge was as full of deep sword cuts as a crimped herring, any one of which would have been sufficient to split open my skull, which my antagonist must have thought unusually hard.[15]

Laurence was transferred onto a British ship in the harbor where he could be cared for by a surgeon. He wrote his next experiences were "the most disagreeable which it has ever been my lot to encounter."[16] Both his arms were bandaged to his sides and he had to be cared for completely by his servant. Then boils enflamed under his bandages, while the temperature hit 95 degrees and his cabin hummed with mosquitoes, keeping him miserable. Without fever, however, Laurence recovered enough in a week to be able to go up on deck, and within two weeks, he was again attending meetings and performing light official duties for the delegation. It was decided he should be the one to carry the official letters about the attack back to the Queen and Foreign Secretary as soon as ships were scheduled to leave, and he found himself back in London on sick leave just two months after he had left.

Whether he knew it or not, Laurence was ending a chapter in his career. He had been formally launched as a diplomat by the Foreign Minister and Queen, and had accepted a very difficult posting in Japan. Then during the failed assassination attempt, he had performed admirably. No one in the delegation would have had anything but praise for his resistance under attack and brave recovery. But now back in London, he had time to assess his options closer to home, and the benefits of the complete independence of action available to him were compelling. His health was returning. He had no financial worries, and his proven writing career could supply him with an ongoing stream of income. He could also be closer to his widowed mother. During this period of convalescence, he kept busy with a series of excursions not too far from home both at the request of the Foreign Ministry and for his own amusement keeping current with the latest political machinations in Europe. These trips began well when, while visiting the British Embassy in Vienna in the Spring of 1862, Laurence chanced to meet his former acquaintance the Prince of Wales. The Prince was setting off on a tour of the Middle East arranged by Queen Victoria and Prince Albert to familiarize their son with the history, cultures and rulers of the region as part of his training to become the future King Edward VII. Since the Prince and Laurence always got on very well, Laurence was invited to join the tour for the next ten days, journeying by train and ship as far as Corfu, with some spirited wild boar hunting with the Prince along the way. In his diary, the Prince noted how Laurence told him the harrowing story of his brush with death in Japan.[17] After parting from the royal party, Laurence traveled again down to Italy to check on the progress of its reunification. Besides his political observations, he also had an amusing interlude when he was somehow mistaken for the nephew of the venerable British statesman, Lord Palmerston. Word was sent ahead as he traveled along one Italian road, and arriving in the next town, Laurence found himself greeted with bands, parades and speeches, which, at first, he had not realized were in his honor. Unable to speak in the local language and explain to the hosts that it was all a mistake, Laurence gracefully went along with all the formalities, however, reporting on the confusion later by letter to Lord Palmerston, who was very much amused.[18]

After such a stimulating interlude, Laurence returned to London and concluded his intoxicating adventures with independence and freedom were a better option for him than returning to diplomacy in Japan. He formally resigned from the diplomatic service, citing "family considerations." He was, after all, the same person who while serving as temporary Superintendent-General of Indian Affairs in Canada wrote "nothing can be a greater curse to a young man wishing to get on than a permanent appointment."[19]

Unofficially, however, Laurence continued to stay very close to his former employers at the Foreign Ministry where he had established himself as someone who could be sent discreetly to assess and report back on the world's changing political scenes. In fact, there would have been very few people available and interested in such work with the same degree of experience with foreign affairs. After all, Laurence had grown up in Asia, traveled and reported extensively on the Americas, and become an expert on the complicated nest of European politics. His web of personal connections included politicians, statesmen, revolutionaries and royalty—all of whom found him enjoyable company. Just keeping in touch with the world's affairs and commenting on them could allow him to fashion a unique career of his own, well paid for by the Foreign Ministry and publishers such as *The Times* and Blackwoods.

Consequently, in the years immediately after his 1861 attack in Japan, Laurence continued "fishing in troubled waters." He covered the 1863 revolt in Poland against its Russian masters where he visited the rebel camps and wrote movingly of how they kept up morale singing songs of national freedom while being surrounded and outnumbered by massed Russian troops about to pounce on them with harsh reprisals. Then he spent time in Schleswig-Holstein where the independent monarchy was being jostled on one side by the Danes and on the other by Prussia. Queen Victoria's sister-in-law, the Duchess of the nearby Duchy of Coburg, asked Victoria to have an "able agent" sent there to give reliable reports on the people's feeling towards its monarchy. The Dutchess continued by specifically requesting that the Foreign Minister send Laurence on the mission—and he went. Soon after, Denmark and Prussia went to war over the province.

Author Laurence Oliphant as Lord Frank Vanecourt,
embossed on the cover of Piccadilly, 1870.

All of this activity was exciting and kept him an authority on the most complicated ongoing political affairs, but the pace became tiring after a few years. By the spring of 1864, he began to lessen his travel and settle into a comfortable notoriety in England where he could remain close to his mother while also enjoying star status as a world traveling author and "man about town." Laurence had ready access to Parliament and his clubs, as well as the townhouses and country estates of his wealthy and powerful friends. He did, however, resist becoming totally consumed by his "plunge" into society. He could see there was a great deal of ignorance, posturing and blind self-interest driving many of the people jostling for positions of power, and he was brave enough to decide to expose them gently, in a cultured sort of way. After many amusing evenings full of conversations with his friends about all this, Laurence and some co-conspirators decided to write and anonymously publish a satirical sheet called *The Owl* lampooning local society and political events. It became a great success. In addition, by early 1865, he started to nurture personal political ambitions by raising his profile in his native territory north of Edinburgh, near the Oliphant's ancestral estate of Condie. He made frequent visits delivering lectures, speaking with voters and printing up pamphlets to circulate the content of his speeches. Finally, he was able to conclude a successful campaign for election as Member of Parliament for the borough of Stirling during the general election of July 1865. Even though he was immediately elevated to the status of an M.P., Parliament itself would not re-convene until seven months later, early in 1866, so Laurence had plenty of time before becoming active in the government.

He expanded his satirical writing, which he had started with *The Owl*, and next wrote a new fictional satirical story published in serial form in *Blackwood's Magazine* in seven consecutive monthly installments from March to September. These later were collected and re-published in one volume as the popular satirical novel *Piccadilly* lampooning the peccadilloes of the fashionable government and society of the town and mimicking Laurence's own journey through London's fashionable society.

In the opening chapter of the novel, its narrator, Lord Frank Vanecourt, is a thinly disguised manifestation of Laurence. Lord Frank rents rooms overlooking the fine mansions surrounding Green Park, from which he can view and depart to participate in the goings on in the nearby townhouses and salons of high society. In following chapters, he meets and skewers missionary bishops, traveling Americans, resident "Hindoos," politicians and the local British elite before meeting and being transported off to America by a mysterious but more sane and moral character who is transparently Thomas Lake

Harris. When he revised the articles into book form later, he even inserted one of the Harris's more turgid and social reform minded poems into the middle of the book, ascribed by Laurence to "the greatest poet of the age, as yet, alas! unknown to fame."[20]

The caricatures in *Piccadilly* are not simply silly and amusing, but rather more depraved and morally bankrupt. For example, we learn there are three reasons that bring men to London society: "Either to find a wife, or to look after one's wife, or look after somebody else's."[21] As far as religious matters go, "the priesthood itself, once an inspiration, has become a trade," and the Church is one "that tends to atheism and that loves corruption."[22] And politics is no better, as towards the end, Lord Frank has concluded:

> I am beginning daily to feel, while in the world, that I am less of it. Already I have cut myself off from the one great source of interest which Parliament offered me... for it was impossible to resist the occasional fits of depression which reduced my mind to the condition of white paper, and the world to that of a doll stuffed with sawdust.[23]

The first installments beginning in March were light and lively, but by installment number six, in August, Lord Frank's tone has become much more serious. He tells his frivolous co-characters in the novel that he has had a major breakthrough, discovering the true path to fulfillment. When they press him to tell them this secret, he declares that it is to "LIVE THE LIFE,"[24] with capital letters as they appeared in *Blackwoods Magazine*. The character Broadbrim replies, "I don't understand you." Then Lord Frank – or actually Laurence – continues:

> Supposing, now, that you and I actually put into practice what all these friends of your mother profess, and... tried to live the inner life ourselves. Supposing, in your case, that your own self interest never entered your head in any one thing you undertook...[25]

The author is parroting here the teachings of Thomas Lake Harris, the prophet of the American community where members were then striving to do just that and "live the life." By the seventh and final installment of *Piccadilly*, appearing in September 1865, Lord Frank has decided to abandon London's insane asylum of society and retire to America "by the next steamer." To help him actually go, he is saved from a bout of utter despair by a mysterious Harris-like stranger who rescues him and escorts him to America by his act of:

> coming in and finding me stretched on my bed, and of lifting me from it by a single touch… but his name I am forbidden to divulge… and the path lay clear before me.[26]

He ends the story saying he has changed from a commentator who could just satirize the insanity, into someone who must now abandon society all together, to find the real life – mirroring exactly what Laurence had decided by the fall of 1865.

Privately, Laurence was also fed up with the sexual dissipation in his personal life, where he was living out sensual excess at high tide. One line of chatter among some of his female critics said he had a personal ambition to "know" a thousand women.[27] Another rumor was that he had seduced Constance, his mother's maid, to Lady Oliphant's great distress.[28] Undoubtedly he was a frequent visitor to the sexual underworld rampant in the London of the 1860's. Even his great friend and fellow sensualist, the Prince of Wales, remarked how Laurence "sugar-doodles the ladies."

In fact, society had become so lascivious at this time that "the great evils" of prostitution and venereal disease were surfacing from hidden whispers into heated debates between crusaders for reform and the authorities. In 1862, a careful survey of illness among the military in key British port cities revealed that 30 percent of serving soldiers and sailors there were incapacitated by venereal disease. Reformers used these results to force the Contagious Diseases Act through Parliament, which, for the few years it remained in effect, allowed police to have any woman accused of having venereal disease examined and, if necessary, forcibly confined for three to nine months for treatment in special hospitals.

There was, however, a double standard for the lower classes and the aristocrats, because there was an "unthinking acceptance" of male sexual license among the elite, and wealthy courtesans were never interfered with. For example, every day crowds in Hyde Park eagerly awaited the passing carriage of immaculately dressed and equestrian minded Catherine Walters, also known as Skittles. They jostled along Rotten Row, the park riding track daily, vying for a glimpse of the great coquette, who was a trend setter for the latest fashion as well as friends with the Prince of Wales, Lords, and, probably, with man-about-town Laurence as well. Although he certainly moved in these circles, Laurence was also surely riddled with guilt for his sins since, as one commentator wrote, "existing within him side by side… was a pagan sensuality and a Calvinist conscience."

So, by this stage in life, in spite of his heroic exploits, popular writing, and elected high office in Parliament, Laurence at 36 was profoundly unsettled by his desultory place in a seemingly pointless world. Signs of that world's descent into chaos were on all sides. And exactly at this moment, some believe Laurence also had a bad health scare, possibly showing some early symptoms of venereal disease himself, with its looming threats of illness and eventual madness. At the same time, his mother, shattered without Sir Anthony, was equally unhappy with her own empty life as well.

Very shortly they would both make a change that would startle and astonish their wide circle of colleagues, family and friends. And, at the center of their new world was their new best friend, Thomas Lake Harris, who in 1865 was back in Britain, in robust good health from country living, and barrel-chested from deep breathing. In a telling sign, his former sponsor, Dr. Garth Wilkinson, recorded in his diary that, when passing each other by chance on the sidewalk, Harris now ignored him, and instead was being escorted everywhere around town by the Oliphants, who were hanging on his every word.

After an intense period of re-engagement one-on-one with Harris, Laurence planned a short visit to the United States in September, hoping to see firsthand the damage from the disastrous Civil War and to gather intelligence for use in his upcoming maiden speech to the House of Commons the following February. He was in New England in October 1865 when Ralph Waldo Emerson reported on October 27 that he had written to invite Laurence for a visit, "if he was still in town."[29] Laurence had another fact-finding mission on his agenda that fall, however, and had gone up to visit the Brotherhood of the New Life in Amenia to see that miracle in action firsthand. Unfortunately there he was taken seriously ill with "blinding headaches." Indeed, he was sick enough to ask that his mother be contacted, and she hurriedly traveled over from Britain to be at her son's side. There have been rumors that Laurence's recurring severe headaches were symptoms of venereal disease – and this indeed could have been the case. His mother's care and the invigorating country air combined to restore his good health. He had recovered enough by December to continue on his way south to New Orleans, as originally planned. Lady Oliphant, however, with nothing in particular awaiting her return to Britain, decided to stay with Harris and join the community. Just as Laurence had been revived, so had she become enlivened by the freshness and the industry of the community and the renewal of her friendship with Emily Fawcett Cuthbert who was already there. So Lady Oliphant and her maid Constance were admitted to the Brotherhood as equals, tasked with laundry and house-cleaning chores. Meanwhile Laurence was told that he himself could not join before proving to Harris that he was resolute in his wish to do so. Harris believed unenlightened people around him generated negative spiritual forces, which in turn became distractions that could hinder his critically important spirit work and Harris sensed Laurence would be arriving with a serious amount of spiritual baggage. He was ordered back to London for at least one year of probation and was told to start to withdraw from his typical occupations, to fill his leisure time with humble, lowly work—such as sewing to mend handkerchiefs—and also to purify any unclean ways to mitigate any symptoms of venereal disease his playboy lifestyle may have scarred him with along the way. Much conflicted, but determined to change his ways, Laurence sailed back to England.

Laurence arrived in London just in time for the new Parliamentary session in early 1866. At that time one of Parliament's top concerns was the perceived Fenian threat from Irish republican patriots in America who were fund raising and conspiring to threaten British interests. By this time, America under President Andrew Johnson was a British ally, and many members of Parliament wanted to pressure Johnson to take action to rein in the Fenians. The debate during the last week of February became heated as speakers bemoaned the lack of reliable intelligence on the topic from America, with one member complaining "he should like to know what our Minister in Washington has been doing." It turns out their concerns were warranted, because two months later, in April 1866, an armed band of 700 Fenians massed on the Maine border to attack New Brunswick and, in June, a force of over 1,000 did attack Canada from Buffalo, New York.

Members of the House of Commons knew in advance that Laurence would be making his maiden speech on this topic and his opportunity to be heard presented itself on February 23. Following the Chancellor of the Exchequer, Laurence took the floor and declared he had personally just returned from America, and he could deliver a firsthand report on the Fenians there. There was no need to worry, he lectured for about ten minutes, because once the Americans had discovered there was "not a gentleman" among the Fenians, they had "denied them any sympathy." The Fenians were just "hewers of wood, drawers of water, the waiters at hotels and men engaged in similar occupations." In short, the Fenians in America were a joke and not to be worried about. Why Laurence decided to address his more experienced colleagues in such a glib and condescending manner is a mystery – or just bad judgment. The next member to speak criticized Laurence's speech as "too jocular" for treating a serious threat to British interests as a jest. There were none of the traditional congratulations given a new member for an opening speech, and the debate just ignored Laurence's comments and moved on. Furthermore, over the months that followed, Laurence really did not make any speeches to Parliament again, and only contributed a quick comment here and there, possibly following Thomas Lake Harris's orders to abandon his usual life.

Meanwhile, Laurence did keep in contact with the Foreign Ministry during early 1866—in particular when he was sought out by a delegation of Japanese students studying in London. They were sent on a secret mission to study the mysterious West by their feudal lord in Satsuma, the southernmost province of Japan. The leaders of the students told Laurence that the forces for modernization were gaining the upper hand in the civil war underway in Japan and that Britain should be aware that the government there was about to change. Laurence then wrote an introductory memo for the students to the current Foreign Minister, Lord Clarendon, who arranged a series of meetings with the Japanese. As a result, the British government played close attention to the potential new regime in Japan and looked for ways to make friends with its emerging leadership.

When Thomas Lake Harris and his deputy Jane Waring (Dovie) returned to London yet again in 1867 to arrange publication for three more of his books, Laurence introduced the students to the prophet. The civil chaos back in Japan was making the funding for the student's' mission uncertain, and Harris stepped forward to help. He offered the boys the chance to spend their summer vacation at the Brotherhood of the New Life in America where they could balance half days of healthy manual labor with half days of lessons relevant to their mission. Six of the boys accepted Harris's invitation and set sail for America as soon as their school courses ended. Laurence also took Harris and Waring to meet his friends the Cowpers—William and Georgiana Cowper-Temple—the step-children of Lord Palmerston who had recently inherited his title and spectacular estate Broadlands near Southampton. The Cowpers were at the highest levels of British society and had been Laurence's best friends for several years—and they would continue to be his closest confidants and letter-writing correspondents. Both had a lively interest in "new religions" and for years sponsored well known "Broadlands Conferences" at their country home. They were also fabulously wealthy, and backed Thomas Lake Harris in several of his ventures in the early years.

Back in Parliament, Laurence's fledgling career was proving even more disillusioning. He had won his seat as a passionate supporter of Mr. Gladstone, a liberal who was championing significant reforms to improve working conditions and extend the voting franchise to more working class men. However, Gladstone was defeated in his efforts to pass a reform bill by the worthy opponent, Mr. Disraeli, who took over power. But after considerable public pressure, in one of the first acts of his new order, Mr. Disraeli re-introduced the reform legislation, only slightly modified, and tried to pass it under his own sponsorship. To Laurence's disgust, Mr. Gladstone and his followers then obstructed its passage at every turn, just as vigorously as they had previously championed it. So Laurence could see both sides were simply playing a sickeningly self-serving game, and neither side seemed to give much of a damn about actual reforms to relieve an oppressed population.

It was in the middle of this legislative wrangling that Laurence's distant cousin and prolific author, Margaret Oliphant, met him one evening in 1867 in a visitors' gallery at the House of Commons. It was late in the day and they were both awaiting the speeches for Disraeli's re-introduction of the reform bill, and although they had met before, Margaret said this occasion led them to the closest conversation they had ever had. Several things from that evening deeply surprised her: first, the degree of utter contempt Laurence had for the politicians; and second, his de-bunking of the spiritualist mediums, rappers and table-turners as quacks. She was also just as surprised by his assertions that exciting new paths to spiritual enlightenment were actually manifesting themselves to those open enough to receive them and that great changes were at hand. Above all, she was startled at how bitter he was. He declared his current life was "unendurable" and something he "could support no longer."[30]

Things were to get much worse. As Laurence walked back to his lonely rooms each night, like Lord Frank in *Piccadilly,* he could see the frivolous elite driving their coaches to the fine houses around Green Park for entertainment. But such delights were no longer for him as he sat down and picked up his sewing for the evening. He became more introverted and longed for the relief he was sure he would find when he was accepted into Harris's Brotherhood. In fact, he became uncommunicative and seemed to disappear for a time. Lady Oliphant had to write from America to Laurence's former editor at *The Times* to find him and prod him to resume his letters. Writing about this dark time later in letters to the Cowpers, Laurence said "I had all the symptoms in my head of softening of the brain" and his letters were all signed "Woodbine," his faerie name[31] inside Harris's Brotherhood. In the spring of 1867, Harris could sense his new disciple was at the breaking point, and, no doubt with the urging of Lady Oliphant, gave permission for Laurence to join his industrious community in Amenia—just in time.

PART TWO:

A NEW LIFE

CHAPTER 5

THE BROTHERHOOD OF
THE NEW LIFE

When Laurence moved in during 1867, the Brotherhood of the New Life was a thriving and very successful community. At its beginning, when Harris came back to New York City from Britain in 1861, he passed the hat among his most loyal followers and bought land for his new Brotherhood of the New Life community in Wassaic, a village in Dutchess County, New York, about 90 miles northeast of the city, near the western Connecticut border. Today that area is a popular choice for weekend homes within easy reach of Manhattan. The combination of country air and easy access to the city by passenger railroad must have been part of the appeal to Harris as he made a tentative beginning. This new haven was to be a restorative country home base for him to make serious advances on the spiritual front, while also spending time away in the city or traveling in the American South or in England.

True to his intention to have simple physical activities as a balance, Harris worked at manual labor himself at Wassaic, spending the days and afternoons carrying stones and building the walls that would become the foundation for the main house where he and his followers would live. Then, during the nights and early mornings, breathing intensely, he visited the spirit world. This balance of labor and mental work would be a signature characteristic at all Harris's future communities, although the great man himself would soon drop the physical activities. After all, he was getting enough exercise in the world beyond.

The first house at Wassaic was set back in the leafy woods away from the main road on a steep hillside overlooking the deep gorge creek of the Wassaic River, which would have added a continuous roar from rushing white water churning down below. An early member recalled the structure as "a very fine one, and known locally as the House in the Woods."[1] At home were Harris, his second wife, and the two sons from his first marriage, together with eight devoted— and invited—right-breathing followers, making twelve in all. No one had progressed towards the divine breath as far as Harris, but each had at least mastered the preliminaries needed to start their own journey. These supporters included his wealthy devotee and heiress Jane Lee Waring, the daughter of a New York stove manufacturer; Mr. and Mrs. James Requa and family from Harris's New York City congregation; and Arthur Cuthbert, a British believer who would become an American citizen and continue as a lifelong Harrisite, writing the great man's biography published much later in 1908. Miss Waring alone contributed the equivalent of $15,000,000 in today's money to the community fund controlled by Harris, so from the start, they were not worried about running out of capital. Cuthbert writes that the group at this time was extremely diverse, with some "of the simplest working class, and others of culture and social position."[2] They included "representatives of the Northern and Southern states of America, also of England, Scotland and Ireland; individuals also of French and German descent."

Seclusion at this "breath-house" allowed Harris to focus his attentions on understanding the new celestial world which became so real for him as he retired every night. Some of the twelve lived there permanently, and others visited as they could, with permanent homes and jobs in the external world keeping them gainfully employed and practical. Commitment to open breathing was the common bond for all the members of the Brotherhood. We are told that the "physical phenomena" related to open breathing "differ a little in every person." However, Harris told his followers that those who succeed have adapted their circumstances to "free themselves from worldliness, and give themselves up to the New Life that will be exacted of them"—so having a sober Christian life according to the prophet's instructions was the way to prepare for receiving the breakthrough.[3] In a letter to Arthur Cuthbert's fiancée (and Lady Oliphant's good friend) Emily Fawcett, one member wrote a description of another sister's experience when first achieving the desired state of first-step open breathing. The sister explained she had been suffering for an extended period from "a deep sense of sin and unworthiness." Finally, she sensed "all her life was brought before her into judgment." She felt "indescribable agitation and grief." At this moment of crisis, open breathing was achieved:

> It begins in the lower part of the abdomen and from thence rises and fills the lungs. When she inhales this breath it feels cold in the throat, the throat seems to expand, and she says this is externally perceptible: it is audible but not painfully so. She feels it as high as the throat and down to the knees. She is only in the first degree of it. In the deepest degrees it is felt from the sole of the foot to the crown of the head. She can only express the sensation as being full of comfort to the spirit and body.[4]

In his book *The Breath of God in Man*, Harris explains the senses become supercharged as the breath of God flows through the frame:

the physical senses by degrees put on a hyper-physical character. The eye detects the moral character in the beams that strike the retina; the ear a moral quality in the sounds that vibrate through the tympanum; the touch the moral quality in the substances, visible or invisible, that thrill in contact with the nerves.[5]

Unfortunately, evil spirits spring into action whenever they sense "a person moves in the direction of open breathing":

they waylay him day and night; they load the brain with a corrupt magical substance; they invade the fine space of the ear with deadly sounds; they cast a cursed dust into the eyes; they inject noisome effluvia into the nostrils; they anoint the lips with secretions of hates in the saliva, and violently, if possible, inject the very quintessence of death into the lungs.[6]

Doing battle to near exhaustion, one then progresses beyond the first stage towards re-birth of the soul at stage seven. Harris never does seem to define the specifics of each step in the process. We know man is "foul" before it starts, and glorious at the end, but we are only told the exact path is different with every person. He did say, at stage four, "faeries are seen," so that would be something to look forward to.[7] Indeed, all along the way is the increasing ability to visualize spirits, to travel to other worlds and generally to become more intimate with the celestial beings.

It was in the presence of the residents in his breathing house in Wassaic, by the spring of 1863, that Harris was able to advance through all seven stages of right breathing, to the point that group member Arthur Cuthbert says: "the old animal soul of the man dies, and a new animal soul, in infantile state, descends into the body directly from the Lord, the new Adam-Eve." Cuthbert reports Harris's achievement of the seventh stage was "the first case in revealed human history," and was a major milestone in the prophet's progress.[8]

After this momentous event, Harris felt he had the obligation to start some light recruiting by reaching out to the wider circle of unenlightened people nearby, and so he started to expand the Brotherhood's operations, albeit in small steps. More substantial new property was bought for the founding members about four miles away around the Mill Pond in the larger village of Amenia, and new members were invited to move into the property in Wassaic. Three large families came from Georgia, escaping that battle-ravaged state and adding the proceeds from the sale of their properties and slaves. Arthur Cuthbert's fiancée, Emily Fawcett, arrived in 1863 from London, reminding Harris of his fledgling British followers Lady Oliphant and Laurence, and the couple were married by Harris and moved in to a pond-side cabin in Amenia.

The growing group operated a mill as their first base of commerce in the community. Jane Waring then planted the Brotherhood's first vineyards on the hillside adjoining the pond and managed all the farming operations, having grown up on a farm with her agriculturist brother George, who had been manager of Horace Greeley's farm at Chappaqua, New York, and lead sanitary engineer for the draining of Manhattan's wetlands and the creation of Central Park.

Showing acumen in business and practical affairs that other utopian leaders sorely lacked, Harris founded the one-room First National Bank of Amenia in the spring of 1863, with himself as president and James Requa as cashier. Cuthbert said "its main feature being only one formidable iron safe, with a combination lock." Later a five-sided stone structure was built and remains the centerpiece of Amenia village's main street today, where it is still operated as a bank. Harris began to invite the villagers into the bank, where lots of chairs and a warm stove were always provided, and then would start to talk about his world-view.[9] In this meeting place, there were no organized services, or regulations to be followed, but rather only the encouragement to become aware of the truth and importance of the revelations given to Harris, and to practice divine breathing at home.

From 1863 to 1865, membership increased to about 35, including some with specialized skills, such as Dr. J. W. Hyde, an expert winemaker from Missouri, who joined with his wife Lucy and son John to take over vineyard operations. The group became a factor in the local elections, with all members voting the same in a block and enacting whatever ordinances they wanted to help their own commune. Their war chest of funding was swelling since joining the Brotherhood meant pledging obedience to Harris and turning over all material wealth to him. No doubt the contents of the safe at The First National Bank of Amenia began to bulge with a very substantial common fund controlled by the prophet for the good of all.

All the members knew the arrival of Lady Oliphant, and the probable future arrival of Laurence, represented a new financial bonanza for the Brotherhood. This led to enthusiastic discussion about possibilities for expansion. While Harris and Jane Lee Waring were over in England in 1867, James Requa, perhaps the most business-savvy member, made a visit to friends in the far west of New York State at the village of Brocton, 400 miles away from Amenia on the shores of Lake Erie. There, he became impressed with the area's ideal soil and climate for growing grapes, as well as the ready availability of distribution using the trains running through the village. He became convinced wine production there was a major commercial opportunity for the Brotherhood. He also identified several contiguous farms, available for purchase, where the start for such a new venture could be made. With encouragement from Lady Oliphant,[10] Requa went immediately over to London and told Harris face-to-face about the opportunity. That led Harris to come back himself, visit Brocton, and then to execute a new ambitious plan: the common fund, newly enriched by the Oliphant money and the future sale of all the properties in Dutchess County at Amenia and Wassaic, would be re-deployed to establish a new headquarters in Brocton.

Showing his acumen in dealing and real-world business, and with James Requa's help, Harris began negotiating and buying up adjoining parcels of land in Brocton. He spent about $250,000 (in 1867 dollars), about forty percent of which came from the Oliphants. In spite of his eccentric religious and spiritual views, all reports attest to Harris's shrewdness and practicality in business matters and he had soon accumulated 1200 contingent acres of prime land. With the Oliphant money, he added about 800 more. Two substantial atlases from the time show the effects of the prophet's purchases. The 1867 *Atlas of Chautauqua County, New York* shows the village of Brocton as a rural hamlet, surrounded by small farms very near Lake Erie, with a dozen or so new businesses setting up for trade along the main street. The Atlas was refreshed in a revised edition in 1881, which then showed a transformation as 15 farms had been amalgamated into two large parcels now captioned in the atlas as owned by the "Brotherhood of the New Life."

The smaller parcel of Brotherhood land was directly in the village itself and included a half-mile stretch of prime commercial property along the main street. The second and largest parcel included over a mile and a half of lush lakeshore property, with seven farmhouses facing the water on adjoining lots. Further inland towards the village were a half dozen more houses, and a giant wine cellar, with a capacity of 65,000 gallons, built into the ground next to the train tracks at the Brocton rail station. A journalist visiting the properties in 1869 described an idyllic setting with a deep valley running through the estate, with a "copious creek" powering a busy sawmill operated by the Brotherhood. Along the northern edge, Lake Erie "stretched like a broad 'ribband of blue.'" He continued, "the land for the most part lies warm to the sun, and… is bountifully supplied with wood and water, and is variegated in surface and in soil."[11]

Harris had particularly high hopes for yield from "Salem" grapes and he invested heavily in planting them. He called his new domain "Salem-on-Erie."

Local residents must have been amazed when the genteel Harrisites started to move in during the late summer of 1867. Not only was there the wild-eyed head of the community to get used to, but the worthies from New York City as well as Europeans—and even a rumored British aristocrat in the form of Lady Oliphant. Then, even more remarkable at the end of the summer, was the arrival of Japanese students set to help with all aspects of the migration. Chinese Asians were somewhat familiar in America, helping to build the railroad east from the Pacific in the late 1860's. But Japanese at the time were literally unknown. Japan had been a closed society for centuries, with citizens forbidden to leave. In fact, he 1860 U.S. Census recorded only 7 Japanese, not counting the diplomatic delegation in Washington.[12] But now six students from leading samurai families were in Brocton. Their leader, Arinori Mori, would grow to represent Japan later in Washington and as ambassador to Great Britain—and the youngest of the group, fifteen-year-old Kanaye Nagasawa, would rise to a major position in the Brotherhood as Harris's deputy and eventual heir. But for now the students would have some heavy lifting and moving to attend to while adding a unique strangeness to Brocton, as if they had landed there from another world.

*

Finally, at the end of July 1867, Laurence departed Parliament and his frequent weekends at assorted British country houses for the Brotherhood of the New Life's remote farms in America. His wealthy friends Georgiana and William Cowper came to see him off at the dock in Liverpool, and gave him a luxurious travel "dressing bag" as a present. Laurence was ecstatic at the thought his new rejuvenation was finally to begin. He wrote to Harris's deputy, Jane Waring, on the morning of his ship's departure from Liverpool:

> I am so happy at the prospect of going to work in the Lord's vineyard and I feel I shall love working in it for its own sake, and not regard it as a hardship or a trial at all. In fact, it would seem a hardship to be doing anything else…[13]

It had been a long wait, with many chances to withdraw his request to join the Brotherhood. Even at journey's end, when he arrived at Amenia, the community member meeting him brought the message he should reconsider whether to continue on to the farms or just go away. Laurence, however, had no doubts, and he climbed up onto the wagon for the ride to the Harris compound where he was put into the poorest possible accommodation in an outdoor shed and told he was not to have any conversation with his mother already there as he started "to live the life." He must have had to change out of his Mayfair suit very quickly to start his new work at manual labor. He had to begin each day at 5 a.m. by cleaning boots and the stable. By late October, Laurence was able to write to the Cowpers again about all of the lessons in humility he was learning as he took orders from a foreman and three more knowledgeable Irish laborers, lessening the "evils" of his pride. He had also tried work peddling grapes at a neighboring village, he said, but said "I was not very successful never having tried my hand as a salesman before."[14] Even though he was at first forbidden to talk to Lady Oliphant, Laurence could "see her out any window" and thus could report on the effect of the communal life on his mother, who had spent much of his childhood as a near invalid on her couch:

> the change in her is quite wonderful, and the separation is not very serious, for I can look at her going about her daily avocations out of

any window, with a light step and a merry laugh, such as I never saw or heard before.[15]

Vine Cliff, Harris's waterfront house in Brocton, New York, sketched by Laurence Oliphant.

Laurence ended the letter talking about the uncertainty of when he would be able to move to Brocton himself, since members could only go as houses became available, and, at the end of October both the bank and the vineyard in Amenia remained to be sold.

As the weather grew colder, the whole community was consumed with migrating in stages to its new quarters in Brocton. By November, Harris himself and Lady Oliphant were permanently settled there, and by early December, Laurence also made the move. Just as in Amenia, his living quarters were two stalls in an unheated shed that became more and more humbling as the winter of 1867 intensified. He had to make any furniture he wanted out of fruit crates he found there. He wrote of "bare hands and icy barrels." On an average day he was up at 5am and worked until 9pm. For example, he pulled heavily laden sleds by horse over the frozen lake. Then at the end of the day he spent an additional hour or two drawing water and delivering it to several of the houses around the campus before bed in his shed.

His mother had settled in at the 24-room lakeshore mansion called Vine Cliff where Harris installed himself and his inner circle. This was a sprawling New England style white clapboard house, with a pillared entry porch adding a grand Palladian effect. When Harris bought it, the major lakefront road went right by its front door. But as the area's largest landowner, and with his powers of persuasion, he convinced the local authorities to re-route the road a hundred yards farther away from the house. Harris then put in elaborate landscaping to seclude the grounds with a labyrinth of walkways where he could meander and meditate. Next, he expanded the house to thirty rooms, including an impressive library and study, as well as a private wing for Mrs. Harris, who was becoming quite eccentric and was kept apart from everybody else. Residents at the Vine Cliff house included Mrs. Harris and Miss Jane Waring; Lady Oliphant and her maid Constance, who worked as equals with housework and gardening; and two of the Japanese—Kanaye Nagasawa and Osui Arai, a new arrival introduced by Arinori Mori to join the students already there. An observer at the time noted Harris was "waited on hand and foot by two Japanese boys" but other sources indicate that the whole household pitched in with serving the master.

By 1868, the Brotherhood had completed its systematic migration. Finally, everyone had been relocated from Amenia to Brocton, and the properties in Amenia and Wassaic were sold. Estimates were of a community of 75 to 100 members,[16] 60 to 70 of whom were adults, and 40 to 50 women. The Japanese samurai contingent numbered more than 10 and the duties of these young men were very different from those afforded by their privileged lives back in Japan. For example the youngest, Kanaye Nagasawa, helped with the dairy and milk production, and all of them worked in the vineyards. The *de facto* leader of the group, twenty-one-year-old Arinori Mori, studied baking and also helped with laundry and housework.[17] Even though he was a samurai, and would scale the highest levels of the next Japanese government, Mori accepted the lowly work happily and indeed would remain a lifelong follower of Harris, although in a rather distant way. He ended his career as Minister of Education in Japan, and was credited with introducing modern educational practices throughout Japan before traditionalists shocked by Japan's metamorphosis into a modern state assassinated him. Meanwhile, Harris kept his promise to provide lessons for the Japanese as well. Instruction began before the end of December at a building designated as a school, with Laurence usually playing the role of teacher for the half-day lessons on language, culture, religion and military affairs. Over the following years, the Japanese group grew to as many as 25 as word went out among other Japanese students about Harris's willingness to house and teach them for free in return for part-time healthy physical labor. In the spirit of the samurai educational code, all the Japanese students in Britain and America for familiarization were very closely connected and so the option of spending time at the Brotherhood was well known among them.

The practical reality was that the Brotherhood operated a very large working farm. As planned, grape growing for wine was the main business—largely for "medicinal purposes" since the wine from their vineyards was supposedly infused with benign ingredients from the spirit world, and could only have healthful effects on its drinkers. Harris made a bet on the "Salem" grape he brought with him from Amenia, a cross between the wild New England grape and the "Golden Chasselas" of Europe. Since most newcomers, like Laurence, had to undergo a kind of cleansing when renouncing the everyday world, Harris made hard physical work the first cure, and the labor of these neophytes surely contributed a major portion of the required agricultural effort. But because many members of the community were from the more genteel ranks of society and strangers to farm employment, sturdy Irish and Swedish farm hands were also hired to make sure the agricultural necessities were addressed.

Besides general members, there were also specialists in the Brotherhood community—expert horticulturists, wine makers, businessmen and at least one doctor. Harris even enticed his New York City lawyer with the gift of a lakeside building lot; soon the lawyer had constructed a gracious summer home where he could be close to hand at least during vacations. It was said the individuals came to Harris for many reasons, but after he put them on their new paths, each successful member grew healthier from their daily exertions and closer to spiritual peace as they followed their resident prophet's instructions to work on their open breathing in the evenings at this well-off and hard working community.

Daily life at the Brotherhood of the New Life was called "the Use" and members expected to be "used" according to the direction of Harris, the Father of the community. Each was to "live the life." In other words, members were not just to "talk" about improving their spiritual states or helping others with brotherly love—they were to "do" it, enriched by Harris's presence. Since members were typically assigned difficult tasks at which they had no experience, life was not without humor. In his memoirs Laurence describes himself one day on a madcap sleigh ride over ice, laughing hysterically as his horses ran wild and a shifting cargo of potatoes went dizzyingly out of control. But soon after, in a letter back to Louis Liesching, his worried family friend from Ceylon days, he wrote, "here I am removed from the whole class of temptations and sins to which I am liable in London" and his mother added this note at the end:

> One thought is constantly with me, and that is, how heartily our beloved
> Sir Anthony would have embraced this life, how he would have found
> so many of the perplexities which troubled him solved. I am reminded
> of him daily, and I am sure we are both doing just as should have made

him happy by remaining here. My head is my weak point, and I am thankful I am able to be useful in other ways.[18]

By Christmas Day 1867, Laurence seems to have made enough progress from his arrival at Amenia in the summer to be invited to the main house at Brocton for Christmas dinner with his mother, Harris and the inner circle. This was the first time he had been able to talk to his mother in over a year.

*

For most newcomers, joining the Brotherhood of the New Life involved an introduction and an interview with Harris. The prophet would assess each candidate personally, and was said to have a gift of deep insight into their hearts and minds, and the hopes they had for a place in the Brotherhood. One member based a fictional character on Harris in a novel about life in the community and described Harris's perceptiveness:

> He knew the minds of most of his disciples better than the owners did. He seemed to seize the key-note of each nature and enter with dominating genius the secret heart of him he would control. He appealed to the most ideal motives, and could always waft before him the helpless crafts whose rudders were too weak for the mastering current of idealism upon which they sailed.[19]

In his own terminology, Harris evaluated each applicant's spiritual "spheres" and "states" closely, because the whole idea of the community was for like-minded and spiritually receptive souls to *help* Harris in his spiritual explorations. Negative or disbelieving beings would only aid the ubiquitous mischief-making earthbound demons intent on thwarting Harris's role in man's restoration.

Once he decided to accept someone, Harris would develop whatever plan he thought necessary to bring that person into closer harmony with the spirit world. Besides taking charge of all the money, Harris assigned the living arrangements. Husbands, wives and children were likely to be split up, with everyone composed into new associations, which over time would be modified again and again. Moves to new quarters could occur at any moment—especially in the middle of the night—and were a regular occurrence. Harris's orders were not to be questioned but accepted essentially as divine guidance. Abandoning entrapments of the past was part of Harris's intent— that's why fashionable dandy Laurence was made a laborer and his pampered mother a maid, isolated from her beloved son.

At Brocton, Harris himself now performed no physical work other than his continuous study, engagement with the spirit world, and writing to define his new religion, which was always framed in the most sensual terms, as in these lines from his poem "Veritas":

In secret watches of the night
I open paths of pure delight
With telepathic touch, I make
Pressures for rest in hearts that ache.

The prophet claimed to be way ahead of all of his followers in experiencing the reality of the spirit world. For example, while most members were not yet able to sense or see them, Harris taught that faeries and mischievous spirit beings were everywhere. To help make this more real, each member was conferred a faerie name by Harris, who was himself known as Faithful or Father. James Requa was Steadfast and Mrs. Requa Golden Rose. Lady Oliphant was Viola and Laurence was Woodbine. Jane Waring, who directed many of the practical affairs of the community, was Dovie. Kanaye Nagasawa's faerie name was Phoenix. Perhaps the loser in the naming game was the eccentric and now largely isolated second Mrs. Harris, who became Lady Pink Ears.

In spite of the whimsical names, the faerie world was far from frivolous and benign. Evil forces—or "infernals"—attempted to impede Harris's progress at every turn. They were demons, and although invisible to members other than Father, Harris preached that they were wreaking havoc at the community:

> The evil ones let things go comparatively smoothly for a time, during which they are preparing some infernal machine which suddenly explodes in our midst, carrying destruction and ruin in its path.[20]

Harris cautioned community members that their "states" might become infected by evil spirits and obstruct the great man's work, though they themselves were unaware of the condition. As a result, some members were ordered to leave suddenly for a time—or permanently. Devoted lifelong member Arthur Cuthbert was sent away for months to work as a lumberjack. Others might be sent on missions abroad, as Oliphant would often be. But Father stayed put and soldiered on with his spiritual work bravely, to the point of exhaustion, determined to fight the infernals and bring humanity to salvation.

He also directed everyone else as co-combatants in fighting the evil spirits. As a result, Harris was not the only one likely to be exhausted up at Brocton. Here is a description of group defense activities as reported by the member Mrs. Hankin:

> Sometimes 'the infernals'... were very active and in that case the community had to watch to save those who were 'infested,' because it was believed that the infernals were more active in sleep. For this reason, in many instances persons were kept almost without sleep for months. One woman, in particular for weeks was only allowed to sleep

from nine o'clock till twelve, all the rest of twenty-four hours being spent in the hardest work.[21]

Once the infested wretch was finally sleeping, vigilant members would have to wait until they observed a deep and sustained heavy breathing. Then all would concentrate on actually visualizing the infesting evil creature. When this incarnation of evil was sufficiently realized, the watchers would pray and shout out, "Bind, him, Lord!" again and again, raising the level of fervor. With all the shouting, the poor possessed patient would be startled into wakefulness, and the whole process would have to unfold again from the beginning. Cases of very bad infestation involved several infernals, which meant the watchers might have to remain awake, watching, praying and shouting all through the night before stumbling away at dawn to resume their daily work.

The infernals scored a victory early on at Brocton when James Requa suddenly took ill and died. He had been a savvy businessman, and his loss dealt the Brotherhood a serious blow. Some years earlier, when commercial adversity first struck him in New York City, he had deftly put all of his affairs in order—and all of his assets in his wife's name—before going bankrupt and joining the Brotherhood. For the move from Amenia to Brocton, he had been deeply involved helping Harris with the various property negotiations, as well as the logistics of the re-location, but by the spring of 1868 those exertions proved too much for his health.

Earlier, Harris had announced to his members that no one in the Brotherhood would "die" while they concentrated on improving their states and preparing for the new world order (which was to come at any moment). To reconcile this pronouncement with Requa's demise, Harris explained that "Steadfast" had "been summoned to the field of invisible service": He had gone to heaven to assist the Brotherhood with celestial reconciliation. Harris saw and spoke to him every night.

In this letter back to the Cowpers in April 1868, just after Mr. Requa's "seeming death," Laurence explains the stress the Brotherhood was under, and the fatigue after yet another re-arrangement of the living quarters:

> Ever since dear Steadfast's death the battle has been fierce, doubtless the infernals thought the occasion one which might be taken advantage of, and there is scarcely one amongst us who has not been conscious of an unusual degree of spiritual struggle. Some days Faithful has passed altogether in bed, Dovie has been confined to her couch for the last three days, but still, I believe that there has been a great deal of ground won. The whole of one establishment consisting of 14 or 15 persons with 3 exceptions has had to be moved to a new house close to Faithful, and as all such moves have to be made at a moment's notice they involve a great deal of confusion. These are the moments when persons states get tried, for at such a time the harmony has to live unbroken through all the inevitable petty annoyances incidental to so many being turned anyhow into an unfurnished house.[22]

Besides working on deep breathing, there was not much "structure" to the religion of the Brotherhood in Brocton. They did not meet for regular services, nor did Harris preach to them except when some new revelation came to him. They did not share communal meals, except on holidays and special Harris-declared celebrations. Then singing and dancing, often directed by Laurence, might be a welcome break in the routine. Favorite songs would be familiar tunes, with poems by Harris substituted for the original lyrics. For example, this verse was to be sung to the tune of "God Save the Queen" or "My Country, 'Tis of Thee:"

> In thy dear blessedness
> Hearts unto hearts caress,
> Holy and clean

Mother and child and bride
Woman ensanctified
Hail thee beatified,
God save the Queen![23]

The Brocton community did eventually form a band, and even fashioned some sort of gymnasium. Otherwise, hard work, deep breathing and the efforts to cleanse one's states were the order of the day. Bodies also had to be de-magnetized by bathing naked together, with vigorous mutual scrubbing to rid any evil forces that had become attached, and especially to keep "lust currents" at bay.

Harris, however, was at a different level. The specifics of such spiritual practices are obscure but centered around respiration and sexual unity between male and female essences. First, through a special process of deep breathing, the adept practitioner would enter into an altered state of consciousness making him or her more open and susceptible to the spirits. From an initial state of simply feeling lightheaded and different, pressure might spread from the solar plexus out to the genitals and extremities, with an accompanying sense of warmth and satisfaction. The entire body would then be consumed with the feeling that a new force had entered it, joined and taken it to another level. Over time—perhaps over many years—the practitioner might evolve to a more sophisticated engagement where the "sensations" took on anthropomorphic shapes, so the adept wasn't just "feeling" the presence of a spirit, but was "seeing" the spirit in a luminescent human shape, as in a "vision." Then besides actually seeing and being present with the envisioned spirit, they might have conversations, and travel with the spirits around the solar system—or even go to heaven. At the highest levels, the practitioner and spirit would have sex.

The sex would come when the person finally found the spirit in heaven who was their personal missing counterpart—the missing part of their unique dual-gender soul, which had been cut in two at birth.

For a man this would be a female spirit, and for a women a male one. Harris could help seekers with the identification process occasionally. For example, Harris told Laurence that the woman Laurence later married, Alice le Strange, was not his true counterpart, and so the couple were forbidden to have normal sex despite their vows.

Harris taught that separation of the genders was the cause of all of man's troubles on earth, and the second coming of Christ would occur only when mankind was ready to re-unite with its missing halves and become complete again in the united image of The Deity—who also manifested a combination of Male and Female attributes. In fact, the prophet proclaimed the Deity had selected Harris to be "the pivotal man" who would first return to heaven and achieve "the Two-in-One" with his own counterpart, and then pass on this knowledge to the benighted members of the chosen Brotherhood of the New Life, paving the way for the new world order when man and spirits would live together in harmony again, as they did before the fall.

While Harris eventually shared this plan within the Brotherhood, few in the community ever achieved this goal, or even got to first base. But some members felt they were advancing along the path. Among them were Lady Oliphant, who at least had visions of Sir Anthony in heaven, and Laurence, who while abstaining from relations with his actual wife claimed very close relations and sex with his counterpart, the spirit named Alawenie. But in these early days in Brocton, while everyone in the Brotherhood was earnestly seeking their own contact and conjunctions with the spirits, there must have been a lot of heavy breathing during the nights but probably not much actual sex. Harris frowned on traditional intercourse among members, with only a few exceptions for couples who, like the Cuthberts, had approved marriages. He wrote:

> We think that generation must cease till the sons and daughters of God
> are prepared for the higher generation, by evolution into structural,

bi-sexual completeness, above the plane of sin, of disease, or natural mortality.[24]

However, Harris himself claimed to spend essentially every night joined in "conjugal bliss" (sic) with his own spirit counterpart, a beautiful blonde spirit called Queen Lily of Lilistan. Meanwhile, it was also revealed to Harris that the widow Mrs. Requa, Golden Rose, was actually her departed husband Steadfast's true counterpart, clearing the way for Rose and Steadfast to have celestial sex. Harris wrote (with his typical flair for pompous obfuscation):

When members of the new kingdom and family have been removed in recent years, it has generally been because the counterpart is also on this side; and it is necessary that one of them should be removed, the one thus removed becoming a ministering angel to the other that is left in the earthsphere: thus the church and family on both sides being essentially one, as they will visibly be one when the evil is removed.[25]

That meant that although the Requas had seemed the closest of companions while married on earth, they could now hope to achieve the true "Two-in-One" together since they were genuine counterparts, on the different levels of earth and heaven. So, a few months after Steadfast's death Harris, to facilitate the Requas making "the Two-in-One," welcomed Golden Rose into his inner circle at Vine Cliff. Over time, Harris and Rose would become closer still, helping each other achieve "the Two-in-One" by lying in bed and rubbing each other with oils, probably naked in each other's arms: Golden Rose breathing, rubbing and reaching out to achieve union with her now celestial late husband Steadfast, and Harris, holding her, reaching out to mate with his own counterpart, Queen Lily, on the other side.

A passage in *Masollam*, the novel Laurence Oliphant published many years later, describes how a typical night's mating session with the prophet began:

(He) undid his shirt-collar and bared the upper part of his chest... she... pressed both her palms upon his temples... slowly moved one hand to his forehead, while she placed the other upon the lower part of the back brain, and again pressed, but in an opposite direction, with the same firm but gentle force. ... Her... respiration underwent a remarkable change. The breathing became deeper, fuller, more prolonged, until her lungs seemed to acquire a power of unnatural expansion, while... (his) appeared altogether to have ceased; his eyes had closed, his whole frame stiffened, as the gentle heaving of his chest subsided into complete quiescence; and, except for a faint colour in his cheeks, which was not the hue of death, he would to the casual observer have presented all the appearance of a corpse.[26]

After half an hour, the participating female would rub Harris with a special fluid, massaging his chest, and as he came to, their breathing was "absolutely synchronous." While in such trances Harris would "penetrate into regions which are closed to the common herd" and even foresee the future. In time, the actions in these sessions would escalate to include the enactment of sex imagined to be with counterpart spirits on the other side.

To encourage the membership to persevere, some journals of personal experience were written and copied for sharing among the fledgling breathers. Here is one passage about the experiences of one sister's first early success:

I slept tolerably well only, but felt quiet and happy and kept feeling the sensations like those you remember I told you I felt in my arms. Well, since I feel them quite often, and they seem to be gradually extending over my body. This morning for the first time, I felt it enter my head and also pass into my thighs. The first time it came into my body, that is the trunk, it seemed to enter through the generative organs, and with it came the thought, this is like sexual intercourse, only infinitely more so, in that every atom of your frame enters into union with another atom to the furthest extremity of your body. I am sure I never had such a thought before, nor supposed that anything could be of such infinite magnitude. I felt infinitely calm and peaceful, nothing turbulent and passionate about it, and my only desire was to constantly pray in thankfulness. If it were indeed what Mrs. R. says it is, my counterpart, I can imagine in some slight degree what may be in store for us all.[27]

So the other female members of the inner circle, such as Jane Waring (Dovie) and Lady Oliphant (Viola), made room for Golden Rose to take a special place in their first family of the Brotherhood, as a kind of diving board to heaven.

CHAPTER 6

FROM A FARM AT BROCTON
TO A WAR IN PARIS

We can only glimpse at the minutiae of daily life at the Brotherhood because the members were deliberately discreet. However, Rosa Emerson, who grew up in the Brotherhood while her parents were briefly members, wrote an 1884 novel called *Among the Chosen* that gives an accurate picture of the goings on from the point of view of a young resident. The Emersons joined the Brotherhood of the New Life from New York City, bringing their daughter, who was described by the child of other members, Robert Martin, as a statuesque beauty, with poise and presence, who had been trained in the theater. He said "it was only natural all the men of the community should have fallen in love with her." As she matured, Harris showed increasing interest in Rosa, perhaps as a potential understudy to Mrs. Requa for the role of putting the prophet in the right mood to achieve "the two-in-one" with Queen Lily at bedtime. Her novel was published many years after she and her parents were free of Harris. It is well written, but reminds this reader today of a soap opera—which may indeed be exactly right for this story!

The main character in Rosa's novel is Rosalie. At the start, she is an older companion living with the young children of the community, who have been separated from their parents and live apart in a kind of limbo world, working in the garden and being scolded for every act of naughtiness, with treatment devoid of any love or affection. In the actual compound in Brocton, the children's house was called "The Bird's Nest." In the novel, one of the children, lonely little Ted, fails to stay clear of the berry bushes and is scolded. Then he is stalked by a wild-eyed woman named Celestia, whom he no longer recognizes as his mother. "Her eyes devoured the child – poor pinched little creature. She was so hungry for him; her heart was aching and starving for him."[1] But they were not allowed to be together.

Meanwhile, Ted's father, Brother Skilful (sic), is lying ill at Father John's lakeside house, and ultimately dies, with his wife forbidden to go to him. Rosalie ponders how it is possible that her own mother, Petra, has grown completely apart from her father, Noble, who has been sent by Father John out into the external world to earn money for the community in New York City. When she eventually sees him, her father seems so sad for the family life he has lost.

Touching on only a few points more in the melodramatic plot of the novel, in one key scene we see Father John lecherously trying to win over Rosalie as a believer in him, saying "You are growing little one, you will be a great blessing to father one of these days. Who knows but you will be his right hand in the great work."[2] But Rosalie will have none of it and, for her resistance, she is re-located from the children's house to much rougher quarters at another community house called "The Farm" where she will have to cook, clean and do manual labor. When she shows strong feelings for a boy her own age named Felix, Father John sends the boy away.

And when her father, Noble, returns for a visit from the city, Father John and his minions press him relentlessly to make out a new will, cutting out his wife and Rosalie, and leaving all to Father John.

At first Noble resists, but ultimately gives in. Soon after, he dies while away working in the city, and when his belongings are sent back to the community, the zealot Celestia discovers bundles of valuable deeds and stocks, together with a new will, re-instating his wife and Rosalie as heirs. Celestia understands what is at stake and burns the will.

Unfortunately, the flaming paper sets fire to the main house where Father John lived. But this turns out to be just as well since Rosalie has just stabbed Father John to death with a dirk brought back from India by Harold—a very Laurence-Oliphant-like English aristocratic member of the community. Evidence of Father John's stabbing death is destroyed by the fire and Rosalie is able to join her young man Felix and live happily ever after, unfortunately without the inheritance from Noble, but that doesn't seem important to her at the time.

Besides the antagonistic sentiments of the novel's main character Rosalie towards her prophet, there is some telling writing along the way. Earnest supporters of Father John say wooden and pompous things like:

> "…the worst is over. Disease and death will pass away, but his children will not pass away. Oh a blessed time is coming, the destruction of the world is at hand, and the new era will open up for the chosen." Susan wondered quietly if they would be among the chosen.[3]

Places similar to the Brotherhood of the New Life's Brocton campus are also described, such as the chapel, with a red carpet leading to the altar. Rosa provides some evocative color commentary in the chapel's description, such as:

> rows of chairs… served to seat Father John's people, when he had anything to say to them. This was not often, for he said they did not live up to the light they already had.[4]

More positive real-world eyewitness accounts of life at the Brotherhood can be found in Laurence Oliphant's letters back to his friends, the Cowpers, as in this section from his letter of May 28, 1869. It acknowledges the Brotherhood's growing notoriety, which has resulted in a "flood of applications" from people wanting to join, even though they have no idea about what life in the community would be like. To handle all the visitors, the Brotherhood opened a hotel, restaurant and even a saloon down by the train station:

> It was quite a new experience for two of our ladies to be cook and chambermaid in a hotel, and for our mild Quaker Mr. Clark to attend the bar but the civilizing effects are already apparent. We sell nothing but beer and wine and not more of that to one person than we think is good for him—and instead of its being a lounge for idle and dissipated "roughs" we make it look as pretty as possible with flowers, etc. and ladies go in and out, so as to invest it with a different character from any other place of the sort. In this way we carry the War into the Enemy's camp, and by boldly taking hold of his own weapons hope to turn them against himself.[5]

Laurence's tone in describing all this demonstrates how positive he is about his busy new life at the Brotherhood. His health seems to have returned and his natural abilities seem to be putting him in somewhat of a leadership position, especially when the task involves interacting with the outside world, including tasks like checking in with wealthy benefactors like the Cowpers. Because the Cowpers were so rich and well connected, in all cases they had to be responded to with respect and understanding, even if the topic seemed trivial compared to the Brotherhood's central task of preparing for the end of the world. In this excerpt from letters, Miss Jane Waring (Dovie) responds to Georgiana Cowper's question whether she can bring her favorite dog along with her to salvation, if indeed she and William Cowper made the decision to join the community at Brocton. Dovie notes that, although the animals are "capable of redemption" as well as men, attention at this critical moment must be focused on reuniting mankind with God. Besides, she notes practically:

> the expense of taking one dog across the Atlantic would feed one more struggling soul in our midst who might otherwise have to wait doggy's pleasure.[6]

On a more serious note, there was a certain amount of "bad press" beginning to circulate about the community. While local neighbors noted the genteel character and quiet religious intensity of the Brotherhood, and had been impressed by the gumption shown at their hotel, restaurant and saloon, there were distressing reports about the community's treatment of its children. Stories circulated about children being taken from their parents, and the parents themselves being separated and made to live as singles with other men and women. And there had been some chance meetings between outsiders and seemingly miserable children who had been met unattended and unsupervised on the grounds. In fact, Harris did neglect the children, having them more likely to work in the gardens or kitchens rather than attend a proper school. Later on, there was disagreement between some of the grown children interviewed about their early years with Harris. James Freeman recalled his days at Brocton as the "brightest" of his childhood. Others remembered Laurence Oliphant visiting the children's house and telling wonderful stories. On the other hand, the two Martin boys thought their parents had been deceived ludicrously by Harris and resented how they had been forced to wash dishes rather than get an education. Young Pitt Buckner, with the faerie name Earnest, assisted in the many nocturnal relocations of members from one house to another. He recalled one time when he had angered Harris on some point and was sent to live in an isolated and empty community home. Harris told him his states had become so bad he must stay far away—or the prophet might become very ill or even die. That night, instead of laboring to improve his states, Earnest sneaked back to Vine Cliff and spent several hours walking in tight circles around the house. When Harris emerged the next day unhurt, Earnest went back to his isolated house in disgust, forever believing Harris was a fake.

Some early members had already left the Brotherhood. The Emersons and their daughter Rosa were banished after Mr. Emerson disagreed with how Harris was running things. Mr. Emerson bought a competing winery back in Dutchess County, closer to New York City. He re-named that vineyard to market "Brotherhood" wines that are still being sold today. In later years the Emersons also said they left because Harris was making improper advances to Rosa, which certainly ties in with the events in Rosa's novel. Another one expelled was Mr. James Fowler who demanded his money back and then exited, leaving his wife and son there. Shortly after, he returned and shot himself dead. Harris said Fowler "was a man of feeble constitution" and had him exhumed from a position next to Mr. Requa in their burying ground. Harris did not want Requa distracted in the celestial realm by the presence of the body of a tortured soul buried near him. And a British family, the Ruxtons, joined and was very disappointed with their experience at Brocton in 1868. Harris was apparently disappointed with them, too, and ordered them away. The Ruxtons complained to the Cowpers about their rough treatment, and Laurence stepped in to write a very long letter back to the Cowpers as the prophet's defender and apologist. He explained the Ruxtons' states were so bad "I helped to hurry them away, just as in principle that a General would hurry away soldiers smitten with plague from the middle of a healthy army." For his own state, Laurence chooses to insert verses from Harris's published hymn, *Christ on the Water*:

A pilgrim to the Land of Love,
I cross the stormy seas,
And still, in voices from above,
My Lord is leading me.

He concludes his defense of the expulsion of the Ruxton family by exhorting the Cowpers to:

> Resist as a positive sin the weakness which now you know so much causes you still to doubt. When such thoughts arise go directly to Christ, and in His name and strength trample them under your feet. God bless and keep you from the snares of the evil ones.[7]

The prospects of the Japanese contingent also shifted. The long-awaited change of government in Japan came as their civil war ended the era of the Shoguns and temporal power was returned to the emperor at the Meiji restoration in 1868, although there would be years of chaos before the new order in Japan settled down. As this new order was announced, almost all of the students—such as the group's leader, Arinori Mori—returned home, where eventually, true to plan, they would be recognized for their valuable exposure to the West and set on career paths to rise quickly through the new government's diplomatic ranks. Mori became a diplomatic leader for the next delegation to Washington, where he wrote a remarkably detailed briefing book explaining many of the mysteries of the west for visiting Japanese dignitaries. But Kanaye Nagasawa was at a much younger and impressionable age. He had grown very close to Father Harris and Dovie (Jane Waring), and they to him, and, quite frankly it was safer for him to remain with them at just that time since all of the privileges of the samurai caste in Japanese society were being removed—including their government stipends—and over a million disenfranchised samurai were seething at their newly impoverished predicament back in Japan. Kanaye was no quitter, and, whether he realized it or not, was on a course of transferring permanent loyalty, and filial love and family commitment to Harris and Dovie. In that sense, it was no surprise he decided to stay at the commune. In their place as surrogate parents, in 1870 Father and Dovie thought it might be a good idea for Kanaye to continue his formal studies—at which he so excelled—and sent him to nearby Cornell University for a time. But he was miserable away from Brocton. He wrote to his "Aunt Dovie" from college that he felt he was in prison. She thought schooling "brought him down" and so he was out of Cornell by the end of 1870. They had correspondence with the school,[8] back and forth, trying to reconcile his school fees with his sudden leaving.

In 1870, Laurence also left Brocton, although not for any dissenting reasons – it was more of a "graduation." His time at Brocton since 1867 had put him (and his mother) in robust good health, made him a devoted follower of Harris, and informally ordained him as an ardent spiritualist practitioner to the degree he was able to practice deep breathing and imagine himself visiting spirits in the celestial realm. Harris's plan for Laurence was to send him back into the external world, where he could earn good money for the community's common fund. So early in 1870, Laurence arrived back in London as suddenly and unexpectedly as he had left. It is important to know while away from Brocton, Laurence believed be still had an active connection with Harris and that he would know instinctively to return, if Harris willed it. He also believed he was under a form of celestial protection through Harris, and that he would be safe from any harm while he was away.

At his return, Laurence's eccentric appearance and reputation for erratic behavior probably ruined his normal job prospects and closed any opportunities for a formal appointment in British diplomacy or government. No doubt, many in London society would have judged him crazy to have devoted himself unabashed to Harris's experiment in the American wilderness. Nevertheless, his good spirits, sense of humor, and overall conviviality all returned with him intact. Margaret Oliphant met him at the time and wrote:

He appeared to have a sort of holiday happiness about him, a delight in talking over the trials and difficulties he had passed through, such as a man who has come triumphantly through a long voyage.[9]

That made it even more impossible for his old friends not to welcome him back into their company for dinners, weekends or conversations at his clubs. Quite simply, everyone wanted to hear firsthand what he had been doing while he had been gone.

To supplement his small allowance from Harris, Laurence was ordered to seek gainful employment. His first attempt was a deliberate effort to make a new start. He paid a leading society tailor £500—a significant sum—to teach him the tailoring trade. He had done quite a lot of sewing while on probation waiting to join at Brocton and it had helped him get used to the humility he would need to survive his rude awakening to manual labor in America. Now he tried to cling to the simple life as he re-entered Piccadilly. But Harris was not pleased at his tailoring choice and sent a curt letter telling him to "try something else." Fortunately, just at this time, more than the usual level of intrigue and unrest blew up across the English Channel with the outbreak of the Franco-Prussian war and Laurence was able to get a well-paying assignment from *The Times* to cover the action. And so, he really was back again, in the thick of things, and characteristically eager to join the fray.

*

The new hostilities started when the dissipated French dictator Napoleon III declared war in mid-July 1870 after years of tension with Prussia, which was intent on continental dominance, inspired by Otto van Bismarck's long-term plans for empire. The alleged reasons were disagreement over the succession to the vacant throne of Spain, plus a falsely fabricated insult to the honor of France "forged" or at least added by someone who made the "slightest sharpening" of the language about France in a telegram written by the Prussian Foreign Ministry to Bismarck.[10] Napoleon III was not alone in his disdain for his German neighbors, however, because anti-German sentiments were rampant in France. Observers attending the Paris opera on the night of the declaration reported that, at the end of the performance, one of the female singers walked onto the stage carrying a flag and announced the good news of war. She then led the happy crowd in a passionate and patriotic singing of the *Marseillaise*. Then everyone spilled out into the Place de l'Opera shouting "On to Berlin!"[11]

Unfortunately a farce unfolded. Although the French had made the first official move with their declaration, they were unable to mobilize as quickly and efficiently as the Germans, who had elaborate railroad scenarios worked out in advance for assembling their forces. France was never able to overcome that initial disadvantage. On September 1st, only seven weeks after the night at the opera, 140,000 French troops surrendered at the Battle of Sedan and Napoleon III himself was captured. The entire war was only to last only a few bloody months, with 250,000 lives lost, and seems to have been characterized by ill-advised rushing around and poorly thought-out maneuvering.

It certainly began in a commotion for Laurence, with orders from *The Times* to proceed at haste to cover the civil unrest brewing in the southern part of France at Lyons. Instead, he found himself immediately embroiled in the chaos of stalled and entangled French trains full of mobilizing French soldiers unable to join their units. The mood in Lyons was grim, showing early signs of what would become a bloody civil war after the fighting with the Prussians ended. And it was in no way safe for a British correspondent, since many of the French felt betrayed that they were facing the Prussians alone without the British, with whom they had been so closely allied in the Crimea. In fact, it was highly likely Laurence would have been shot as a spy for a government on friendly terms with the Germans, if his true identity and purpose had been discovered. At one assembly in Lyons, whispers went around that an English spy was in the room, and it was only by standing like everyone else and screaming in French that the intruder must be found and shot, that Laurence was eventually able to make his escape.[12]

Fortunately, Laurence's orders from *The Times* changed, and he was told to try to join the Prussian headquarters staff at Versailles, on the perimeter of the bitter siege of Paris, which had begun on September 19 when the last train was allowed out of the capital. True to his nature in earlier reporting, Laurence was not happy simply to stay at the command center and rely on dinner conversations with staff officers for his reporting. He was intent on being in the thick of the fighting.

For this writer, it is almost impossible to believe the ease with which an English gentleman could move around from one warring side to another in the midst of a savage and bloody war. But Laurence was the same person who had impulsively joined the street mobs during the Italian-Austrian fighting while traveling with his parents on their European grand tour decades earlier, and who directed 200 men to build a cannon battery in the dark of night while reporting from the Crimean War. In fact, although he had just spent more than two years in what at the time might be called the American wilderness, he was still unbelievably well connected. For example, he left for his new assignment in such haste that he had not obtained an official "press pass" to join the Prussian headquarters (but it was probably just as well he didn't have one with him while dealing with the French). So to ensure his access, along the way he decided to send a personal telegraph to his earlier acquaintance, Otto von Bismarck. Although Bismarck didn't help because he did not want a liberal British journalist around, Laurence was welcomed to dinner with his old friend Crown Prince Frederick of Prussia who provided an insider's view of what was going on. In return, Laurence gave the prince encouraging reports of rebellious activities in the south of France that might aid in the fall of Napoleon III's regime from internal sources after the hostilities ended. Finally the chaos of a quick departure from Versailles by the occupying Prussian headquarters staff made Laurence's lack of credentials simply one more aspect of the chaos and missing belongings engulfing everyone, and he was able to join them unchallenged and send back dispatches to *The Times* with a unique and intimate perspective on the German operations.

I think the mystery of why *The Times* would pay top wages to someone who could have been characterized as a Brocton lunatic can be explained by the quality of his descriptive writing posted back to the newspaper each day. Here is a snippet from the report on the German movements around the Loire Valley as published in *The Times* on November 26, 1870:

Yesterday morning the Head-Quarters of the Grand Duke of Mechlenburg left Angerville a little after day-break, and accompanied the bulk of the army in an easterly direction across the immense unbroken plains which characterize the scenery of this part of France. Traversed by excellent macadamized roads in every direction, and dotted over with isolated villages and farmhouses, the greatest facilities are afforded for moving and quartering large bodies of troops...The inhabitants are collected in villages two to three miles apart from each other, and so exactly similar that at the end of the day's march there is nothing to indicate that one is not still at the beginning of it; the same cluster of ancient stone cottages huddled around the same old church, with its dilapidated gabled tower and clock that does not go; the same grand chateau or mansion at one end of the hamlet, and horsepond at the other, with the Mairie and blacksmith's shop in the middle; the same group of surly-looking men in blouses collected in a knot at the door of the little tavern, which is hermetically sealed and doing its best not to be supposed to be a house of entertainment for men and beast; the same frightened old women standing at the cottage doors and forbidding the younger ones to show themselves; and, lastly, the same soldiers that fought at Woerth and Sedan, plodding cheerily on, toughened by hard fighting and long marching, and thoroughly versed in all the most delicate mysteries of campaigning in an enemy's country. As we pass the first villages without occupying them, or doing more than make the necessary requisitions for provisions from the inhabitants, they seem to breathe again with relief. We have not proved to be the tigers and wild beasts they had anticipated; and though they would evidently rather not have seen us, it is probable, should we ever be forced to pay another visit, that a larger number will be found at home.[13]

When the two armies did become engaged, Laurence's days were spent up close with the action on the battlefield, driving around the battle zone with a driver and his own covered coach, with bullets and cannonballs flying. The winter became one of the most severe in living memory, with terrible suffering through the country and its besieged capital city. Here is one description of Laurence trying to find his coach one icy evening, after spending two days on the battlefield, with the first night huddled safely in the protection of an occupied house nearby:

I had some trouble in finding my carriage. I had left it at a well-defined position on the battle-field the day before, but to reach it I had to walk for more than a mile over a plain where the carcasses of men and horses were not merely thickly strewn but frozen into all sorts of fantastic attitudes. The thermometer had been 16 degrees below the freezing point on the previous night, and men only slightly wounded, who had not been able to crawl to their comrades, had been frozen to death. One man was stiff in a sitting position, with both his arms lifted straight above his head, as though his last moments had been spent in an invocation, and it gave one a shudder in the clear moonlight to approach him. Others were crumpled up in death agony, and so frozen. In places, many together, French and Germans were mingled, not because they had been at close quarters, but because the same ground had first been occupied by one and then by the other, perhaps at an interval of half a day. I think I was more comfortable with bullets pinging in my ears, than walking the distorted shadows of these dead and stiffened men; and it was quite a relief to see a haystack on fire, and a regiment warming themselves at it, and my prudent coachman within comfortable distance of the ruddy blaze.[14]

The cold was described as "unendurable" throughout the battle zone, and Laurence was glad to be assigned to spend Christmas back at the German headquarters outside Versailles. His room-mate was William Howard Russell, the senior correspondent for *The Times*, who was getting ill, and Laurence's own nights were troubled by deep unrest and sleepwalking. However, their situation was not to be complained of in light of the dreadful conditions being endured by the residents of Paris, who by Christmas Day were in the 98th day of their siege. The herds of sheep and cattle that had been hurried into the fields around the Bois de Boulogne in September were a distant memory.[15] All of the animals in the city had been eaten, including the popular pair of elephants at the Paris Zoo, Castor and Pollux.[16] Rats were delicacies sold at top prices, but the hunger was not as bad as the cold.

Unlike many diplomats, the American Ambassador, Elihu B. Washburne, did not flee the city. He sent his family away to the safety of Belgium, and remained with only his oldest son, maintaining embassy operations and giving shelter and comfort to as many of the citizens as possible. One night, more than one hundred souls slept in the American embassy. He was even single-handedly responsible for demanding and paying for dozens of special trains to safely transport all German-national residents out of the city to safety. His Christmas Day diary entry begins:

> Never has a sadder Christmas dawned on any city. Cold, hunger, agony, grief, despair sit enthroned at every habitation on Paris. It is the coldest day of the season and the fuel is very short... The sufferings... exceed by far anything we have seen... The government is seizing every horse it can lay its hands on with remorseless impartiality. The omnibus horse, the cab horse, the work horse, the fancy horse, all go alike in mournful procession to the butcher's block...[17]

But sadly, the worst was yet to come. Finally, the city surrendered on January 27, 1871, the 131st day of the siege. After the Armistice was signed between the two countries, Laurence snuck into Paris on February 1st—something forbidden to journalists by Bismarck, but Laurence was intent on reporting on conditions inside the city and the likely revolution which would ultimately end the Second Empire of Napoleon III and usher in the French Third Republic.

The Times directed Laurence to rent central quarters in the city, appropriate for interviewing all sides of the dispute in a private home, rather than out in the streets or hotels, which were all uncomfortably dangerous for everyone. Laurence sent dispatches on February 15 warning of the possible tensions between the French National Guard, all of whom were about to become unemployed with the recent peace, and the regular army, which was supporting the unpopular defeated government. The Prussians formally marched into the city on March 1st, and then marched out again, disrespectfully, through the Arc de Triomphe on March 3rd, and, with their departure, any sense of civil order was then gone. On March 18 forces of the army attempted to remove cannon at the heights of Montmartre under control of the National Guard, and bloody chaos erupted. Two retired generals strolling nearby were seized by the mob, shot dead and urinated on by the crowd. Everywhere people were storming barricades and dying in the street, while Laurence kept reporting as events unfolded on the days of the Paris Commune.[18]

The two sides in the chaos were divided as those still somehow in support of their disgraced leader, Napoleon III, who had started the late war, versus those eager to install a new republic. On March 22, Laurence was out watching the action in the Place Vendome as a young Army officer seized a tri-color flag of France and led an unarmed mob in an attack on a National Guard barricade. Some National Guardsmen fled to spare the crowd, but others fired point blank into the mob. Laurence went into a nearby doorway and climbed the stairs for a better view. He was looking on from a window, when a bullet went through his hair. Finally, it seems, he paid some attention to his perilous situation. As legend has it, Laurence took this close call as a signal that his celestial "protection" was being withdrawn by Harris, and he was subtly being told to leave. He later wrote:

> I had turned into a home to avoid a charge of soldiery, and a bullet grazed my hair. I took it as a sign that my protection was removed and got away as soon as I could manage to do so.

Indeed, he left Paris for Brocton that night. While the bullet triggered his departure, he had been planning a trip back since had also received distressing news from Brocton earlier in the same week that his mother was very ill there. He had arranged for his post to be covered by another correspondent for *The Times* temporarily while he hurried "home," but he had the definite plan to return again soon.

On April 7, 1871, Laurence re-entered Brocton at the end of the same cold and miserable winter he had left in Paris. He found the Brotherhood going through challenges. Mr. Fowler's suicide had been picked up and given substantial local newspaper coverage. And Laurence's mother, Lady Oliphant or Viola as she was called with her faerie name, was indeed unwell, probably from overwork at manual labor and real suffering caused by her forced separation from her son, as much as from any disease. She had even been forbidden to say goodbye to Laurence the year before when he left, and nor was she ever told where he had gone.

The young samurai community member, Kanaye Nagasawa, kept a personal diary from these months in early 1871, through the winter and into early spring, which is among the papers preserved at the Gaye LeBaron archive at Sonoma State University in California. The original is written in beautiful Japanese calligraphy, no doubt learned from his father, and there is a typed English-language translation. It was a dark and cold winter, and the Harrisites at Brocton were wretched—especially Kanaye. The mood is set right from his entry in the diary for the start of the year, on January 1, 1871, in a faltering translation, and not written in Kanaye's own English-language words, but in those of some struggling translator:

> I never spend before such sad and unhappy New Year's Day... as I examined my heart deeply I discovered all my past act(s)... were from selfhood. But my earnest aspiration is to use higher and deeper in the Lord with self-abnegation commencing with the new year.[19]

Kanaye goes on to record a daily repetition of terrible weather—as bad as it had been in Paris—combined with minor illnesses, such as colds, earaches and toothaches among the residents of the commune, with Dovie and Harris frequently making trips to the dentist off campus. Besides these temporal challenges, the spiritual spheres of the members are also in chaos, with some being sent away by Harris, and others being moved around from house to house in the middle of the night, with Kanaye usually doing the notifying, and "Earnest" Pitt Buckner handling the physical moves. One January morning Mrs. Requa seems cheered up after a celestial visit the night before with her dead husband, James, but even she complains about being pestered by the spheres of Laurence Oliphant and Jonathan Lay. On February 11, Father said the Faeries had a council and were complaining that Mrs. Requa should keep herself more quiet. Perhaps she was making too much noise as Father and she made their nightly gyrations together to move into heaven for "conjugal" visits with the deceased James Requa and Queen Lily?

On April 7, Kanaye writes in his diary that Uncle Woodbine, also known as Laurence Oliphant, was expected back from Paris, after his bullet-through-the-hair experience. Father, Dovie, Golden Rose (Mrs. Requa) and Kanaye all went down to the train to meet Laurence and then went to dinner at the Brotherhood hotel in the town, as they did frequently. The night of April 9, Kanaye reports Father and Uncle Woodbine were up talking about going to Europe until two o'clock in the morning. The next day, Arinori Mori wrote from his post in the Japanese delegation to Washington asking about Uncle Woodbine and noting several of the original students had joined him at the U.S. capital. On April 15, Father and Woodbine are talking a lot about the war in France, and the diary ends a few days later.

The diary ended because Laurence was ordered to return to Paris, taking Lady Oliphant with him since she seemed to respond to Laurence's presence as a medicine to get well again. Father, Dovie, Golden Rose and Kanaye were off shortly on what must have been a breathtakingly exciting Spring visit to Europe for Kanaye and a welcome change of pace from the dreadful winter in Brocton. The prophet himself wanted to get the heck away from all the needy souls in Brocton, and use their money to update himself on the state of mankind in Europe in the final days of the Franco-Prussian war. Since the turmoil in Paris to him was the work of evil demons, Harris needed to see if the situation was grave enough to foretell the end of the world and judgment day.

On landing in Britain, Kanaye re-traced his steps to visit his old secondary school in Aberdeen, Scotland, which he had attended for two years after first arriving in Britain, while the Harris party relaxed in luxury near Southampton at Broadlands with the Cowpers. Then Kanaye caught up with Harris and his entourage in time to go over to Paris. The Oliphants had taken a nice house on rue du Centre (now rue Lamennais), which was a small street just off Avenue de Friedland, one of the spoke boulevards fanning out from the Arc de Triomphe at Place de L'Etoile. This effectively placed them in the middle of everything. *The Times* formalized Laurence's appointment as their chief French correspondent during this critical time the new French government was reforming and order was being restored. He had a large salary, and all expenses paid. A French colleague of Laurence in those days, Henri de Blowitz, recalled the house as a beehive of activity, with Laurence receiving telegrams by the moment and responding with telegrams that magically appeared a day later in the front pages of *The Times*.

Laurence and his mother were ready as hosts when Harris and his inner circle arrived on their tour to assess the condition of mankind in France. The small group stopped in at Paris before eventually continuing on to Switzerland. They arrived at a dramatic time in the fighting, in the very last days of the Commune known now as "La Semaine Sangleant," or "The Week of Blood." Now certain that the passionate insurgent Communards had to be stopped in their takeover of Paris and atrocities against the supporters of Napoleon III's Second Republic, the defeated French regular army camped at Versailles marched into the capital to restore order. Jane Waring ("Dovie") wrote back to the members at Brocton:

> Beloved ones – It is a long time since I passed the happiest day of our absence from you in writing letters home from Broadlands. Since then Father has been in almost incessant combat in the French spheres. We entered Paris while the fires were still burning and the blood stains were on the pavements and prisoners guarded by bayonets were marched through the streets at all hours, a fearful scene of human passions and contrast to which all our aims must lead if we are faithful.

Miss Waring then shared a poem written by Harris about the conditions the traveling group encountered in Paris:

We entered the stately city
Through pathways where shot and shell
Had made of the beautiful Boulevard
A cavernous track through Hell.

The marble arches were shattered,
The pavements with blood were red,
When the gory breast of the commune
Lay gasping and well-nigh dead.

We counted the last pulsations
Of its fierce inhuman heart
In thunderous verberations
From the cannon upon Mountmart

Women with smoky tresses
Unsexed for a vile misuse
Were flinging through shrine and palace
The torch of the Petreleuse.

Girt by the flaming ruins
Pierced by the dripping blades
We saw where the dead were lying
Under the barricades.

Cold from the sulphurous heaven
The rains began to fall
Ashes and smoke and burning
Were wrapped as a somber pall.

There where the fire fiends reveled
Blasting with one curse and ban
We read with a strange new meaning
The creed of the Artisan.[20]

Soon the insurgents of the Commune reached a desperate state behind their barricades, and decided more dire action was needed. In addition, there was a sentiment that, if their cause was to be lost, they were going to be sure to take the usually delightful city with them. On May 24, 1871, the Communards decided to torch the city. In a later interview, Kanaye recalled "I saw people setting fire to a big hotel in Paris." Of course, the burning was also observed by Laurence and the other *Times* correspondents who telegraphed their reports to London for the May 25th edition. In reports shortly after noon, the Chateau of the Tuileries, the mansion of the Minister of War and the buildings and inner courts of the Finance Ministry were torched. Updates at 5pm contained the fears of the horrified reporters focused on the fate of the buildings at the east end of the Tuileries Gardens and around the Place de la Concorde at the west end. The printed *Times* report read:

The Louvre is not wholly gone, and perhaps the fire will not reach all its Courts. As well as we can make out through the flame and smoke rushing across the gardens of the Tuileries, the fire has reached the Palais Royale. Everyone is now crying out "The Palais Royale burns!" and we ascertain that it does. We cannot see Notre Dame or the Hotel Dieu. It is probable that both are fast becoming ashes. Not an instant passes without an explosion. Stones and timber and iron are flying high into the air, and falling to the earth with terrible crashes. The very trees are on fire. They are crackling, and their leaves and branches are like tinder. The buildings in the Place de la Concorde reflect the flames, and every stone in them is like bright gold. Montmartre is still outside the circle of the flame; but the little wind that is blowing carries the smoke up to it, and in the clear heavens it rises black as Milton's Pandemonium.

In the words of American Ambassador Washburne, "the rage of the soldiers and the people knows no bounds. No punishment is too great, or too speedy"[21] for the guilty who were responsible for defacing Paris with fire. Retaliation by the army killed an estimated 20,000 to 25,000 people. It was said the Seine ran red with blood. But, in spite of these dark hours, the city did recover. The saner members of the population who had fled Paris before the worst of the fighting came back in. The Venus de Milo statue, which had been removed for safekeeping, was re-installed in the Louvre, and repairs and re-building were begun wherever restoration was possible. By early June, the Harris troop left Paris for Switzerland, letting the Oliphants catch their breath.

During the ensuing period of recovery, Laurence's house was always full of the most important visitors jockeying for positions of power and seeking the latest news and gossip. It also became a lively center for the expatriate scene. During that heady time, Lady Oliphant developed the habit of going coach riding in the afternoons with her English next-door neighbor, Lady Wynne-Finch, and that lady's daughter from a previous marriage, Alice le Strange.

Alice's unusual surname was from her deceased father, Henry le Strange, head of an ancient British family with its family seat in Hunstanton, Norfolk, on the cliff-lined eastern coast

Alice Oliphant in her twenties.

of England. The family name probably dates from around the fourteenth century when the Norman aristocracy in England gave it to one of Alice's ancestors, because he was "a stranger," not from Normandy but instead from Brittany, further to the west of France. When Alice's father Henry inherited ten thousand acres in Norfolk, including breathtaking coastline, he developed what became a very popular Victorian seaside resort, easily accessible by train for short and long holidays. He also indulged a passionate hobby restoring old churches, which was very popular among the upper crust levels of English society at the time. When Henry died at age 47, his younger widow re-married Mr. Wynne-Finch, a Member of Parliament for Wales, but she loved to spend time in Paris, becoming a longtime expatriate resident. Now Lady Wynne-Finch and Alice were living next to Laurence and Lady Oliphant.

At 26 years old, Alice was both a stunning well-educated beauty and a thoughtful and spiritual person. She had been born in the middle of Paris, on rue Saint Honoré, and grew up to be an accomplished musician and artist, and well-experienced in society, although she had not found any young man who could be her match. Much of society she found shallow, dilettantish and annoying—and she had no passion for any of the tepid religions popular at the time. On the ladies' long carriage rides, she loved to hear Lady Oliphant's stories of life back in Brocton and the peace it brought. When Laurence was also added to the mix—a well-known author and the fearless war correspondent for Britain's leading newspaper—perhaps it was not surprising that the two young people became attracted to each other and fell head over heels in love. Alice was wealthy from an inheritance from her late father, but she was more than aware of the requirement that she would have to submit to Harris's teachings and "live the life" on his terms. Undaunted, she wrote her own letter of introduction to the prophet, noting she intended to make all her property "payable to you."

Not only was all of this a worry to her mother and brothers, it was also a shock to the prophet and his inner circle who were by now back in Brocton. Sometime earlier, Harris's prohibition on Laurence marrying had been removed, probably in recognition of his recovery to full health and his loyalty to Harris—but this particular development was unexpected. After a good deal of back and forth with the prophet in Brocton, and the suspicious and reluctant le Strange family, the couple finally received permission from all sides to marry. The ceremony took place at St. George's chapel in Hanover Square, London, in June 1872, with both parties listing their residence as the Cowpers' London town house in Curzon Street. They were soul mates from the start, although with some peculiarities to the relationship. Harris informed them they were not true counterparts (since they were both still on earth) and warned that sexual intercourse would only aid the demons. Consequently, marriage started deeper efforts on sexual purity for Laurence who later said:

> I learnt self-control by sleeping with my beloved and beautiful Alice in my arms (for twelve years) without claiming the rights of a husband. We lived together as brother and sister. I am a passionate lover, and so it was difficult, very difficult.[22]

Nevertheless, they were very happy. Laurence and Alice decided a belated honeymoon trip was in order, and headed to the Atlantic coast of southern France for a six-week holiday. They crossed over into Spain and traveled along its northern coast, visiting San Sebastian and Bilbao. "By chance" there the couple met the new King of Spain and joined his party "in his magnificent ironclad frigate" slowly sailing out to Corunna at the extreme northwest corner of Spain just above Portugal. There they joined a British fleet of seven ships where the King was hosted by Admiral Yelverton for several days of festivities in honor of the royal visit to the fleet.[23]

The experience of traveling with the King, including Alice sitting next to him for dinner every night for more than a week, was extremely diverting for the couple. Like many of Laurence's adventures, it is not quite clear whether this was a randomly planned holiday trip, as he claimed, or whether he was on some mission from *The Times* or the Foreign Ministry. The monarch in question would have been the new Spanish king, Amadeo, second son of Victor Emmanuel of Italy, who had just been installed on the vacant throne at the end of the Franco-Prussian war. According to Anne Taylor in her book on Laurence, "England, France and Prussia kept a close eye" on Amadeo, and at this time, Laurence might have been the English eye.[24] Both Laurence and Alice liked the young king very much, although in fact he did not last long and abdicated soon after. It was also a bonus that Alice's younger brother, Charles le Strange, was an officer in the Admiral's circle and had a chance to observe how well the newlyweds got on together. Charles's reports back to the rest of his family smoothed the way for an on-going positive relationship for the newlyweds with Alice's parents and siblings, and that was a great comfort later.

But a pleasant interlude was ending. Without barricades and bullets through his hair, Laurence was bored by normal work, and Harris wanted them all back in Brocton. Alice, after all, had not yet begun to "live the life" and had to go through the usual humbling orientation to join the Brotherhood. No doubt Harris wanted to make sure he could assert his complete control over her. So, in the summer of 1873, Laurence resigned his job with *The Times* and returned with Alice and his mother to Brocton.

We don't know exactly what Alice had expected, but there is a story that, on first arrival at Brocton, Harris ordered her to "bathe in the earth" and the speculation was that she was perhaps buried up to her neck in the earth and only dug out at nightfall. Hopefully this is an allegorical tale and not the "actual" reception for the young woman who had just entertained the King of Spain for a week. However, the prophet would indeed have wanted her to start "living the life" by shedding the entrapments of the past, and concentrating on purifying her "states," so some rough challenges must have been put in front of her.

The couple was now split up and set back on two individual paths by Harris, as he did with so many married couples. Alice was to "live the life" at the Brotherhood, while Laurence was to take on a series of missions to make money for the common good out in the external world. Occasionally, Harris allowed them to re-unite and go off together. For example, by September of 1873 – fourteen months after their wedding — Laurence gave his publisher, John Blackwood, an update on their activities and moods:

> I have been spending three weeks on Long Island, at a lovely spot about thirty miles from New York… fishing, boating, bathing and otherwise putting my wife and myself into robust condition… My wife and mother are both very well, and desire to give their kindest regards to yourself and Mrs. Blackwood. The latter is very happy, and says she finds her time at Brocton all she came for, and enjoys the general novelty and brightness of American life.[25]

Obviously, Laurence and Alice enjoyed spending time in each other's company immensely. Unfortunately, since part of their separation meant not corresponding too regularly, there is not much record of Alice's early years in the Brotherhood. But it turns out Harris had plans for each of them that would keep them apart for a very long time.

CHAPTER 7

LIVING APART

The next years began a prolonged period of prosperity – and even riches – for the Brotherhood. Not satisfied with that success, however, Harris kept his earthbound eyes open for new opportunities, particularly watching how developments in Victorian technology could bring important new openings for the working members, like Laurence Oliphant, to earn even more. Laurence was equally interested in new possibilities, and together their attentions turned towards one of the most romantic and well-publicized ventures of the era – the transatlantic submarine telegraph cable.

That riveting drama had been unfolding for almost two decades by the time Laurence and Alice returned to Brocton. It started in 1856, when successful American businessman Cyrus Field began pitching his visionary idea to connect America and Britain. Unlike the rest of the world, America was still separated by a two-week information delay, because news between New York and London, for example, had to be carried by shipping. That put American government, business and citizens out of step with the rest of the world. Cyrus Field's idea was simple: lay a telegraph cable under water across the Atlantic, along the shallow shelf stretching from Ireland to Newfoundland, and eliminate the information handicap. No longer would America be isolated—it would be aware of changing events, and could react almost as soon as the rest of the world. Field was prone to fast action, even if the scientific and geographical challenges were immense. Because he under-estimated those difficulties, it would take him a decade, from his first pitches to investors, to finally making it all happen, with millions of dollars risked, lost, and won back along the way.

At the beginning, no one ship could carry 2,700 miles of cable, so two had to be used—the first laying cable from America, meeting with a second doing the same from Europe, with serious splicing in mid-ocean. In 1858, they did indeed successfully link up, and the first official communication sent was a joyous exchange between Queen Victoria and American President James Buchanan on August 16. Copies of the messages were framed as collectible certificates, and for one month that summer, telegraph signals flashed between the two continents as bands played, parades marched, and champagne glasses clinked. And then all went quiet, victim to unknown "technical difficulties." Cynics even sensationalized the early success as a likely scam to dupe investors.

But Field was not to be stopped. He lobbied for more money to replace lost investments, and by 1866, after the Civil War, a giant ship called the *Great Eastern* was fitted out for the task, capable of carrying all the cable. It could simply go in one direction, lay the cable, and keep in constant touch with the shores it had departed. After some wrenching failures and fixes in mid-ocean, the ship finally reached the Canadian side with the telegraph signals still working back to Ireland. In fact, it delivered a signal that would remain constant for the next 25 years, restoring Field to riches and good reputation. Several corporate entities had been formed and bust along the way, but the last hastily-configured conglomerate that had finally done it was called the Anglo-American Cable Company, and at the time Harris and Laurence spotted their potential opportunity, Anglo-American enjoyed a lucrative monopoly on all transatlantic cable traffic.

Laurence knew a lot about Canadian law, both from being a colonial lawyer in Ceylon and from his experience as personal secretary to Canada's Governor General Lord Elgin. In fact, he had actually written most of the international Canadian-American trade agreements back in the early 1850's. Since the Anglo-American cable came ashore in Newfoundland, Laurence knew Canadian law should have given the province "ownership" rights, as it would for anything else coming up onto its shores. At the time, Canadian law also forbade monopolies. So if he could craft and introduce new legislation more in tune with the existing law, and help push it through the provincial legislature, the monopoly would be broken, and other companies could take a share of the cable business. In addition, there might be an "All-American" opportunity to take business away from the British-controlled traffic between Newfoundland and Ireland by feeding the transatlantic signals directly to the United States. Whereas the Anglo-American signals made landfall in Newfoundland and then traveled over landlines to the United States, another company could possibly route the international transmissions the whole way to America under water. There was also some relevant new technology since Siemens Brothers & Company in London had developed an enhanced underwater cable with a large central core wire surrounded by a ring of smaller ones, improving the speed of transmission.

To explore this opportunity in the winter of 1873-4, Harris dispatched Laurence to Toronto and even allowed him to take Alice along. Laurence renewed many of the acquaintances he had made as personal secretary to Governor-General Lord Elgin years before. His specific task was to develop the new legislation that became called "An Act to Regulate the Construction and Maintenance of Marine Electric Telegraphs." On their return to Brocton, Laurence wrote to his publisher, John Blackwood:

I am coaching a bill through the Dominion Legislature, which has for its object the extinction of the existing cable monopoly… rather late in life, I am learning business in a school, which as they say, requires one to keep one's "eyes skinned," and if you should want any sharp Wall Street practice exposed or moral detective work done, I am qualifying myself rapidly for the occupation.[1]

Laurence was good at this work and his new legislation was "read" for a vote before the Canadian Senate in May 1874. Forces aligned with the entrenched Anglo-American monopoly lobbied hard to have the bill thrown out by having it referred to London where Anglo-American hoped the government would override the breaking up of the monopoly by its Canadian colonists. Company representatives gave testimony at the Parliamentary inquest in London that the bill would adversely impact the financial interests of many British subjects not resident in Canada. But, after the Indian Mutiny, Britain was happier with "responsible government" for its colonies, letting them govern themselves, and both the British Privy Council and the Earl of Carnarvon, who was Secretary of State for the Colonies, decided there was no practical reason to interfere with the Canadian Parliament's local jurisdiction for this bill. It was allowed to proceed to a vote in 1875 and was passed. The monopoly was indeed broken.

Meanwhile, in anticipation of the bill's success, Laurence was set up as Manager at the Wall Street offices of the Direct United States Cable Company, a new company backed by Siemens, where he now would "exercise an autocratic control over an army of clerks and operators." The company's mission was to steal share from Anglo-American, so he armed himself with on-the-job training on how clever business people in New York, like Jay Gould, were operating, as they put conglomerates together, manipulated stock and generally behaved as what he might have called "swindlers" in his life in London. Soon Laurence was holding his own in the new Wall Street world where "my only weapon is a guileless innocence, which disconcerts them, as they don't know whether I am precious deep or precious flat."

For the practical logistics of the enterprise, Laurence also managed planning for laying the new "direct-to-America" submarine cable, which was a two-step affair. First, in the summer of 1874, a new ship called *C. S. Faraday,* built by Siemens specifically for the task, laid a relatively short 550 nautical mile cable underwater from Tor Bay, Nova Scotia, down to Rye Beach, New Hampshire, assisted at the end by another ship, the steamer *Ambassador.* The completion of this task was an occasion for great celebration, with cannon firing a salute at Rye Beach. Then, in the following summer of 1875, the *Faraday* laid the 2,400-mile transatlantic link between Tor Bay and Ireland. To the dismay of Anglo-American, the new cable successfully started operation in September.

While Laurence was totally absorbed managing all the details of the cable work, Alice and Lady Oliphant teamed up together as they were immersed in the day to day chores of the Brotherhood of the New Life back in Brocton. They lived in isolation together, away from the other members, and no more of their details are known until sometime early in 1876 when Lady Oliphant sent an update on the previous year's activities to Georgiana Cowper, their wealthy friend back in England who was very concerned about the long silence from them:

> Alice (Lowry's wife) has been going through the ordeal, a very hard one, of putting off all the old and much-admired refinement, polish, intellectual charm, etc. ... She is very brave and true, and fights hard against herself. She and I lived together in a cottage for eight months, quite alone except for the help of a boy to do what was too hard for us, and that only about an hour in the day. It was our own wish: we wanted to realize something of the lives of our hard-working sisters in the world, the cooks, housemaids, etc., and to learn to do things for ourselves.[2]

Lady Oliphant goes on to say they cooked, washed and ironed, while she herself actually raised more than one hundred chickens! Just before she sent this letter, their cottage interlude was ended as both herself and Alice were ordered back into Vine Cliff, Harris's main house where the prophet was making real progress in the celestial realm. I suppose, in the twisted world of Harris's community, the forced separation of Alice and Laurence at this point was understandable in that Alice needed to work through her own orientation to the Brotherhood, while Laurence had his hands full on Wall Street. In addition, the separation was consistent with how Harris usually split up married couples so that "scortation," the prophet's favorite word for lewdness and fornication, would not interfere with their progress towards the higher life. But now months apart were turning into years, and neither of them could suspect how long their separation would continue.

*

Harris had been writing prolifically during his early years in Brocton. In 1867 alone he published three new books: *The Arcana of Christianity: The Apocalypse, The Breath of God with Man*, and *The Great Republic: A Poem of the Sun*. Meanwhile, the most devout of his followers, such as future biographers Arthur C. Cuthbert and C. W. Pearce (also known as Respiro), were keeping close eyes on the prophet's evolving revelations, hoping to discern when they might all reach the actual point when the spirits would return to earth and live among them. The early transitions Harris made were clear enough: from his youth as a Universalist minister, to his years as a trance-dictating spiritualist poet, and then to his period of claiming to be the new Swedenborg. But the new revelations, and all his new published works written in Brocton, took the prophet to somewhat confusing new ground, which Cuthbert struggled to explain, and which I will attempt to summarize.

Recapping Harris's key milestones, as I understand them, it had been back in 1853 that Harris had his first vision of Lily in the celestial realm and then began to share frequent glimpses of her with the readers of his trance poetry, such as *Lyric of the Morning Land* (1854). Then, sometime around 1862, while at the "breath house" in Wassaic, Harris achieved the seventh stage of open breathing and was re-born into a new celestial aware soul, but only in an "infantile state." Over the next ten years, this new state developed until Harris was able to visit heaven and pursue his counterpart Queen Lily through a kind of courtship. He continued giving followers more glimpses of progress in his ongoing poetry. Now, in the early 1870s in Brocton, in a cataclysmic event, apparently replete with celestial orgasm, Harris graduated to a complete spiritual and sexual union with Lily, so that her spirit at times entered into and remained resident in Harris's own body on earth, restoring their joint being to the same half-male and half-female nature as the Deity's true nature. Rather unhelpfully, Cuthbert explains that, until now:

> the upper kingdom had not begun to descend into what is known as the "interspace," which had been formerly occupied by evil or impurified spirits between Heaven and Earth...

But now, all that has changed as "Lily has descended to the full degree of consciousness in Thomas Lake Harris's frame."[3]

All of this elevated Harris, as a single individual, to a unique half-human and half-spirit nature from which he could show followers the path for their own return to this desired state. And when all of the chosen attained the same state as Harris, then the reunion of split souls would be complete, and heaven and earth would be back to where we all were before the fall of Adam in the Garden of Eden.

On a finer point, at this time when he has rejoined with Lily, Harris also achieved more understanding about the goals of their partnership for everyone else. Just as Harris has been living in a community of right-breathing souls at the Brotherhood of the New Life in the terrestrial realm, Lily has been leading a spirit community of her own in heaven. And just as he is now the earthbound "pivotal man" who first united fully with the spirit world, Lily is the "pivotal celestial woman" who is leading lesser spirits on the celestial side to make their own link-ups on earth. It seems they are rather like the two ships laying cable separately from Europe and America, with the goal of splicing together in the middle of the ocean. In fact, Lily is the Queen of a whole marching column of lesser young spirits behind her, now ready to become two-in-one with more of the terrestrial faithful at the Brotherhood of the New Life. Lily has been training the young spirits in their own celestial community, like Brocton, which was located on an island in a heavenly zone called the "sea of the golden islands." And just as Lily has now joined with Harris, these other spirit students with her are ready to team up with the other earthbound members of the Brotherhood to whatever degree the Broctonites can receive them. This meant that while the pivotal man Harris and the pivotal celestial female Lily can join with each other in the fullest degree, everyone else in the Brotherhood can now meet up with their own, less adept but still wonderful student counterparts from the other side right there in the neighborhood, so to speak. So everyone in the Brotherhood was directed to intensify their work on open breathing to join with their waiting counterparts to whatever degree they could manage. Certainly some other members would eventually claim to have achieved "the two-in-one" to the ultimate degree—like Oliphant, for example, who later wrote he had joined with his imagined counterpart Alawenie—but from the early 1870's on, everyone else had their marching orders to have a go, even if the attempt felt less than earth shattering.

While this all sounded fairly dignified, there was, unfortunately, a somewhat comic aspect to one method Harris deployed at this time to summon Lily to join him in their unified state, and that was the power of music, even though Harris never learned to play an instrument. Her "electro-vital" nature, apparently, was particularly attuned to music, albeit not music as it was listened to on the earthly level. Not to be deterred, Harris acquired a fine piano, had it perfectly tuned, and then sat down to play it, as Cuthbert says "by sheer influx," as the vibrations from the other world channeled through him. Cuthbert continues, "Perhaps the absence of artificial training was a real advantage, so far as the supreme end in view was concerned." So Harris would bang away at the keyboard, generating what he claimed to be music of the sort valued in heaven, and he continued doing so for many weeks "in the presence and hearing of sisters well trained in music, whose ears seemed in no way shocked by such inartificial strains."

Then when the musical stairway appeared, "the electro-vital form of Lily herself came down, "in full substantial embodiment!" One can only imagine how all this sounded. But now Lily was truly with him, and it was not only through feeling herself within him that Harris would know it. Cuthbert claims Harris could actually see, touch and hear her materialized in front of him—that is, until she felt too cold, and then:

> she had quickly to withdraw again into the beloved one's form, for the deadly cold of the world, as she stepped out, struck with such a chill into her as was beyond endurance.[4]

*

As if the wonderful arrival of Lily and the other counterpart spirit beings was not enough, changes on the terrestrial plain were also afoot. The Brocton community was getting too crowded for Harris. Whenever a new member joined, the prophet would have to pitch in with fighting the infernal demons attacking the novice. With the population of the Brotherhood now well over one hundred, this must have been an epic burden for Harris, and an irritating distraction from him making the most of his god-like union with Lily. On a much more mundane level, the Brocton climate, lakeshore near Buffalo, was very harsh in winter, and the ageing prophet probably felt the cold more keenly than when he first arrived eight years before.

And so, a new plan took shape. The newly accomplished horticulturalist, Kanaye Nagasawa, had been studying the many articles and pamphlets then in circulation about the heaven-like climate of California, especially for winemaking. At the same time, Harris himself had been reading articles by the lumberman, Colonel James Armstrong, about the wonders of Sonoma County on the edge of the great wine country.[5] Soon Harris had a powerful vision of himself standing amid giant sequoia trees and listening to the not-too-far-off sounds of the sea. In addition, dramatic improvements in travel had been brought by another wonder of the Victorian world: the transcontinental railroad, recently inaugurated for service in November 1869. And so Harris decided to heed the oft-quoted exhortation of his former parishioner, Horace Greeley, "go west, young man, go west," and, in 1875, a migration of the Brotherhood's leadership to California began to be planned. The new headquarters of the Brotherhood would be established with a much smaller group, each of whom would be on higher spiritual levels closer to their own spiritual reunions, so Harris would have fewer evil demons to fight. Meanwhile, the less enlightened could soldier on trying to advance themselves back East at Lake Brocton or on their assignments out in the world to make money. In addition, the new enclave on the West Coast would have to be more than a collection of simple farmhouses. It would have to be a setting appropriate for the senior spirits relocating from heaven, and possibly even comfortable enough for the Deity as a new Garden of Eden. All of these advances would have to be subsidized by the operations in Brocton and from withdrawals from the Brotherhood's "common fund" until the California campus could become a moneymaker as well. While they worked out the travel details, Harris hired New York City architects to come up with appropriate plans.

*

The new transcontinental railroad came out of the growing pains of the new United States of America, then less than one hundred years old, and its need for a safe and reliable system of transportation to bind it together, especially after its disastrous Civil War. By 1875, a transcontinental service was well established with essentially two very different ways to make the journey. The first was by "emigrant trains" designed to haul virtually desperate and destitute settlers to new lives out West. On these, the emigrants journeyed in a rail car described by passenger Robert Louis Stevenson as a "long, narrow wooden box, like a flat-roofed Noah's ark, with a stove and a convenience, one at either end, a passage down the middle, and transverse benches upon either hand." The emigrants were soon "miserable" and the cars would soon "stink abominably."[6] The second way to make the crossing was by luxury train, usually populated by wealthy tourists who wanted to experience such a fast, safe and novel way to move west while also observing the poor emigrants and recent settlers as if they were monkeys in a zoo. At the 1876 Centennial Exposition celebrating America's one hundred years, the Pullman Company exhibited a car with an elaborate salon and fully equipped kitchen so that its passengers could glide along on overstuffed furniture, with meals served on fine china, and sofas converted to luxurious bedding, all made up by uniformed ebony-skinned attendants.

There can be no doubt as to which sort of travel arrangements were made for Thomas Lake Harris, the "pivotal man" intent on establishing a new haven suitable for the spirits to join, who would have traveled in the highest style. The advance party he led for the Brotherhood was deliberately small—just himself, Mrs. Requa, her eleven year old son Amodio, and the two Japanese, Kanaye Nagasawa and Osui Arai. They would all have been dressed in the finest apparel for their entry into this new territory, signaling the high seriousness of their mission and the level of service they expected. Chinese were well known in San Francisco at the time. In fact, the city had its own unique Chinatown. Those Asians had arrived during the Gold Rush, and built the railroad with hard labor. Now most had small businesses, or worked as household help or laborers. They were entirely different from the regal Japanese samurai accompanying Harris, and the newcomers would have attracted a lot of attention wherever they went.

Kanaye Nagasawa had been corresponding with the Japanese Consul in San Francisco, Takagi Saburo who had been in the original Japanese delegation to Washington with Arinori Mori, Kanaye's friend and a former resident at Brocton. Kanaye had been writing Takagi for help sourcing possible wine-growing land for the Brotherhood. Takagi identified a site near Santa Rosa in Sonoma County. He met Harris and his small entourage when they arrived in Oakland in early spring, 1875. He had booked "suites" for them at the Cosmopolitan Hotel in downtown San Francisco, one of the city's best hotels. At the Cosmopolitan, an elevator—one of only two in the city—would have raised Harris and his attendants up to their accommodations, where they would have found other technical wonders as well, such as hot and cold running water and inside bathrooms.[7] They rested in the city a few days, and no doubt would have explored the town to assess their new environment.

They would have found a city that had morphed into something truly "cosmopolitan," as the name of their hotel implied, due to the many fortunes and investments made there in the twenty-five years following the California Gold Rush of 1849. As Jules Verne described it in his 1872 novel *Around the World in 80 Days*:

> San Francisco was no longer the legendary city of 1849—a city of banditti, assassins, and incendiaries, who had flocked hither in crowds in pursuit of plunder; a paradise of outlaws, where they gambled with gold-dust, a revolver in one hand and a bowie-knife in the other: it was now a great commercial emporium...there were silk hats and black coats everywhere worn by a multitude of nervously active, gentlemanly-looking men. Some of the streets... were lined with splendid and spacious stores, which exposed in their windows the products of the entire world.[8]

After a few days in San Francisco, Harris and his group boarded carriages of the five-year-old San Francisco and Northern Pacific Coast Railroad and headed about 60 miles north to Santa Rosa. There the land was a lush paradise of microclimates, each shaped by the variety of its elevation, its distance from the sea and its relationship to the mountains to the east and west. Many of these provided ideal environments for vineyards and, although the area was growing in population, there was still plenty of room. The 1850 Census counted 560 inhabitants in Sonoma County. This grew almost forty-fold to over 20,000 by the time Harris arrived in 1875—but that number is only equivalent to 4 percent of the one half million souls living there today – so there was still plenty of near virgin land to be purchased. Once in Santa Rosa, Harris was no longer sightseeing. He was seeking a "world headquarters for the regeneration of humankind" and he had an appointment to see specific land owned by the family of rancher Henderson P. Holmes. He also had the cash he needed with him.

Sonoma County would have been well known by reputation to Harris and Kanaye Nagasawa as the center of the fast-growing California wine industry. They would have both seen, while in Brocton, articles such as the one published in the popular 1864 *Harpers Weekly* news magazine entitled "Wine-Making in California" which calculated California alone had 40 percent of the total acreage suitable for growing wine grapes in all of Europe. Soon Harris was successful in his negotiations for buying the Henderson land by late spring, 1875. The properties were in the rolling hills above the Santa Rosa plain where there was in a "cold belt" ideal for growing grapes. As soon as the property transactions were concluded, Nagasawa spent his days walking and studying every corner of the thousand-plus acre holdings for prime vineyard sites, while building on the site began almost immediately.

First, in July, came tents for the construction equipment and a four-room bungalow for Harris and his advance party. Harris and Mrs. Requa slept inside, traveling to heaven at bedtime, while her son and the Japanese boys set up a makeshift tent made up of boards leaning against the house. Then work started on the main mansion, for which Harris now had ambitious architectural plans in hand, drawn up by New York architect and Harrisite, Louis Cowles. The construction budget alone for this first permanent building was roughly equivalent to $1,200,000 in today's money. The design was for a twenty-room English manor house, with a dining room capable of seating 100 people. Ingredients included ornate fireplaces of marble and cast iron, hot and cold running water, water closets and an 8,000-volume library—undoubtedly the largest private one in California and including all of Laurence's personal books. Gaslights bathed the house in a soft light at night, and Harrisites from all over the world shipped in antiques and rarities for their prophet's sanctuary.

It was ready for occupation by November. Reviewing the results, the *Sonoma Democrat* of 27 November 1875 said "Mr. Harris came from New York… and commenced immediately to erect a residence which surpasses anything in Santa Clara County for its architectural beauty and magnificent design." The name of the new estate became the Fountaingrove Ranch.

Later, the next two buildings to come would be the "Commandery" for the men, followed by the "Familistry" designed to house the women of the community, although the separation of sexes could not be rigorously enforced, even by Harris. The Commandery was built of amber Redwood, with ten manly verandas jutting from its three floors. The Familistry was primarily white and was described as "less stilted in its furnishings and design than the main house." There were large communal bathrooms in each where naked members were later rumored to wash and rub each other's bodies all over each morning to "de-magnetize." All over the grounds there were elaborate landscaping and fountains. Ornamental shrubs and flowers were planted in abundance, and glass greenhouses ensured a never-ending supply.

While the three main buildings and elaborate landscaping were rising quickly, the agriculturalists were much more cautious. At first, energies were focused on running a horse and dairy farm and planting wheat. Grape planting had to wait because the native American phylloxera lice, lethal to European grape vines, were active in California at the time. These hearty insects "spring full-winged from the aphid eggs deposited on the upper roots of the condemned vines,"[9] and if they spread to new vines on the ranch, the result would be disastrous. So far Santa Rosa had been spared, but Brocton wine expert Dr. John W. Hyde and his deputy, Kanaye Nagasawa, decided to wait a bit more before launching the vineyards. As a separate task, Hyde was asked to personally oversee the construction of a printing operation, housed with presses in its own standalone building on the ranch. This was finished during the first year and stood ready for action as an important part of Harris's evolving plans. Although the vineyards would have to wait, the Fountaingrove spread was soon truly magnificent. One history of the county wrote "No one passes over the highway leading from Santa Rosa to Healdsburg without noticing with great interest the Fountain Grove estate... and the palatial residence of Mr. Harris."

Thomas Lake Harris surrounded by some of his
female devotees, with Alice Oliphant at his side.

So, by 1876, the Brotherhood was split between its first followers remaining in the humble collection of farms at Brocton or out in the world, like Laurence, and the elite of the Brotherhood strolling around the palatial grounds at Fountaingrove. Harris and Lily stayed out in California. Very few of the loyal Broctonites received orders to re-locate to Fountaingrove, with the rationale their "states" were not sufficiently advanced to be in the close vicinity of the prophet at this critical time, although their money and all of the earnings of Brocton were most welcome. Jane Waring, Mrs. Harris and a few others did move west when the main house was ready, and a few more came when the Commandery and Familistry were completed. However, Lady Oliphant, Laurence and most of the other New Yorkers never did get invitations to re-locate.

By the fall of 1876, when Laurence was fully engaged with the cable business in New York City, Harris considered his immediate flock and decided it was time for Laurence's pretty and spirited wife Alice to make the trip to relocate to Fountaingrove. She was told to set out in October in order to complete the journey before snow in the high mountain passes might make travel difficult. On the long train ride across the country, Alice must have been quivering with excitement in anticipation of the great events she would help unfold. She had already been working directly with Harris on his great celestial work just before he left Brocton for California. On arrival Alice was ordered into the newly finished main house, signifying she was to be one of the few intimates of Harris's most inner circle. Laurence must have been dismayed that the prophet judged Alice's "states" much more advanced than his own, while he remained on Wall Street, laboring at the Direct United States Cable Company, over two thousand miles away from his young wife. On a more mundane level, perhaps Mrs. Requa was losing her allure for helping Harris merge with Lily in the celestial realm at bedtime and a willing younger and prettier devotee could help?

*

I suspect that Alice was indeed brought out to be Harris's muse and spark for moving on to the next great spiritual transition he made –

the one he thought would be the culmination of his religious journey. I also believe Alice did replace Mrs. Requa in her nocturnal gyrations with the prophet. And if she did do that, I think she would have been honored to have such an elevated role and would have accepted it without a fuss. After all, she was not shy and she would be doing the work of the Lord, who was about to arrive shortly.

Now in the years from 1876 to 1878, Harris was perhaps at his most confident about his growing powers and his leadership role between the spirits and the earthbound mankind. He ordered everything around him to become elevated. He wanted all of the faithful at Fountaingrove to feel "the counterpartal presence and to make the household conscious continually that this was literally the residence of angels and faeries, celestial royalties and nobilities." Mrs. Harris, who was preoccupied with faeries, took time to bestow appropriate names upon her favorite faeries, such as Prince Wisdom, Sir Sunbeam Courage, Lady Precious Pearl, and so on. Harris referred to himself with the regal name of Chrysantheus, and to Lily as Chrysanthea, and their former "brothers" could now address them as King and Queen. The men and women of Fountaingrove were to address each other as "Sir Knights" and "Ladies," and behave towards each other with a courtly decorum suitable for their aristocratic roles in the new cosmic order.

The members in both Brocton and California sensed there was a great change taking place as Harris, Alice and the others in the inner circle were sequestered in the main house at Fountaingrove. Alice herself shared the anticipation of a momentous event. Just before she left Brocton for California, she broke a two-year letter-writing silence ordered by Harris to sneak out a quick update to Laurence enclosing also a letter to the Cowpers, the Oliphants' wealthy friends who had lent herself and Laurence their London townhouse after their wedding four years before. Laurence forwarded the letter to the Cowpers with a preface explaining Alice was going to be playing a central role in the momentous news about to break, and she did not want that to startle them when they heard it. She wrote that the two years of her silence were "more than wonderful," but now she wanted them to prepare for a revelation—which she apparently had prior knowledge of, and indeed had been an active part of—but she "cannot bring myself to trust it to the post." She was bristling with excitement as she continued cryptically:

> I will only say to you that things more wonderful than any imaginings become the simple realities of everyday experience. And I need not write for I do not doubt that the writings will soon be to you, as they are to us all, all in all.

Now, after that veiled heads-up from Alice, Harris made the apocalyptic announcement. It had been revealed to Harris that while, until now, most of his work had been known only to his followers, he had now been told, by Jesus himself, to circulate his next book widely to the greater public because of its significance. In fact, Jesus himself, the male half of the divine two-in-one, had made his Second Coming, manifesting himself to Harris, with God's female half nearby, and telling the prophet that Harris and Lily were the new king and queen of mankind on earth. Cuthbert reported that Christ's remarkable Second Coming to Fountaingrove took place during the earliest days in Santa Rosa, perhaps even when Harris was still living in the temporary bungalow before the main house was finished. Cuthbert wrote, ending in capital letters:

> And here it was, even in those roughest, earliest days, that it pleased the Lord Jesus to make his second advent to the Earth in full ultimation of form. The record of that great event is all given in what must be regarded as the most important of all the books. It is designated in full, "THE LORD, THE TWO-IN-ONE, DECLARED, MANIFESTED, AND GLORIFIED."[10]

This book, entitled as in the capital letters above, was published on the printing presses of the Brotherhood. It detailed the appearance of Jesus to Harris and Lily—Chrysantheus and Chrysanthea—and recorded the initial series of meetings and conversations between them all. Lily, indeed, was also made even more fully realized, brought to life most powerfully through the participation of Alice. Perhaps the words of this holy testimony itself should be used to describe the morning of the first day of these interactions:

> In the morning there appeared with Lily (Chrysanthea) a company of celestial wives, such as had all been taken from the natural world as infants like herself, and they were all singing a nuptial song of the marriage of Earth and Skies, while a shower of golden rain diffused fragrance and softness in the atmosphere. Chrysantheus put forth his hand to take the raindrops where they fell, and they condensed in his palm like grains of sugared wheat. And one said, "Eat," whereupon he tasted them. At this moment, one of the matrons cried, "Let us go into the house, for this rain betokens that a great tornado of judgment respiration is speedily to sweep through the Earth below us, and Lily (Chrysanthea) and Chrysantheus require that we should assist them in making preparations.
>
> OUR LORD MANIFESTED AS PRINTER[11]
>
> After they had returned fully into the natural world, the Lord Jesus came into their bedchamber wearing upon his head a printer's cap. The sleeves of His under-raiment were rolled up above the elbows, and a printer's apron was tied over His other garments above the waist.

It turns out that Jesus, in a printer's outfit, was signaling to Harris and Lily that he felt the best way to communicate the great new tidings of his Second Coming to the unsuspecting world was through a printed book, so that the message could be received gently and understood in its fullness over time. In this way, the "word" of the Lord would actually come through writing to mankind, and "as the words go forth, the Holy Ghost shall accompany them"—and that is why Harris's written pronouncements are so sacred. This, apparently, was thought to be a preferred method of communication with humanity over simply appearing in the skies surrounded by a heavenly throng of archangels, for example. Harris and Lily also agreed the more low-key publishing approach was the most suitable, and now the blessed book itself rolled off the community's presses.

Inside are even more transcripts of conversations between Harris, the Deity, and Lily over several meetings. The traditional Christian churches are attacked. Sacerdotal knowledge of the Way is not something that grows from deacon to minister to bishop to archbishop—that is only done for "the exploitation and oppression of Humanity." Trade unionists were also demonized and Jesus and Harris met a group of them when visiting Hell. Surely all this would provoke a revolution as the world learnt the Second Coming of Christ has arrived? But, amazingly to the Californians, there was only silence— and their own abject disappointment at the lack of impact the work achieved in the marketplace. For some reason they could not fathom, the volume was not instantly embraced as actually announcing the end of the world and the long prophesized Second Coming of Christ. In fact, it was ignored—and worse, as some reactions even dared to be negative. For example, Laurence—overjoyed at all these goings on—sent Louis Liesching, his boyhood friend in Ceylon, a copy hot off the Brotherhood's presses. Liesching was a loyal lifelong friend and an open-minded student of religion. In writing about the book, Liesching could not even include a quotation because he found it all "so blasphemous, so foul, so coarse" that it could only be "a warning, how far away the keenest intellects, the most refined natures, the most shrewd minds nay be led when once they abandon their reason and moral sense to the guidance of another." Liesching also ridicules the postscript to the public, which asked for feedback, reading

> Chrysantheus and Chrysanthea do not receive guests at present but communications from friends may be addressed, if from gentlemen, to Mr. T. L. Harris; and if from ladies, to Mrs. Lily C. Harris, Fountain Grove, Cal.[12]

In total dejection at the great book being ignored, Cuthbert reported:

> After this great book, declarative of the Divine Kingdom had been given and distributed as widely as there was call for it throughout the world, it ere long became apparent that the world in general was not yet prepared for its ostensible embodiment among any of its peoples. Its own state was too directly adverse: therefore no further writings were published. After this, all were printed privately for friends.[13]

The reason for the world's lack of responsiveness was soon revealed to Harris. Among the peoples of the world, truly dreadful states prevailed, particularly when it came to sexual matters. As a result, they were unable to receive Harris's glorious message. So the voice of the prophet became something only the faithful, such as Cuthbert and the benighted flock back on the East Coast, would hear as Harris circulated his "private" updates among believers. The floodgates were opened as Harris composed prose and poetry daily for those few who were ready to receive such messages. Arthur Cuthbert reported that each of the poems eventually published as *The Golden Child* in 1878 started appearing daily "one by one on the breakfast table, beautifully written in Mr. Harris's own hand," beginning in the autumn of 1876. When the Fountaingrove printing presses went operational, Cuthbert reported there was a backlog of 1500 large manuscript pages to be dealt with immediately, and apparently the flow continued unabated. These works all flew off the printing presses operated by printer Osui Arai. But in spite of these private pieces, no further attempt at publicizing the Second Coming more widely to outsiders would be attempted for the next fifteen years. Meanwhile, Laurence in New York City and all of the so-called "members" in Brocton were left on the sidelines of the Second Coming, and, as they forwarded more money to Harris, wondered why they had not at least been elevated to "courtier status" similar to all the Knights and Ladies at Fountaingrove. That snub would soon sow the seeds of great discontent.

PART THREE:

A NEW MISSION

CHAPTER 8

EMBRACING A NEW QUEST

In 1876, while Harris was strategizing with Jesus, and Fountaingrove was becoming a true earthly paradise, Laurence was entering a career crisis. He had re-invented himself and his religion at Brocton and then flourished back in the world reporting for *The Times* in Paris, finally courting and marrying Alice. But now he was adrift in New York trying to make a go of the Direct United States Cable Company. Although he won the early rounds against Anglo-American, the management of the former monopoly would not give up, and a fierce battle between the two firms continued in back rooms in lower Manhattan. What's more, while the "swindlers" were scheming, Laurence was very lonely, missing his wife Alice, and worried about his future.

As a backup plan, in case his cable career evaporated, Laurence also explored an opportunity to move back into personal diplomacy, his first love. An interesting possibility presented itself when Laurence met his cousin, Arthur Oliphant, during a visit to London on cable company business. Arthur was personal secretary to Sir Salah Jung, the Prime Minister of the Indian princely state of Hyderabad. Back in 1798, Hyderabad and other Indian states had entered into a protective alliance with the Britain's East India Company, and later, in the 1860s,

Britain helpfully interceded in the state's favor when a dissolute monarch brought it near bankruptcy. However, the cost of that bailout was the transfer of revenues from the state's most prosperous Berar region to the British. Now years later, Sir Salah Jung helped restore the state to fiscal health, and wanted to write a new constitution, restoring the Berar wealth to its native rulers. Britain watched affairs in Hyderabad very closely because it was a Muslim stronghold in the middle of a predominantly Hindu India, and might be more likely to push for independence, possibly leading to trouble.

Sir Salah Jung could be very charming and charismatic. He impressed the visiting Prince of Wales in India, to the extent he was then invited to come to England. During the minister's subsequent visit there in 1876, Jung was lionized by society and politicians alike. However, positive opinions of him from the Queen and Prince of Wales differed with more cautious assessments made by Lord Salisbury, the Secretary of State for India, and Lord Lytton, the British Viceroy of India. Salisbury and Lytton were leery of Sir Salah Jung's continuing growth in power.

Jung met Laurence during his London visit, possibly at the suggestion of his secretary, Arthur Oliphant, or even through an introduction by the Prince of Wales. Based on Laurence's experience writing treaties for Lord Elgin, and his skillful coaching of the cable bill through the Canadian parliament, Jung hoped Laurence would help with writing and implementing his state's new constitution. The minister even invited Laurence to attend an upcoming Council meeting in Hyderabad where the assembly would be drafting a new constitution. But when the Viceroy, Lord Lytton, learned Laurence had in fact already written a draft constitution before any Council meeting took place, he complained to Salisbury that Arthur and Laurence seemed to be meddling intriguers, and asked that Arthur be dismissed and Laurence banned from India. Although details of this behind-the-scenes maneuvering are not completely known,

Arthur did, in fact, suddenly lose his job as Jung's secretary, and the opportunity for Laurence to help write the constitution also fell through.[1]   Laurence was told Lytton "would not sanction the employment of any European in such a post." Shortly after, Jung was out of favor amid reports he had been manufacturing muskets and bringing in armed men to Hyderabad.[2]

Dejectedly, in a letter from New York dated 10 January 1877, Laurence wrote to the Cowpers that his Indian opportunity was dead, his cable future uncertain and, most importantly, that he was missing Alice since she had obeyed the summons from Harris to move out to California in the previous October.   He planned to go out to Fountaingrove very shortly to see her, but meanwhile he was going to stay in New York until "the fate" of the cable company was decided at an early February shareholders' meeting. If that meeting went against him, Laurence was going to be out of a job. It is important to remember that although Laurence's earthly work was not satisfying, both he and Alice were very much settled in their spiritual lives, confident in the leadership Harris gave the Brotherhood and resolute in the belief that Harris was close to achieving great things for all of mankind, themselves included.   He finished the letter to the Cowpers noting the imminent spiritual apocalypse Harris and all of his disciples were expecting: "The horizon looks pretty stormy both here and in the East and matters seem approaching their climax."

When Laurence next wrote to the Cowpers six months later, his cable company job was over. The Anglo-American "swindlers" had taken over Direct US Cable and fired Laurence. He was in despair with no certain plans or instructions received from Harris to direct his future. He spent a week recovering and fishing in Canada and wrote:

> I am now on the point of returning to New York – but whether I shall have to go to England or shall be permitted first to take a run to California, or do neither one without the other, is beyond my knowledge...[3]

He reported he had heard from other members of the Brotherhood that Alice in California and his mother in Brocton were well, although both communities were on edge, expecting earth shattering developments, in spite of the fact Harris's announcement of the Second Coming of Christ had not achieved its desired impact. Living arrangements at Fountaingrove seemed to have changed as Harris continued his practice of mixing people into new groups whenever he deemed it necessary. Both Harris's loyal devotee Jane Waring and Alice now were out of the main house living on their own together somewhere on the Fountaingrove campus. Laurence wrote:

> I hear that she (Alice) is well and happy and progressing. She and Dovie (Jane Waring) live in a cottage quite alone by themselves and surely two such natures ought to work out something—They work principally in the garden for demagnetizing purposes, and then of course have their cooking and household work, washing etc. to do besides.[4]

Back in Brocton, Laurence continued, he believed his mother was "in more robust health than I ever knew her considering that I have always regarded her as an invalid and that she spent most of her time on a couch."

The focus at both Fountaingrove and Brocton was on the long-awaited fuller manifestation of Lily—hopefully in a form all the members would be able see and interact with as Harris claimed he did. Laurence finished his letter ruminating on how different his life would be after the great change took place. Then he would leave the distractions of Wall Street to return to "the intense spiritual atmosphere" of the Brotherhood, and resume closer relations with his wife, who he knew was spiritually busy, but whom he missed very much. He had only been able to visit his "brothers" in Brocton twice during the previous year and heard only about once a month from California, but never from Alice herself who remained under a communication ban from Harris.

This was all a very uncertain "limbo" time for Laurence, now aged forty-eight, with no job, no prospects and no wife. It was a time his cousin, Margaret Oliphant, called his "vague years." He did continue to write and keep some money coming in, publishing two short satirical pieces in *Blackwoods Magazine*, "Autobiography of a Joint- Stock Company" (July 1876), and "Tender Recollections of Irene Macgillicuddy" (December-January 1877-8). The first told the rise and fall of a fictitious swindler-filled enterprise of the sort he most recently left in New York. The second profiled the new fresh-mannered and confident sort of American girl who, in the fashion of the times, was hooking up with becharmed English aristocrats thunderstruck by the novelty of the American worldview. The two pieces were successfully received on both sides of the Atlantic and gave their author money and some slight diversion from his troubles.

But finally, in spring 1878, he could resist no longer and he made his first pilgrimage to Santa Rosa, without an invitation or permission from Harris. Incredibly, Harris had him turned away from Fountaingrove and refused to let him even see Alice, let alone talk to her. While it may seem absurd that Harris would not allow Laurence to see his wife after such a long absence and his cross-country journey, the prophet was obeyed without question by all of his followers, and that included Alice and Laurence. He was also maniacally protective of his home environment and the "states" of those around him. At this exact time, Harris and Alice would have been consumed in the vortex of important revelations that Harris believed himself to be experiencing, and indeed he was almost reaching his own breaking point. He had worked himself to exhaustion, by day generally writing revelations about society from the "Male" side of his celestial self, while by night devoting himself to passionate interactions with his "Female" side.

Laurence was crushed at being repulsed from Foutaingrove without seeing Alice. He retreated to the nearby home of his friends Mr. and Mrs. J. D. Walker of San Raphael, about twenty-five miles away towards San Francisco. He had met the Walkers in New York City years earlier when he did them a favor that cemented their friendship for life. Mrs. Walker had been about to travel to England with friends when she became ill and was delayed in New York a brief time. She was dreading making the voyage alone with her children. Since Laurence was also about to go to England, he offered on the spot to change his own crossing plans so he could accompany Mrs. Walker and her brood on the transatlantic journey, which he did. Now, in distress, he appeared in Mr. Walker's San Francisco office and stayed with them in San Raphael for a few weeks while he negotiated with Harris for a chance to meet Alice. When he realized that was not going to happen, he resumed his lonely vagabond life. He left for New York, and then made several trips back and forth to his base of friends in England, including Alice's brothers. Seeing them would have been a bit awkward since Alice's silence was a source of strain with her family as well, and her overall embargo on communications cast a cloud over everyone.

Soon after Laurence's visit, however, Alice had her own falling out with Harris. Although she probably had been the prophet's new bedtime companion for diving off into the celestial realm with Queen Lily, Alice must have strayed too far from the great man's instructions. Alice was suddenly banished temporarily from Fountaingrove, without property or money. This sort of thing happened to Cuthbert when he was sent off to work as a lumberjack. It would also happen to Jane Waring for a time when the prophet thought her "states" needed to improve. Just as Laurence had been sent out to work in Europe in 1871 and later on Wall Street, Alice was now ordered to move through another stage in her orientation, back in the outside world, but still under the order of "no communication" with Laurence or her family in England. This was probably due to Harris's own need to be alone after his great book announcing the Second Coming failed to empower him to reign over the kingdom of earth.

Thinking positively, and still under the influence of Harris, Alice decided to use the experience to establish herself as an independent woman. At first, she settled in the nearby working-class town of Vallejo and offered her services publicly as a teacher of drawing and music. When friends at Fountaingrove wrote to Laurence about these new developments, he reached out to the Walkers for assistance. Mrs. Walker then found Alice and convinced her to take up a better paying teaching position at a school run by friends of the Walkers in Benicia, where she would also be nearer to them. There Alice stayed, wanting to succeed and prove she could be self-sufficient for her immediate future. Laurence gave her that space, but no doubt wondered whether he still had a wife, or if he had lost her forever to the strange world of the Brotherhood of the New Life into which he had introduced her.

*

Meanwhile, alone and back in England during 1878, Laurence discovered a new mission, which was to occupy him, and Alice, for the rest of their lives. Even while he labored several years on business in the age of the robber barons, Laurence always kept his keen interest in politics and wars, especially when the battlefields were nearby in Europe, where he spent so much time as a journalist, war correspondent, and amateur diplomat. His years at the cable company ran parallel with the savage events of the 1877-1878 Russian and Ottoman war, which in many ways continued the tensions of the Crimean War, enflaming the Balkans between the power plays of Russia from the north and the Ottoman Empire to the south, very much de-stabilizing the region that would later erupt into The Great War of World War I.

The Ottoman Empire, ruled by the Sultan in Constantinople, had just lost this latest Russian war. The peace gave Russia authority over several troublesome Balkan provinces the Sultan was ill-equipped and under-resourced to control. Indeed, fearing Russian expansion, the British had sent a fleet to persuade the Russian victors to stop their advance before Constantinople and to make a preliminary treaty with the Sultan at the village of San Stefano, just eleven miles west of the capital. Further agreements on the fate of the region were settled in talks between all the major European powers at a special conference called the Congress of Berlin. The details of those discussions would have fueled the post-dinner conversations of Laurence and his fellow club members in London, amid brandies and cigars on his lonely evenings in England during 1878.

Laurence's contribution to the situation was arrived at through a process of "deduction" which he describes in the introduction to his 1880 book, *The Land of Gilead*. The weakened Ottoman Empire still retained title to provinces like Palestine all the way down through Asia Minor, including territories surrounding the Suez Canal, very recently opened, and now a vital route for British transport from Europe to India and beyond. However, vast parts of that Ottoman domain, to Laurence's view, remained undeveloped and unpopulated. As a result, there was, in fact, very little to prevent Russian expansion southwards into Africa as soon as the appetites of the recent combatants were sharpened for another war. Nor did the Sultan have the economic means to strengthen these scattered territories by bankrolling any new population to give his realm more structure and stability. At the same time, refugees from the recent hostilities had migrated up into Europe and filled the city streets as new and impoverished groups of unwanted immigrants. While Laurence's idea would not address all of these problems, he felt that it could be an example of how one small part of the picture could be dramatically improved, and that token success might encourage the Sultan to take similar additional steps to become a stronger deterrent to Russian expansion.

The idea was to re-locate one of the persecuted communities from Europe into an undeveloped part of the Ottoman Empire.

The refugees would make a new start and become a colony of new Ottoman citizens, paying taxes, and contributing to the Sultan's stability. Laurence evaluated the options. First, he considered displaced Christians – but these often argued among themselves, and were already very troublesome to the Turks. They would be a difficult group to get approved by the Turkish as a new colony. Similarly troublesome issues surrounded re-locating the displaced Muslims who also fled north into Europe from the fighting. In addition, both the Christian and the Muslim refugees were penniless and would require financial support to become established, and the Sultan was in no position to invest after losing the 1877-1878 war. And so, continuing his process of elimination, Laurence arrived at the conclusion that there was only one group then under persecution in Europe, who would be both enthusiastic about re-locating and establishing a colony in an Ottoman province, while also agreeing to live peacefully under the administration of the Sultan. In fact, there would also be a possibility that certain sympathetic Europeans and others might finance the whole venture. Ticking all of these boxes for Laurence was the idea to establish a homeland for the Jews somewhere in the Turkish province of Palestine.[5] He reasoned that the appeal to the Jewish would be immediate, since it would mean restoration to their biblical homeland. In addition, many wealthy and established European Jews, such as the Rothschilds and British philanthropist Sir Moses Montefiore, might find supporting such a re-location a worthwhile and fulfilling investment. And there never had been any trouble from the Jewish minority presently resident in the Ottoman Empire. In fact, they were recognized as a productive and valuable part of the Sultan's population, and were fully protected as citizens under the current Turkish law.

Probably because it was such a *really good* idea, Laurence's notion started to gather considerable support. His own social connections—together with the free time he had for dinner parties, country weekends, and evenings at his clubs—allowed him to refine and sell in his thinking to very important and influential friends and acquaintances. By November 1878, Queen Victoria's daughter, Princess Helena-Christian, whom Laurence had known since childhood, wrote to the Prime Minister Disraeli, urging him to give a hearing to Laurence's thinking on an idea very close to her own heart—establishing a homeland for the Jews in Palestine.[6] And, later that month, Laurence was invited to a small house party hosted by the Prince of Wales at the Royal Estate at Sandringham. The Prince's guest list was "the Prime Minister, Lord Beaconsfield [Benjamin Disraeli]; the Foreign Secretary, Lord Salisbury; the Duke of Sutherland; the Austrian Ambassador, Count Breust; and Laurence Oliphant"—and the topic was Palestine.[7]

Zionism, or advocacy for restoring the Jewish people to their biblical homeland, has been the aspiration of many for thousands of years. For the Jews, in their hearts and their daily prayers, it was the dream of a persecuted and powerless people. But there have also been staunch Christian advocates, who believed it was a sacred right, expressed in biblical prophecies, and even a necessary prerequisite for setting up the final sequence of events leading up to the millennial thousand years of peace before the Second Coming of Christ and the end of the world. In the mid-nineteenth century, British leaders like Lord Shaftsbury in 1840 described himself as "an instrument" to restore the Jewish people, having lobbied to open a British Consulate in Jerusalem two years before in 1838. Prime Minister Benjamin Disraeli was Jewish himself and was an enthusiastic supporter. Even Mormon leader Joseph Smith dispatched an emissary named Oren Hyde to Palestine[8] in 1841 to make sure there was a clear connection between his new sect and the Jews in the Promised Land. But Laurence Oliphant was one of the rarest early Zionists because he was practical enough to focus on making it actually happen: by finding a potential site for the relocated people; getting diplomatic agreements in place to allow them to move there; and even looking for real money to pay for it all. That's why he—and his wife, Alice—are still remembered and honored in Israel today, making this last chapter about to unfold in his life perhaps the most unexpected and important one.

Starting from the end of 1878, with Alice still under Harris's orders as a teacher in California, in short order Laurence received informal approval from the British Foreign Ministry to develop the idea into specific plans. He decided to go to Palestine to identify a specific location for a new colony. He was given letters of introduction to ensure on-the-ground support from British Ambassadors and Consuls in the relevant regions. He was also asked to begin his travels by visiting Paris to brief the French Foreign Minister on the scheme to make sure the French understood this was a mission in support of Turkish stability and not some kind of British power play. By the end of 1878, the French also agreed with the merits of the idea, and Laurence was ready to take the next steps of, first, visiting Palestine to find a location for the colony, and then convincing the Sultan and the European Jewish leaders that it was all a good idea.

By January 1879, Laurence was on his way to Beirut to meet an old friend who had been living in the country for four years, Captain Owen Phibbs. Phibbs would prove a great travel companion, knowing the languages and customs of the people – although he would be going for the first time to the specific areas around the Dead Sea that Laurence wanted to see first. The plan was to be resourceful and avoid the expense of assembling an armed and well-provisioned caravan of followers. Essentially, they wanted to look poor, in order to avoid paying any "blackmail" for information. In fact, they took very little money with them, wanting instead to throw themselves on the local traditions of hospitality for strangers. They engaged only two servants and a boy, and set off with horses and a mule, and without any tent, on what could be characterized as a camping trip, rather than an expedition, to explore the largely undeveloped interior territories of Palestine which at the time were sparsely populated by native Arab tribes. They also carried letters of introduction from the British government to ensure good treatment from any Ottoman officials they might meet.

Laurence captured their exploits in a new book called *The Land of Gilead*. The narrative gives a blow-by-blow diary of their travels, written not as a travel guide for future explorers, but as a case book proving that there was indeed attractive, undeveloped and unpopulated land in abundance, which could in short order be transformed into a profitable agricultural community. Furthermore, Laurence showed how a well-located community could easily be connected to cities and shipping ports by a potentially profitable new railroad. This book would become a tool for selling in the plan, so Laurence could verbally introduce his proposal for the colony to any influencer or potential investor, and then hand over the written casebook to substantiate his claims and close the sale.

At the start, Laurence and Phibbs meandered through dry and largely deserted lands, although they discovered the landscape was dotted with the remains of ancient cisterns and rock-hewn storage rooms that could be restored to the condition needed to support resident populations. In short, Laurence painted a picture of land with real development possibilities, which could, in his opinion, be cleared of the few Arabs who roamed there, and repopulated with more ambitious and well-subsidized colonists.

Laurence finally came into an area of "at least a million, or possibly a million and a half acres" located along the boundaries of the northwest corner of today's kingdom of Jordan. The terrain is geologically unusual, making a steep vertical rise from the salty water of the Dead Sea 1,000 feet below sea level, rising to a level plain at 4,000 feet above sea level. Because of the diverse elevations, Laurence extolled the cornucopia of different agricultural crops an ambitious colony might produce there:

The valley of the Jordan would act as an enormous hothouse for the new colony. Here might be cultivated palms, cotton, indigo, sugar, rice, sorghum, besides bananas, pineapples, yams, sweet potatoes and other field and garden produce. Rising a little higher, the country is adapted to tobacco, maize, castor-oil, millet, flax, sesamum, melons, gourds, cumin, coriander, anise, okra, brinjals, pomegranates, oranges, figs – and so up to the plains, where wheat, barley, beans and lentils of various sorts, with olives and vines, would form the staple products. Gilead especially is essentially a country of wine and oil…[9]

Besides all these crops, Laurence concludes his lecture to the reader by reminding that the "chemical and mineral deposits" within the Dead Sea would also be a natural resource bonanza, especially if a railroad could connect this land of abundance to cities and ports for distribution, which could be done, Laurence believed, "entirely free from any engineering difficulties."[10] Other profitable trade for the rail line could become the transport of pilgrims to Mecca and the connection of a line to the Suez Canal, facilitating increased trade for Egypt. He concludes that, in Gilead, he had "gazed from its highest peak in its mountains over a Land of Promise." His next steps would be to sell his proposal to the Sultan… and then the Jews.

The critical mission of his scouting trip was completed with the discovery of this agricultural haven in Gilead, and after brief visits to Jerusalem and Haifa, Laurence turned his attention to the Ottoman officials nearby in Damascus. There the Governor General of Syria was an old friend of the Prince of Wales—and an acquaintance of Laurence—named Midhat Pasha. Midhat listened to every aspect of the proposal during Laurence's three-week stay with him. He not only thought it could work, but also promised all appropriate support to the colonists from his government locally, should they start to appear. All that was needed now was the blessing of the Sultan, before selling the idea to the leadership of the Jewish refugees strung out across Northern Europe.

With that goal in mind, Laurence arrived in Constantinople in May 1879 and was warmly received by the British Ambassador who made him an amusing and most welcome fixture at all the British-led entertainments that spring and summer. Margaret Oliphant paints a vivid picture of the diplomatic community on their summer break just outside Constantinople at Therapia, a supremely picturesque setting where the summer palaces and crusader castles line the shores of Asia and Europe facing each other across the water. Laurence was among friends:

> *attachés* and secretaries of legation, flitting round their former brother in the craft, and careful ambassadors not scorning to take counsel with the sage, yet visionary, the man of the world who had been everywhere and seen most things under the sun, yet whose heart was all in some inconceivable mystery of religion, at which these gentlemen did not know whether to laugh or to frown.[11]

It turned out the diplomatic community did both "and it did not matter to him what they did, who was equally ready to laugh with them, or to fight for the faith that was in him."

The British Ambassador promised to use his influence to get Laurence a hearing from the Sultan, but it ended up taking most of one year to achieve it. Meanwhile, Laurence was able to present the project to the Grand Vizier and the Minister of Public Works, as well as a majority of the Sultan's cabinet. Their only feedback was to make it crystal clear to any colonists that they would have to become loyal subjects of the Sultan and not secretly harbor any dreams of independence. As he waited, Laurence was able to report back to his Prime Minister, Benjamin Disraeli, that all seemed to be going well. But other events soon started to get in Laurence's way. He wrote back to his publisher Blackwood that his mission was not the top priority for the Turkish and British governments at the time – they were preoccupied with enforcing the messy implementation of the Treaty of Berlin after the Russian and Ottoman War.

Finally, however, the audience with the Sultan was arranged[12] in April 1880 as a small dinner party where Laurence could make his case, supported by the British Ambassador and other members of that delegation. The Sultan heard him out, but said, unfortunately, that his ministers and cabinet were all against it, although the monarch himself thought it interesting. Laurence protested, helpfully at first, that he actually knew from dialogue with the ministers from the Grand Vizier to the head of Public Works that there was strong support, and that his majesty must perhaps be mistaken. That path of conversation did not go down well, and in a very short time observers later reported the conversation between Laurence and the Sultan became very "hot." In fact the British diplomats had to literally step in so Laurence would disengage. Reportedly, the Sultan urgently sent a snuffbox as a gift to Laurence in the anteroom where he was cooling down, but it was some time before Laurence could be persuaded to accept it. He left muttering about lies and corruption and indeed later published some rather ill advised letters in the English press expanding on his opinions. At any rate, the project was definitely de-railed. Friends thought that Laurence had "put a stopper in it himself" by becoming overly enthused and mentioning to the Sultan that the return of the Jews to their biblical homeland would also hasten the Second Coming of Christ and the prophesized end of the world. That was something the Sultan had no interest in facilitating.

No doubt muttering insults about the Turks to himself, Laurence returned to England to re-group and at least tend to getting his book *The Land of Gilead* published while he planned his next move. There also had been a change at the top of the British government, with Disraeli leaving his office as Prime Minister in April 1880, after his defeat in general elections. However, far from any thought of abandoning the mission for a Jewish homeland in Palestine, Laurence found new events unfolding across Eastern Europe only strengthened his resolve to continue the fight.

From his base at the Athenaeum Club on Pall Mall, Laurence became an avid reader and correspondent with the London *Jewish Chronicle*, the leading weekly newspaper on Jewish affairs, still published today. On June 11, 1880, the editors of the *Chronicle* reported on Laurence's impasse with the Sultan as follows:

> Although Mr. Laurence Oliphant has returned from Constantinople without having obtained the signature of the Sultan to the Iradé authorising the formation of a company for the purpose of colonising the fertile and unoccupied lands east of the Jordan with Jews, he by no means despairs of ultimate success.[13]

The paper goes on to explain that the Sultan, and the "fanatical clique" that surrounds him, are suspicious and against every plan suggested by the many foreign governments tinkering with the future of the decaying Ottoman Empire.

On September 3, the paper reported on Laurence reading a "highly interesting" scientific paper on his travels in Gilead at the meeting of the British Association for the Advancement of Science that "met with applause." Then the late summer editions of the *Chronicle* were full of disturbing reports of persecution and atrocities involving the Jews of Russia and Romania. For example, new Romanian edicts had banned many Jewish merchants from trading in local villages, causing widespread poverty and suffering among previously quite well off families. One society of one hundred early Zionist families organized itself in Bucharest to emigrate en masse and wrote an open letter to the *Chronicle* seeking £1,000 in order to buy suitable land in Palestine.

Laurence responded with his own reply published in the *Chronicle* in September 1880. He made three key points. First, he noted a far greater sum could be raised among sympathizers in England. Second, he told the Bucharest Committee they did not need to buy land as a prerequisite for emigrating. With his knowledge of local law, he wrote:

> The Roumanian association are probably not aware that by the Ottoman Colonization Law they are entitled to take up and cultivate any amount of unoccupied land they may desire without purchase, on condition of becoming Turkish subjects, and that there are in the Caimakamliks of Tiberias and Jenim about 200,000 acres of most eligible land for the purpose.[14]

Alice after reuniting with Laurence.

And finally he says if they essentially send an emissary to London in person, he will personally make everything happen for the one hundred families to move. This began a period of several years when the oppressed Jewry of Europe, and their sympathizers in wealthier countries, made Laurence a kind of superstar in the Jewish quest for salvation, and he became quite famous for his advocacy. The Romanian group wrote back in the *Chronicle* of the joy of reading his letter (translated):

> We will not describe in detail the enthusiastic joy which the cheering and precious words of your correspondent caused us—words full of confidence and hope, and breathing the deepest sentiments of patriotism.[15]

Despite his growing fame with the desperate and grateful Jews, Laurence had had the wind knocked out of his sails by his encounter with the Sultan. He complained of headaches, and had a haggard and sickly look about him. He was decidedly not himself and had been working on his "mission" to the point of exhaustion, without attaining success. In fact, he was dangerously close to a mental breaking point. His distant cousin and future biographer Margaret Oliphant had several chances to meet with him that summer. In one disturbing encounter he shared with the real reason for his forced separation from Alice, which kept them both at arm's length while they remained under the influence of their prophet, Thomas Lake Harris. Harris told them that Alice was not, indeed, his true celestial counterpart, and Laurence had confirmed this with his own investigations. He stated his counterpart was actually a spirit named Alawenie, in the celestial realm, and in fact she had been collaborating with him on a few verses, which he shyly shared with Margaret. Apparently they were sadly lacking—something that later delighted the supporters of the smooth-versifying Harris, who later published some, "fortunately preserved for the derision of posterity."[16] Margaret said that conversation "was the only time I ever saw him exhibit any signs of insanity."[17]

*

As Laurence teetered on the edge of falling apart, help was on the way. It was just at this time, while visiting his wife's family in Norfolk, that Laurence received word Alice was returning to England, to be with him. To get word to her and about her, Laurence had often written to the Walkers in California. She probably knew about his mission to Palestine, and she also knew he was in poor health. Frankly, he could very much use her assistance, if she could distance herself from Harris's influence, which still somehow controlled her life, even though she had been living and working independently as a teacher for more than two years. She had not even seen or heard from Harris during that time, until he gave her parting orders when she left California. From his sickbed suffering from scarlet fever, Harris reminded Alice she was not Laurence's true counterpart, and cautioned her to refrain from "scortation," Harris's favorite word for fornication. Probably feeling she had proved her ability to succeed on her own, Alice decided it was time to "come home"—at least for a visit—to her worried family and especially to Laurence.

As soon as she arrived on English soil on November 1st, 1880, she wrote to her mother that she would be home in Norfolk soon, where she hoped to recover quickly from coughing and bronchitis she had caught on her travels. She reminded her mother that "I have always exacted of Laurence that he should leave me free to make my own personal experiments that I may think needful for my usefulness in the world."[18]

But she wasn't going to be allowed much time to recover since her oldest brother Hamon, the lord of the family estate at Hunstanton, wanted her and Laurence to make an appearance at an upcoming royal ball at Sandringham, right in the immediate neighborhood of the Le Strange estate. A royal ball, with all the prying eyes of aristocrats and Norfolk gentry focused on her, would be quite a change from lessons with her music and art pupils in California, but she was ready for it. Alice knew her absence distressed her family and caused a lot of gossip and speculation about her long estrangement from Laurence. She continues in the letter to tell her mother that her return to England will stop the wagging tongues of gossip about the couple, and that her time in California importantly has helped her prove she can be "a producer in the social scheme, unaided by any social connections."

And so she was back, ready to stoke the fires of Laurence's own spirit, and to resume her place in his high society. She did endure the ball at Sandringham, and she also met Laurence's cousin Margaret Oiphant in person for the first time, who described Alice as a "vivacious beauty." She continued:

> She was by this time at the full height of life, the *mezzo del cammin*, and a little worn with delicate health and many labours; but so sweet, so bright, so gay in her profound seriousness, so tender in her complete independence, that all the charms of paradox were added to those of nature.[19]

She had also acquired a slight American accent, which Margaret found absolutely charming in a well-bred English woman of her class, noting it enhanced her "brilliant" conversation. Margaret concluded:

> the extraordinary mixture in her of the finest culture of the Old World and the freedom and strange experiences of the New—the latter acquired, not in the sophisticated places where New York or Boston holds the mirror up to London or Paris, but in the Far West, and in the primitive country districts, where all is individual and strange—was more fascinating, amusing and curious than words can say.[20]

As the cold, wet dreariness of an English winter began to close in on haggard Laurence and coughing Alice, their English doctors gave the couple a familiar prescription for the time, ordering them to a sunny climate for recovery and convalescence. Happy as newlyweds, they set out for a holiday in Egypt—not to the well-traveled destinations of the time, but to a remote oasis "in the Libyan desert" called Medinet al Fayoum.

Laurence made his money with his pen and was one of the most popular authors in the Blackwoods' catalog, which was bound into the back of each of their books. There he was listed alphabetically alongside his cousin Margaret (who was a great deal more prolific even than him). So although this trip was for the health of himself and Alice, the plan was for their observations to form a series of articles in *Blackwoods Magazine*, and perhaps afterwards, a book. Since any subject about traveling to Egypt, as Laurence writes in his preface to that eventual book, *The Land of Khemi*, "has been so thoroughly exhausted by the various works which have been published… and the country is now so largely frequented by invalids, and so overrun by tourists," the two reunited travelers sought out a base camp in the middle of nowhere. Here they hoped to indulge a yearning for amateur archaeological sleuthing among unvisited ruins, with intimate conversations and dinners with the local sheiks. The new book was thus offered to:

> encourage visitors to depart a little from the beaten track, as proving that, even in a country so well worn by the feet of tourists, there are other things to do down in the valley of the hill besides living in Shepheard's Hotel and going straight up to the Second Cataract and back.[21]

Even though, as invalids, their "capacity for enduring fatigue was somewhat limited," they embraced their reunited holiday with delight and gusto.

No tourist amenities awaited visitors at the oasis of Medinet al Fayoon, although they were able to make their arrival there in the comparative comfort of a First Class rail carriage, which was so little-used by the locals that it had to be cleared of freight and mountains of dust before they could enter it. Since the Egyptian ruler was a friend of the Prince of Wales, the government offered Laurence and Alice rooms at the local palace as a base camp, although they arrived late the first night and had to be temporarily put up in a tent replete with oriental carpets and torches in the sand. Once settled in, they made their excursions by donkeys, camels and, although it was not the local custom, by canal boat. In search of a local pyramid he found mentioned in one of the history books he had brought along, Laurence described how they set out on one typical adventure:

> It was on a warm lovely morning in February that we spread ourselves on the carpet on the stern of the boat, and, towed by two sturdy *fellahin*, made our way amongst the current at the rate of about three miles an hour.[22]

This sets the relaxing tone for the book's chapters covering several months of rest and relaxation, giving the reader a ringside seat at two Coptic weddings, a funeral, and a disastrous rain-soaked excursion by camels into the desert. Laurence and Alice enjoyed each other's company immensely in this exotic setting and both enjoyed sketching to capture the dreamlike setting they found themselves in:

> The climate was soft and temperate; the view from our place of residence over the Nile, with precipitious limestone cliffs rising out of the palm trees, presented a constantly renewing variety of marvelous effects of light and shade, which it was a constant source of delight to watch and attempt to put on paper.[23]

In another incident, a recovered Laurence out on his own insists on being lowered by his servants into a dark opening in the desert, partially blocked by sand, which turns out to lead to an entry passageway and a warren of corridors and chambers under the desert. He and one servant then tried to explore it all, but were repulsed:

> … I was literally overpowered and driven back by the bats. They charged us in dense whirling battalions, banging into one's face, putting

out the candles, thumping on one's head, and creating as much draught as if a fanning machine was at work.[24]

He seemed to be back in his youth, hunting on the high ground of Nuwara Eliya in Ceylon or storming the walls at the siege of Canton. It was even later suggested Laurence asked Alice to have a child together at this time, but she demurred because of Harris's explicit orders to her.

But the days of Harris's influence over the two were numbered. With virtually all their strength returning by spring, Alice and Laurence had their reverie interrupted by a stark communication from Harris in California, who was now in a frenzy of fund-raising to finance the completion of Fountaingrove as a terrestrial haven for his counterpart, Queen Lily, and the other celestials, who apparently were about to arrive very soon. Harris was demanding that Laurence and Alice immediately send him a legal order making all of their unassigned property over to the prophet. He was also making similar demands of all his abandoned flock in Brocton. In later years, Laurence would recall the moment, and his thoughts at the time, summed up in the word "Enough!" Practically, in order to comply with Harris's demands, Laurence and Alice would have had to go to their friend, the British Consul in Cairo, and ask his assistance drafting a legally binding document. Perhaps the embarrassment of involving that friend in such a bizarre transaction was also a deterrent to action. Also, Laurence was apparently hearing grumblings from his friends, the Buckners and the Martins, still resident at the Brocton commune who, along with Laurence's mother, were resentful of never being invited to join the great man at his palatial Californian estate, where rumors told of distressing, pretentious and licentious goings-on. Finally, Laurence and Alice would need to recover their money already invested with Harris in order to have a financial foundation for their future.

As a result, Laurence and Alice decided it was time to leave their Egyptian revel, and return to sort everything out. They went first to England. There Laurence installed Alice in a rented cottage at Windsor, very close to his cousin Margaret Oliphant, who was now a very good friend to both. Alice would stay in Britain and work with his publishers on reviewing and correcting the pages being prepared for the new book, *The Land of Khemi*, and Laurence would travel back to America, stopping first to see his friends and his mother, still at Brocton, New York, and then continuing on to meet with Harris in California. He told his publisher, John Blackwood, that he expected to be back around the end of the year.[25]

Alice was very happy with this arrangement, and was a treasured companion to Margaret, who described how much she enjoyed Alice as a neighbor:

> There was no weariness where such an intimate and companion was. To old and young she was alike delightful—not too wise for the girls, not too serious for the boys; ready to talk, to laugh, to play on the piano almost anything they asked her for; to fall into beautiful discourse one moment upon the love and service of mankind, to which she felt herself dedicated, and to break off the next moment into some homely jest of the family.[26]

With Alice secure, Laurence set off, first to Brocton and then to confront Harris in California—but an unexpected surprise awaited him.

CHAPTER 9

BREAKING WITH HARRIS

As Laurence settled Alice in Windsor and began his eastward journey to Brocton and then Fountaingrove, he might not have known how much the insulated and other-worldly community around Thomas Lake Harris had changed. Both Laurence and Alice had been "out in the world" for years, while the prophet and his elite followers spent most of their time in a strange fairyland cocoon we can hardly imagine. Fortunately, we have a firsthand description of living the life in the California Brotherhood at that time. In the spring of 1881, while the Oliphants were recuperating in Egypt and writing *The Land of Khemi*, one young woman supplicant came and left a journal of her experiences entitled *Experiences of a Sister in the New Life*. The content was copied out by members and circulated among new and potential recruits.

The journal is written as letters to an unknown correspondent. The author apparently came from San Francisco, and was later joined by her sister. Entries were dated. Here is a section from her first day at Fountaingrove, May 16, 1881, as she settled down to rest, tired from meetings with Harris and his harem at Aestivossa, the main house:

I am the first one who has slept in the house besides the people who belong here for four years. I occupied the room Mr. H. usually does. I slept tolerably well only, but felt quiet and happy and kept feeling the sensations like those you remember I told you I felt in my arms. Well, since I feel them quite often, and they seem to be gradually extending over my body. This morning for the first time, I felt it enter my head and also pass into my thighs. The first time it came into my body, that is the trunk, it seemed to enter through the generative organs, and with it came the thought, this is like sexual intercourse, only infinitely more so, in that every atom of your frame enters into union with another atom to the furthest extremity of your body. I am sure I never had such a thought before, nor supposed that anything could be of such infinite magnitude. I felt infinitely calm and peaceful, nothing turbulent and passionate about it, and my only desire was to constantly pray in thankfulness. If it were indeed what Mrs. R. says it is, my counterpart, I can imagine in some slight degree what may be in store for us all.[1]

The writer tells us the whole community was on edge, nervously awaiting the end of the world and the transition over to the new life with the spirits. Harris told her in a conversation that "on 28th of January the giests (sic) of every human being left the bodies, so you, nor I, nor anyone else are any longer as we formerly were." On the last day of the present world experience, coming soon, the changes will start in the morning, with the day "growing gradually darker and darker," until everyone will lie down and the "wicked will crumble into a handful of dust." Meanwhile, everyone who is worthy should calm themselves and prepare.

As the first weeks of the young woman's visit to Fountaingrove continued, more changes took place. She wrote:

Did I tell you about the wonderful flutter in my breast that there is all the time? Well I woke with it one morning and very soon something began singing 'In your breast Love has come to build its nest.' The next day it changed to 'In your breast, Love's happy nest, singing birds have built their nest.[2]

These singers must, of course, have been the faeries who were concentrated all around the property in Fountaingrove, and probably everywhere, but actively manifesting themselves to Harris and his community members. Then Mr. Cuthbert took the young lady on a guided tour, including the Commandery. She found it bright and pleasant, but "very close quarters for 100 people to live in." In particular, she reported:

> They have a very large bathroom and there they literally wash each other's feet and the rest of their bodies as well. Our father says that before we can be in any true condition we must all be so innocent that we can stand naked before each other without a thought of shame and wash and dress each other.[3]

As her initiation continued, by June she could recognize her true counterpart entering into her and infusing her entire body with the pleasurable sensations:

> I have felt my counterpart too and it is all so very strange that I scarce know how to tell about it. One morning I woke with feeling a strange sensation in my arms, it seemed as if something were flowing in and filling them up as it were... since then I have felt the same something gradually extending all over.[4]

Next came play dates with the faeries, who apparently found an entry point into her body at one breast and then built a house there, and made a garden and planted fruit trees. Soon there were baby fays, and then many more baby fays. One day in June she wrote:

Lately I have imagined a little fay; he is about as large as the point of a pin who came out of the tip of the first finger of my left hand, and talks to me; he is exquisitely dressed; yesterday he told me about new babies.[5]

The quotes from the journal continue on through the fall and winter in a similar vein, so to speak, ending with the narrator expressing a feeling of distance and detachment from the world around her in her entry of October 19, 1881:

I now at all times have a strange feeling as if I were far away from those I am talking to or come in contact with; it seems as if there were something in the atmosphere which shuts me off from them. Nothing seems real; I do things because I must but I am not in them.[6]

Whether this young woman was real or imagined, her testimony was popular among active and would-be Harrisites, providing an incentive to continue deep breathing and demagnetizing through communal body washing, in hope their counterparts would soon arrive and provide the sensations described in the journal.

*

When Laurence arrived in Brocton around June 1881, he was shocked to find his mother terminally ill. He sent out for the best medical attention for her, but the doctors had no success. He had not written or heard from her directly for years, based on Harris's edicts. He had remembered her at Brocton in the most robust health of her life, enjoying the gardening and even her chores. Spiritually, he had thought she would be at peace, enjoying celestial liaisons with her counterpart in heaven, the late Sir Anthony Oliphant, who had been the love of her life. Now instead he found her dejected, diagnosed with cancer, and bed-ridden in the midst of a community that was increasingly fed up with the distant Harris and quickly on its way to becoming unraveled.

The Broctonites were particularly troubled on two fronts,[7] as described by Robert Martin who grew up in the Brocton community, writing about his parents at the time. First, there were rumors—"at first remote, and somewhat vague"—that Harris was allowing himself sexual "privileges" relating to an "illicit act" that was frowned on in ordinary society, and allowing other members in California the same permission. Since the rules at Brocton had always been of the highest moral and sexual probity, this was very upsetting. Secondly, since the California community had been formed, the Broctonites were continually beset by requests for "money, money, money—and more money." Laurence had already experienced Harris's growing interest in money—at any cost. He wrote later of Harris that "he wished me to use, as it seemed to me dishonourably, the knowledge I gained by occupying an inner place in a certain business centre, in order to make a large sum of money, and was angry when I refused."

During the early summer days of his visit with his fellow members at Brocton, Laurence was able to catch up with his friends. He probably explained his own spiritual progress, in that he believed he was in daily touch with his own counterpart in the celestial sphere, the wonderful Alawenie, meaning he had also attained a similar level of access to heaven as Father Harris. Harris had always maintained that Alice was not his true counterpart, so Laurence had apparently concocted Alawenie to take that place. Alice herself was also advanced to the highest levels of occult experience, and had indeed accompanied Harris on his heavy breathing approach to the reported Second Coming. The friends in Brocton would also have shared their stories of the relentless financial pressures they had been receiving from their distant so-called Father in luxurious California. No doubt within a short time, Laurence, Dr. Martin and the others began to wonder whether they all would be better off seceding from Harris's extortionate leadership, recovering the ownership of the farms they worked, and carrying on the "wonderful work begun" with the spirit world themselves.

This brief reunion was cut short, however. As Lady Oliphant's health continued to worsen, Laurence decided it was time to go to Fountaingrove to meet with Harris and to bring his mother with him. Perhaps he thought the prophet might redeem himself by curing his mother, or at least by comforting her and setting her mind at peace. It is not clear whether Laurence had made the decision to break with Harris at this point, or whether he still wanted a chance to discuss his future in person with the prophet, as well as presenting the concerns of the Brocton members. He also needed to explain the decision he and Alice had made to send no more money for Fountaingrove because they needed to fund their mission in Palestine, an undertaking Laurence may have been hoping that Harris would support.

What happened at Fountaingrove, however, was something completely different. Harris was essentially furious that Laurence had turned up at his door, disturbing the prophet's spiritual states with his extremely needful mother—who the great man actually refused to see. At the meeting in the main house at Fountaingrove, Laurence had also been shocked at the sight of a watch belonging to Sir Anthony Oliphant being worn by Mrs. Requa, Harris's "Golden Rose," as well as a ring of his mother's on another resident's hand. The situation then escalated on three fronts during the summer and fall of 1881. First, Laurence told Harris that Queen Lily was a fraud perpetrated by evil earth-bound spirits, as revealed to Laurence by his counterpart, the celestial spirit Alawenie. Laurence demanded they all immediately engage in a four-in-one session, where Laurence and Alawenie would join with Harris and the bogus counterpart Queen Lily to expose the true spiritual situation and avert disaster and ruin. Secondly, Laurence delivered an ultimatum that Harris must immediately abandon Fountaingrove and go with the Oliphants to Palestine. Finally, as if the other points were not wild enough to the mind of the prophet, Laurence announced he was representing everyone back in Brocton, and they all wanted their money from the common fund returned immediately. The Oliphants were then summarily thrown off the ranch.

Harris was incredulous at these demands. He was possibly then at the height of his self-confidence, believing he was the "pivotal man" who was destined to deliver mankind to salvation. After all, he had already declared Jesus Christ had come back to earth in his Second Coming and was now resident in Harris's own body – so in effect, he believed he was the Deity himself. He had just been writing letters to his loyal members that the end was indeed nigh and that they should all prepare accordingly. And on the mundane terrestrial front, all the hard work of Kanaye Nagasawa and the elite Brotherhood of the New Life members at Santa Rosa was making Fountaingrove, and its winery, into a fantastically successful venture, in fine shape to survive the turmoil of the final days in order to provide a headquarters to the spirits who would be resident there with Harris during the new world order. So he was completely incensed that Laurence and his dying mother had interfered by showing up uninvited to press their ridiculous celestial and terrestrial demands. After he recovered somewhat from the shock, Harris sent a telegram back to Alice in England demanding that she sign a declaration Laurence was insane, so Harris could have him committed to a lunatic asylum. But, back in England, the Oliphants' wealthy and powerful friends, the Cowpers, had gotten wind of the arguments in America and swept up Alice from her cottage in Windsor into their own care. She probably received Harris's demands regarding Laurence while staying with them at their Broadlands estate near Southampton. Both Alice and the Cowpers agreed that denying Harris's demands was the right course, and did not reply.

Laurence, meanwhile out on his own in California, had to focus on his mother as Lady Oliphant's cancer moved into its final stages. Laurence decided to take her 20 miles north of Santa Rosa to the healthful geo-thermal springs at Geyserville. The steam venting from the fissures in a canyon there originally were thought to be "The Gates of Hades" when first discovered in 1847 but now they were a popular spa with invalids. They made it about halfway, to the hamlet of Cloverdale, and soon were directed to the home of a well-known "nature healer" there who began to "treat" Lady Oliphant's cancer. Laurence also sent word to the Walkers in San Raphael, who arrived to find Laurence at his mother's bedside just as the end approached. Mrs. Walker did not believe in any of Laurence's spiritual ideas, but she later told Margaret Oliphant that she could sense a violent storm in the air just over the bed, as if some epic battle was taking place. On October 25 1881, Lady Oliphant suddenly regained consciousness and told them that she had just seen Sir Anthony with a host of angels and that she was now at peace. She then died.

Laurence was obviously shattered by his mother's ordeal and death. After he buried his mother at the highest point of land in the Cloverdale cemetery, the Walkers took him back to recover in San Raphael. He explained the whole situation to Mr. Walker, who was a practical and successful businessman, and a man of great influence in California. He advised Laurence that legal action was the only practical way to force Harris to a settlement and took on the task of preparing suits to recover the funds of the Oliphants and the other Broctonites. The prophet was furious at this, but was in no position to have litigation and publicity about Fountaingrove hit the papers, especially not on the eve of the anticipated arrival of all the celestials from the other world. So after a good deal of negotiation, Harris settled up with the Oliphants, signing a deed over to Pitt Buckner who was designated as Laurence's property manager in New York and making Laurence the largest landowner in Brocton with 900 of the 2,000 acres.

Harris did, however, make a final effort to bring the other Broctonites back into the fold after settling with Laurence. He traveled back to New York without any warning to reason with the rest of his disgruntled flock. He hoped to use his force of personality to being them back into his fold – but no one would see him. He also was concerned about his oldest son, John, who lived at Brocton and was then seriously ill. Arthur Cuthbert went with him and wrote:

> We came unexpectedly: they had time to close the doors and lock them, when they got a glimpse of us approaching. They shut us out in the cold and refused to speak with us. The one thing they feared, above all others, was our gaining access to any one of their number by direct personal presence and speech. The day was piercingly cold, and it was the height of cruelty to shut our dear Father out exposed to it.[8]

The visitors were shivering inside a horse-drawn coach—a gift to Harris in happier times from Laurence who had bought it in Paris and shipped it back to Brocton. Its former owner had been Louis Napoleon himself, who had used it for hunting. It was somehow a fitting reminder of just what the California Brotherhood lost by breaking its connection with the Oliphants. Finally, Dr. Martin came outside and allowed Harris and Cuthbert to drive over to shelter in the house that Cuthbert "legally" owned within the complicated financial affairs of the Brotherhood. The next day, the Broctonites sent Pitt Buckner ("Earnest") over to lay out the details of all the Broctonite claims since, in the words of Robert Martin, he "could be depended upon to get whatever was coming, as he always figured pretty close financially" and was "true as steel." The fiercely loyal Arthur Cuthbert later reported that the young man was so flustered in the prophet's presence that he began to sweat profusely as he stated the New Yorkers' claims, but he did not waiver. Cuthbert even lost his wife in the discussions. She was at Brocton then, but he was not allowed to see her, and she decided to throw in her own lot with Laurence and the estranged members, demanding her own money back. Mrs. Cuthbert believed "the pivotal centre has departed from Father and abides with Mr. Oliphant" who would be her new leader. The anger on both sides was intense. In fact, Harris's son died subsequently without ever having met with his father again—a circumstance about which Harris later complained bitterly, although he had little to do with the boy while he lived.

The financial situation was dire as well since land values in Brocton had fallen dramatically since the properties were bought. For example, a farm purchased for $15,000 ten years earlier would at that time bring only $5,000, if a forced sale was required. As a result, all of the land at Brocton eventually had to be liquidated to satisfy the demands of the former members there, with nothing legally remaining for the loyal Harrisites who had also invested there. Their shares in the common fund became almost worthless. An angry James Freeman, whose family had joined with Harris back in the happy days in Wassaic wrote of Laurence:

> by extracting from a small community of people (who sought the same life of purity and innocence as he professed to seek) all he had invested, [Oliphant] caused great loss to others... My father lost three fourths of what he had advanced and died an uncomplaining sufferer.[9]

Harris summarized the whole affair from his viewpoint in a letter of December 22, 1881:

> I have just escaped with life and property from the meshes of a long-plotted, subtle and complicated conspiracy; having for its object my personal and financial ruin, with the destruction of the work of my life, and of all the interests entrusted to my charge... The remains of my poor family in Brocton think me suddenly blinded and astray... as Mr.Oliphant, who has become a medium and makes a head for

them, writes automatically through his hand that unless I yield to his direction and go at once under his charge to Palestine forthwith, I shall be destroyed and the whole human race will perish with me.[10]

Harris took the opportunity to reassure his correspondent, that in spite of this attack, the end of the world is not quite yet upon them, and that Fountaingrove was continuing to plant vineyards and orchards "on a great scale" so as to restore it to wealth in a few years. He also wrote to William Cowper that he had been left "penniless" from demands of Laurence Oliphant for money, deeds, property, and more from Mrs. Cuthbert, and Mrs. Fowler and "that man Martin, a refugee with his dying wife and wretched child." He was probably hoping for a handout from the Cowpers, but he didn't get one. Laurence later wrote about the break:

> I had reason to believe he had entirely abandoned the early purpose of his life, and was selling for gold and his own private ends the gifts with which God entrusted him for the service of humanity, thus converting him from a religious reformer into a religious imposter.[11]

All that remained was for Laurence to say goodbye to California and retrace his steps back to Alice, but at this exact moment he did not know what her reaction would be to all that had occurred. Perhaps he had taken everything too far in making such a complete break with Harris? Possibly he feared Alice had been viewing her return to Europe as an interlude to see her family and to aid Laurence in his recovery to health, but she herself had not renounced Harris, and possibly even intended to return to California and re-connect with the prophet? Laurence did not know about Alice's refusal to sign a declaration that he was insane for Harris, nor did he know she was insulated in the protection of the Cowpers, who also had rejected Harris. In fact, Alice had also made her own break with Harris independently, with far less drama than Laurence. So, not knowing all that, Laurence shirked communicating directly with Alice as he left San Francisco in December 1881, taking a somewhat roundabout route home to England.

From Santa Rosa, Laurence took a southern railway east through Texas, gathering cowboy stories which he would write up into articles for *Blackwoods Magazine* and yet another popular book. At New Orleans, he transferred to travel on a ship through the islands to Havana, and then finally made the transatlantic crossing. Full of dread and uncertainty, he rejoiced at the sight of Alice waiting for him at the dock in Liverpool in late January 1882, ready to give him her complete and unconditional support for their future. For their reunion, the Cowpers had the couple whisked away to a seaside holiday house they owned near Torquay so the Oliphants could recover before again stepping out into the glare of their notoriety in the British society of the day. For Laurence, some fourteen years of subservience to his wild-eyed prophet had ended, and the couple's happiest years in their already overflowing life adventure were about to begin.

Harris would quickly get to work blackening the reputations of the Oliphants among his faithful. Alice had deliberately misled him, he claimed, trying to impersonate the Lily Queen through black magic. He said the negative energy sent his way from her cottage at Fountaingrove had weakened him with scarlet fever – and nearly killed him. Laurence and Lady Oliphant coming to challenge Harris at Fountaingrove were, in the words of member Samuel Clark in a February 1882 letter, "the two chief ones among the traitors," and after they:

> met him and called him a liar, thief and other epithets it was easier for him to fight their sphere internally, as after this in combat he could meet them face to face.

In fighting them, Harris claimed to have caused Lady Oliphant's death, and foolish Laurence, "instead of looking upon it as a judgment, called it a glorious translation."[12]

Laurence was a traitor who had led the Broctonites astray with his demon-infested teachings and twisted claims to have achieved the two-in-one with his absurd alleged counterpart Alawenie. Harris also decided to attack Laurence's new preoccupation with helping the persecuted Jews in Europe establish a colony in Palestine. In his 1882 book *Declarations of the Divine One-Twain*, the character of the Divine Mother is addressing Harris about the Oliphants:

> That wretched one, who sought to drag you into his own slavery of the Jews, was inspired by the magic of the Jew, that endeavored to destroy the evolution of Our concept in the Aryan seed. The day of the Jew is over... hence, in Our coming, the name of Israel will be obliterated, and the last remains, both of its familism and religionism, will be caused to disappear.[13]

Apparently, Harris would not have been much help working on the Oliphants' philanthropic and humanitarian Zionist mission.

After the break, several Brocton members remained loyal to Harris. Cuthbert wrote "Mr. Daplyn, Mr. and Mrs. A. R. Buckner and their three young children, and Mr. Freeman, a gentleman of the South, who also owned one of the Brocton farms," came out to live at Fountaingrove, while the older Mr. Buckner sided with the Oliphants.[14] However, when the dust began to settle, most of the Broctonites had escaped, and only their faith in Harris was lost. According to Robert Martin, everyone else's principles and belief in "the ultimate object to be gained did not waiver" and Laurence and Alice were regarded as leaders to take the place of Harris.[15] Indeed, many of the Broctonites would later use their money returned by Harris to join the Oliphants in Palestine, as the next chapter in their story began to unfold.

CHAPTER 10

MIGRATING EAST

In January 1882, just as Laurence and Alice were back together after breaking-up with Harris, new atrocities against Eastern European Jews were widely publicized in the mainstream British press for the first time. First to emerge were details about the Christmas Day riots at the Church of the Holy Cross in Warsaw. There, cries of "fire" startled Christians during holiday church services. As they rushed to investigate, many were crushed to death, including the popular Countess Alexandrovsky. At the doors, churchgoers were fed lies about false shouts of "fire!" allegedly made by Jewish pickpockets trying to escape arrest. Drunken rabble from taverns were brought to swell the crowds, and then all were steered to Jewish districts for vengeance. Incredibly, the exact same "drama" replayed simultaneously at three other churches around the city, even including the detail of the fictitious pickpockets. Whole streets were burned, women and girls were raped, and by the end of three days more than 6,500 families were destitute. At the investigations later, sworn testimony described the crowds being choreographed by men speaking Russian.[1] The distraught widower Count Alexandrovsky testified the Jews were innocent.

Second, just during the same time, two articles broke in *The Times* illuminating the disturbances in Russia after the assassination of Czar Alexander II in the previous March, more than nine months before. During his reign, Alexander freed the serfs and kept a comparatively tolerant policy towards the Jews. Until January, the troubles after his death had been only mentioned as "riots" in terse telegrams finding their way abroad, or in short notes in specialized papers such as London's *Jewish Chronicle*. Now *The Times* gave graphic eyewitness details in the mainstream press:

> During the past eight months, a track of country, equal in area to the British Isles and France combined, stretching from the Baltic to the Black Sea, has been the scene of horrors hitherto only been perpetrated in medieval days during times of war. Men ruthlessly murdered, tender infants dashed to death, or roasted alive in their own homes, married women the prey of a brutal lust that has often caused their death, and young girls violated in the sight of their relatives by soldiers who should have been the guardians of their honour.[2]

In fact, as in Warsaw, these Russian riots were not spontaneous. Many were "advertised" in advance, and "scheduled" for holidays or other times working people would be at leisure. *The Times* told the events of April 27, 1881, in Elizabethgrad as an example. Before any trouble began, emissaries from the Jewish leadership, who had seen advance notices for the "riots," petitioned the Governor of the province for protection, to no avail. Then events unfolded. A staged argument about religion in a bar escalated into a brawl until the mob took over the establishment and drank the place dry. Everyone then poured out into the streets and headed for the Jewish quarter where shops and warehouses were destroyed. Jewish resistance only enflamed the mob and made matters worse. Several Jewish men were killed and many young girls were raped or threw themselves from windows to escape violation. During two days of riots five hundred houses and one hundred shops were destroyed.[3]   Similar stories filled out the columns, painting a picture of a vast region inflamed by the basest form of cruelty. Incendiary arson against Jewish buildings became so common that new Russian slang was used to describe flames coloring city skylines as "the red cock crows."[4]

This dramatic story telling in *The Times* woke up the best sentiments in the British people. They felt they could make a difference. The January 13 editorial in the *Jewish Chronicle* wrote:

> We are glad to see that at last English public opinion is waking to a sense of the full extent and character of the Russian persecution of the Jews. The Warsaw riots have at last roused public attention, and during the past week almost every London newspaper of importance have devoted a portion of its columns to the sorrows of Russian Jews.[5]

But the editorial continued on a practical note, reminding readers that Parliament would reconvene in only three weeks, and then legislative attention may be diverted to domestic concerns. So the time for action to aid the Jews would have to be *now*.

The causes of the Russian atrocities are debatable. It seems they were a combination of deliberate agitation by activists circulating bogus edicts, allegedly from the new Czar, ordering the seizure of Jewish property and the expulsion of Jewish populations from the towns, together with festering popular resentment at Jewish control of inns, drinking places, shops and money-lending. But whatever the reasons, many Jews in Russia, Poland and Romania simply abandoned any thought of assimilating into those communities and decided to leave.

Displaced whole populations of Jewish villages roamed the countryside, or slowly starved cowering in basements of their former towns. Those who could move without coming under attack fled across nearby borders, crossing over into cities like Brody, a gateway to safe haven in the Austrian Empire. Refugee camps began overflowing in Galicia, the region bordered by today's southeast Ukraine and southwest Poland, where many would-be emigrants were corralled. All told, between 1881 and the start of World War I, an estimated 2,500,000 Jews from these regions moved west. Many dreamed of going to America and arrived in Northern Europe and England as staging points, even if they did not have sufficient funds for transatlantic crossings. Hundreds arrived in London daily.[6]

Several philanthropic efforts were already in place to aid suffering Jews before the new reporting appeared. For example, in London the Russo-Jewish Committee, led by Sir N. M. de Rothschild, had a mission to find solutions, but it was now attracting critics, fed up with the relative inaction of the committee in the face of such urgent need. The initial violence was bad enough, but now salvation itself was being bungled.[7]

Outraged by the delays in light of *The Times* reports, and to give immediate aid, a public British assembly of luminaries in religion, culture and philanthropy—including the Bishop of London, poet Robert Browning and the Dowager Lady de Rothschild—met to find a solution on February 1, 1882, at London's Mansion House, the traditional headquarters of the Lord Mayor of London. Their remarks were widely reported and the *Jewish Chronicle* printed a special supplement with full coverage. As a result of the assembly, a Mansion House Fund was established and grew quickly to almost £10,000,000 in today's money. With Laurence and Alice now free of Harris, and already committed to a mission to establish a homeland for the Jews in Palestine, it was inevitable for them to become deeply involved. Here was a chance to move from voices quietly arguing for a Jewish colony in Palestine to an active role in relief aid to thousands of people consumed by disaster. It was an incredible opportunity for Laurence and Alice to dive in and really make an important difference in world affairs.

On February 15, a new letter from Laurence was published in *The Times*. He argued while popular sentiment assumed the preferred destination for all emigrants was America, re-locating some to their ancestral home in Palestine would have the added benefit of reinvigorating them with their history and destiny. Many Jewish leaders were afraid families sent to America would soon forget their historical roots and simply be assimilated into the great American melting pot. Practically, Laurence also pointed out that more care should be taken to ensure that the right Jews were sent to the right places. Those who were capable of succeeding in an agricultural colony would best be sent to Palestine. Other less agriculturally capable Jews should be categorized by their abilities in the trades for jobs in Europe—and even beggars should be identified so they could receive the total support and charity they needed to survive. Finally, he recommended representatives of the Mansion House Fund go immediately to the refugee camps to make on-site assessments and immediate payments for emigration costs.

The effect of this letter in the ghettoes of Eastern Europe was electric, as word spread that "Lord" Oliphant was back[8] from his setback with the Sultan, and was ready, with cash and immense practical good sense, to save them all once again. New assemblies like the Mansion House meeting were repeated in Birmingham and Oxford, gathering grass roots support. In America, similar meetings took place in Washington, Philadelphia and New Orleans. To put pressure on Eastern European governments to stabilize their local societies, President Chester A. Arthur sent a letter to the new Czar.[9]

Meanwhile, Laurence was drafted onto the Mansion House Fund leadership and attended the follow-up meetings in late February and March. The *Jewish Chronicle* reported a "special subcommittee" was formed and passed a resolution:

sending Mr. Laurence Oliphant with or without a second commissioner, to Galicia, to classify the refugees according to their several callings, and after such classification to select those for colonization those who being farmers, mechanics, operatives or labourers, would be serviceable in agricultural settlements; next to select those who, belonging to other trades would not be serviceable in agricultural settlement, but might find employment in Europe or in the British colonies; and finally to deal with residuum in each mode as might be found desirable.[10]

The needs were urgent, and things were not proceeding smoothly. Stories of misplaced refugees were starting to appear. One family was taken out of Eastern Europe and relocated at significant expense to America, only to demand to be brought back to Russia because of the chaotic arrangements in the New World.[11] Consequently, the Mansion House Committee also directed the envoys traveling to the camps should first "proceed in turn to Paris, Berlin, Vienna, Lemberg and Brody." Their specific mission would be to stop the local organizations sending any more Jews to inappropriate places before arrangements to receive them could be made.

This was a mission custom-tailored to the talents of the Oliphants and the engagement must have been electric for Laurence and Alice. Now instead of waiting for their own salvation and reunion with angels, they were, in a very practical way, actively saving a large population of downtrodden and desperate people. The satisfaction that they were actually making a difference must have been very gratifying. Laurence and Alice prepared to travel along the designated itinerary to meet local Committees, to brief their influential friends and other sympathizers, and to make assessments and cash outlays. Just before they set out from London, Margaret Oliphant visited them at their lodgings:

> They were all packed and ready for their start, not knowing precisely where Providence might lead them before they came back, but facing

all the hazards of the future with a pleasant confidence—a confidence, no doubt, springing partly from an over sanguine and buoyant nature, but chiefly from the sense of the great work which they felt to be in their hands, and which they were sure of the guidance of God to enable them.[12]

The first stage of the journey brought them to Paris, where more and more reports of Jewish enthusiasm for their mission reached them in response to articles in the *Jewish Chronicle*. In fact, this was only the beginning of a tide of popular sentiment that would soon elevate the couple to the status of messiahs themselves in the eyes of the miserable and desperate outcasts they served. Traveling on to Berlin, Alice was troubled by recurring headaches whenever she became tired. She wrote home she was glad they only had two meetings there for her to attend. One was with an old friend of Laurence from his early diplomatic days, Odo Russell, who was now British Ambassador, and the other with the Crown Prince and Princess of Prussia, both of whom were very supportive of the mission.

Besides briefing the wealthy and influential on plans to help the Jews, the travelers also met with Jewish leaders who were most eager to size up Laurence and Alice and understand their true motives. In Vienna, Laurence met Peretz Smolenskin, a famous Hebrew language novelist and publisher of the most widely read Jewish monthly magazine in Europe, *Ha Shahar*, or *The Dawn*. Smolenskin was one of the greatest early Zionists, and he was dead set against sending refugee Jews to America, where he feared their immersion into America would obliterate their Jewish culture. Laurence felt exactly the same way, and was excited to have a meeting of the minds with a leading Jewish thinker. Laurence urged Smolenskin to join them on the remainder of their mission, and come to settle with the colony in Palestine. Smolenskin was all for it, but was not in good health, and so he promised to do all he could to support the Oliphants and their mission in his publication. He was to die of tuberculosis within the next few years.

By April, Laurence and Alice arrived at the Austrian refugee centers in Lemberg and Brody. They were met with crowds and ovations everywhere. 1,200 refugees were already at Brody, with more on the way. By the end of May, there were over 12,000. Urgently, Laurence had to work through the mandate of the Mansion House Fund Committee sorting the desperate Jews by those fit for an agricultural community, and those who were not, and then handing out the necessary money. There were not many Jewish farmers since Russian law prohibited Jews from owning land. Groups of emigrants organized themselves into "Oliphant Committees" to present themselves to Laurence and argue for the specific aid they wanted to receive. Laurence did not like the work, because he was convinced it was doomed to fail since no satisfactory arrangements were being made fast enough to receive such a volume of emigrants at their designated destinations.

More Jewish leaders of early Zionism came to meet him. One was Samuel Mohilever, rabbi of Bialystok (today the largest city in northeastern Poland) as well as a champion of Jewish immigration to Palestine, which he believed was "the foundation of the existence of our people." He reminded Jewish sects differing on specific religious practices to overcome separatist feelings and remember all Jews were bonded by their common heritage. During his life he also won over the Rothschild family to the Palestine cause, leading to their investments in several start-up settlements. The rabbi liked the Oliphants and, although they were Gentiles, he thought them welcome agents for facilitating the Jewish return to the Promised Land.

Laurence was also visited by a delegation of students who founded the BILU movement (named for an acronym for a famous verse in *Isaiah* which, in Hebrew, says "Let the house of Jacob go!"). These intense young early Zionists were committed to starting an agricultural colony in Palestine – which they did, in spite of great difficulties – and they also gave their support to the Oliphant mission.

Finally, after three weeks of sorting and bankrolling refugees, as well as meeting with Jewish leaders, Laurence was delighted to welcome two other Mansion House Fund Commissioners to the front lines and then to resign his own committee responsibilities in order to work on the logistics for actually creating a colony to receive immigrants in Palestine. The Fund voted him "a very cordial vote of thanks for his services" on the front lines of the hotspots. Laurence wrote to his friend William Cowper:

> I was detained at Lemberg for three weeks through the bungling chiefly
> of the Mansion House Committee, whose intentions are better than
> their executive faculty.[13]

The Oliphants were ready to move on, and Laurence and Alice left the camps at Brody headed south to Jassy, Romania. The *Jewish Chronicle's* correspondent in Jassy wrote:

> Mr. Oliphant was received here with much enthusiasm by the Jewish
> population. His journey from Lemberg to Jassy was more like a march
> of triumph than anything else, for everywhere on his way thither the
> same manifestations of joy were noticeable.[14]

Along their route, they couldn't resist the opportunity to call at the palace of the Chassidim ultra-orthodox Jewish sect for an audience with their regal leader, the renowned Rabbi of Sadagora.[15] They had heard of this "miracle worker," and reported on his visit in his article "Jewish Tales and Jewish Reform" in the November 1882 edition of *Blackwoods Magazine*. In the beginning, the founder of this sect had the insight during a cholera epidemic that the Jewish God was a god of vengeance, and so the sickness must have been a punishment for the sins of the community. He then declared various rules of atonement—including designating a sick "child of atonement" who should be allowed to die—and, as the epidemic lessened, was revered as an intermediary to God and a broker for divine forgiveness. The first rabbi embraced this designation as a regal calling, and positioned himself, not unlike Thomas Lake Harris, as the connector between the Deity and His earth-bound followers. Money, gifts and other treasures poured in, and the Rabbi of Sadagora constructed a large and impressive palace, and ruled there with his court. By the time Laurence and Alice visited, the son of the original Rabbi was in power, in his early old age. Of his father, Laurence wrote:

> it was said he had upon his palms of his hands the stamp of the royal line of David. This mark was the outline of a lion imprinted upon the skin and it was a sign that his mission was from God.[16]

The palace of the rabbi was located on the edge of the Austrian Empire near the provincial capital of Czernowitz. The contrast between the poverty in the refugee camps and the luxuries of this holy compound must have been jarring. Laurence records more details of their visit, from the moment they were met at the train station by a hansom carriage driven by "coachman and groom with caftan and curls." A crowd lined the streets as they paraded to the rabbi's palace where they were separated, with Alice going off with court wives, and Laurence led to an audience with the great man himself. Laurence shared refreshments with the rabbi, served on trays with vessels of solid gold. After describing the encounter, Laurence wrote:

> I did not call on him in order to test his powers of divination, my visit did not enlighten me on that point. What I did desire to substantiate was the fact of his influence, and of that I have obtained indisputable evidence. That it is widespread there is also little doubt.[17]

After their remarkable meeting, winning another Jewish leader over to their cause, Laurence and Alice continued south into Romania by train. Their first stop was Jassy where Laurence was expected to attend a meeting of dozens of local Romanian emigration committees, all with great interest in relocating to Palestine. On the day he arrived:

> the whole day, a large concourse of people had been gathering round Mr. Oliphant's hotel at the Bingplatz, watching for an opportunity to have at least a glimpse of his person, so much, it seems, was he held in general esteem by the populations.[18]

On May 3, Laurence spoke to the conference and declared America to be a very less preferable destination to Palestine. He pledged to do everything in this personal power to raise funds and receive permissions for emigration to the Holy Land. The assembly was forming a Central Committee and offered Laurence its Presidency, which he declined in favor of Honorary membership instead. He did, however, commit to representing the Central Committee in Constantinople, and received their "power of attorney" to act for them in negotiations with the Ottomans. Leaving Jassy, Laurence and Alice exhaustedly continued south to Bucharest and then on to Constantinople. The *Jewish Chronicle* reported Laurence's future plans were "leaving for Palestine where he is intending to settle down for some time to watch over the purchase and selections of land."[19] But first, they were to pause in Constantinople, with diplomatic lobbying focused on securing the Sultan's permission for Jewish settlements in the Holy Land.

After spending all winter and spring traversing wet northern Europe and classifying and financing desperate emigrants, Laurence and Alice must have been grateful for a respite in the balmy late spring and summer at Constantinople and its enclave of diplomatic summer houses along the water at Therapia. Here are some excerpts from Alice's letters home describing their holiday-like surroundings to friends and family:[20]

"This is a lovely spot," Mrs. Laurence writes to her sister, "as indeed every spot along the Bosphorus seems to be; and we have chosen rooms in a house that is a little way up the abrupt slope. Our ground-floor is at the height of two or three tall houses above the shore, and we are at the top of it, which enables us to look up and down the Straits from our windows."

"Count Conti, whom H. and E. will remember at Washington, is a very old friend of Laurence's, and he has completed my comfort here by giving me a key to the door at the top of the embassy garden, which is just opposite the house, so that I have his hanging terraces to myself, and a short cut down upon the line of houses where most people live at the water's edge, and to which the scramble down the street is stony and roundabout."

"The gardens of the French and English embassies, also climbing the slopes above their palaces, are indescribable for beauty. Periodical garden receptions have begun at both, where all the diplomatic world take tea, and tennis and talk; and one can come and go freely enough not to find it a fatigue to see the world."

"Lady Dufferin has arranged for my bathing with them (in an enclosure with a false bottom, the deep water frightening weak swimmers otherwise) and will send the children's donkey for me, and send me back every day; so I am not absolutely dependent on a change of place for my bathing now…"

While Alice enjoyed the respite, Laurence worked to convince the Turks to let Jews settle in Palestine. Unfortunately, other recent events made that virtually impossible. In 1881, a disgruntled Army Colonel named Urabi Pasha had taken control of Egypt in a coup d'etat. A joint British and French fleet went to bring order and restore proper authority, arriving at the coast near Alexandria in May 1882—about the same time Laurence returned to Constantinople. Refugees fled from Cairo to Alexandria earlier, and on June 11 a "riot," or massacre, took place and 50 Europeans were killed. On July 11, the British warships began a two-day bombardment of Alexandria, and rebels decided to torch the parts of the town that remained standing, so little would be left to fall into British and French hands. The British marines then took the city and re-installed the overthrown monarch to power. More battles followed before a complete British victory in September, and a formal British occupation of Egypt, which continued from 1882 through to 1922, with a British military presence persisting even until 1954.

The most likely reasons behind the joint British and French actions were concern over continued British access to the Suez Canal for trade with India, and action to protect other investments in Egypt. But the impact on the Ottoman Sultan was obvious as he and his advisors worried they might be the next territory the British would decide to "protect." Laurence's lobbying for the Sultan to sponsor a new colony of emigrants into his realm, funded largely by British and other northern European interests, seemed a thinly veiled recipe for a takeover, and no progress could be made. Laurence wrote:

> The very name of an Englishman is enough to rouse the Sultan's present opposition, and the influence of the British Ambassador is entirely negative – in other words, it would ruin any cause he attempted to advocate.[21]

Meanwhile, Laurence and Alice personally did all they could to help the suffering Jews. At their own expense, they relocated over 40 refugees to the former Brotherhood of the New Life properties in Brocton, New York. Since recovering that land from Harris, Pitt

Buckner had become Laurence's on-site manager, and the Oliphants asked that special arrangements be made to give the new settlers every chance for success:

> all the first year's expenses will have to be bourne by our property before their labour can begin to make them independent. We gave orders to have their Sabbaths and all food and special observances respected, of course.[22]

Laurence kept writing articles to make money and also maintained a flood of correspondence with the emigration committees back in Romania, Austria, Russia as well as the sympathizers they visited in Vienna, Berlin, Paris and London. To help, he employed a remarkable twenty-six year old secretary, Naphtali Herz Imber, who spoke eleven languages and could write in five, including Hebrew.[23] Imber originally found the Oliphants to see for himself if they actually were Gentiles interested in a Jewish homeland in Palestine. When they first met in Constantinople, Imber and the Oliphants had a heated discussion, until Laurence realized that not only did Imber not want anything from him, but that he also believed in a combined male and female God, based on his study of the Jewish Talmud. When this came out, Laurence and Alice exchanged surprised glances with each other and immediately invited Imber to join them as secretary. They thought he was sent by God to help them. For a while, they all got on rather well. Imber wrote:

> He called himself a rolling stone. I, too, have been a rolling stone. And if rolling stones gather no moss, they at least knock up against one another; and that is how I had the privilege of knowing him.[24]

While he was with the Oliphants, Imber ensured his lasting fame by writing the poem "Ha Tikvah" about the feelings of love from a desperate people for their ancestral homeland. Later set to music, it became the moving soundtrack of the film Exodus, and in 2004 was adopted as the Israeli national anthem.[25] Here is the poem's opening verse and refrain, translated from the Hebrew:

> As long as in the heart, within,
> A Jewish soul still yearns
> And onward, towards the ends of the east,
> An eye still locks towards Zion,
>
> Our hope is not yet lost,
> The ancient hope,
> To return to the land of our fathers,
> The city where David encamped.

Next, their friend from the Brotherhood of the New Life, Emily Fawcett Cuthbert joined them, after separating from her husband, Arthur, who remained fiercely loyal to Harris. Alice wrote home with some humor to describe their growing entourage:

> Our little household often makes me laugh at its heterogeneity: our three selves (cosmo-English), a little Polish Hebrew, and Hebrew scholar required for the Hebrew and German and Roumanian correspondence that Laurence has, and a steady old Greek man-cook, who takes charge of the kitchen, marketing, and table, and does a little housemaiding.[26]

They were all "hard at work" learning the languages they would need in the days ahead – especially German and Hebrew, the languages of most Eastern European Jews. The rest of their days were filled with reading, riding and swimming until the cold weather of October arrived. And all the time, Laurence looked for ways to sell in his message to the skeptical Turks.

As summer turned into late fall, the Oliphant troop relocated to the fashionable offshore island of Prinkipo – Prince's Island — just south of Constantinople. While the Sultan and his advisors would not listen to any British requests, Laurence did make a friend and ally of the American Ambassador to the Ottoman Empire, Lew Wallace, who was himself a sympathizer to the Jewish people, as he proved in his novel *Ben-Hur*. That book, published in 1880, eventually became the best-selling American novel of the nineteenth century, beating *Uncle Tom's Cabin* for the honor. Wallace's willingness to help in the event of any changes in policy from the Sultan's court probably made the Oliphants' next move easier in Laurence's mind. The island weather was turning cold, and Alice was complaining of headaches from the coal heater at the house, and so they de-camped from Turkey south to sunnier Palestine and the picturesque sea-front town of Haifa. They wanted to settle in and establish a base for themselves at the gateway of the Promised Land.

CHAPTER 11

THE PROMISED LAND

The Oliphants arrived at Haifa, in December 1882. It was a long-awaited coming home to the land where they had been laboring to bring so many other wandering souls. Haifa then was an Arab town with a total population of about 4,500 sitting in the southern jaw of a long natural harbor on the Mediterranean Sea looking out to the east, with the rising slopes of Mount Carmel to the west, and the town of Acre to the north. It was a natural haven, with many ships at anchor in its waters, and a telegraph line through Acre connecting it to the rest of the world. Sunny blue skies, warm water and a clutch of stone white-washed houses with domed roofs made it naturally inviting to the weary travelers. But, on top of all that, some fourteen years earlier, a colony of pious Germans had emigrated there, to await the Second Coming. Their leaders had split with the traditional Lutheran Church that they felt had become mired in dogmatic quarrels, while they believed no messiah would return to earth until people actually lived by the basic principles Christ had espoused for daily life. Ironically, just like Thomas Lake Harris, they wanted their community to "live the life" of Christians instead of debate about principles.

To make themselves feel at home, the settlers built a traditional German village one mile north of the Arab town, with the customary grid of tree-lined streets and stone houses, with gardens and verandas, and red-tile roofs to bake comfortably in the sun until the early shade was cast by Mount Carmel. By 1882, about 350 Germans lived in this Templar Society, and the second-best house was empty. Its owner, Karl Oldorf, had moved on to another branch of the same colony about 60 miles south in Jaffa. Alice and Laurence fell in love with the property's spacious two floors, basement and garden and immediately rented it for one year, after which they bought it. On January 20, 1883, Laurence wrote in his column for the *New York Sun*:

> I know of no locality in the East which offers greater attractions of position, climate, and association than this spot. Thanks to the efforts of the colonists, it has become an oasis of civilization in the wilderness of Oriental barbarism, where the invalid in search of health, or the tourist on the lookout for a comfortable resting-place on his travels, will find good accommodation, and all the necessaries, if not the luxuries, of civilized life.[1]

Oliphant house in Haifa.

Indeed it would have been difficult to find any other settlement then in Palestine more suited to welcoming the exotic Oliphants and their entourage. Laurence continued:

> The whole settlement contains about sixty houses... The English, American and German consuls are all colonists. There is a skilled physician, architect and engineer in the colony, an excellent hotel, a school, and meeting-house.[2]

He ended with a more practical pitch to his New York readers noting there was an olive-oil soap factory in Haifa exporting to their city. The soap "may be purchased in New York by such of your readers as have a fancy to wash their hands with soap direct from the Holy Land, made from the oil of olives of Carmel, at F. B. Nichols's, 62 William Street." The Oliphants' next-door neighbors were a distinguished German family, headed by Jakob Schumacher, "a stonemason, engineer and designer [who] was Vice-Consul for America in northern Palestine."[3] His son, Gottlieb, had just returned from University in Stuttgart. Together with his father, these two neighbors became Laurence's partners in many projects, such as laying out the route for a proposed railway, designing a jetty for landing refugees in Haifa harbor and making maps to chart their many explorations throughout the adjoining territories.

Alice also made their new home the centerpiece from which she would build out a more democratic commune than that of Thomas Lake Harris. It would not be run by a despotic male prophet, but by an enlightened male and female of equal status, like Laurence and Alice. Their creed was "simple" and "informal" because it was only through their works, through giving daily testimony of their love and desire to be of service "that they could demonstrate their theory of equal counterparts – which they considered their real message to the world." In addition, they would continue to explore open breathing, sexual mysticism, sensuality and the other-worldly principles she and Laurence embraced in Brocton and California.

They engaged in an aggressive renovation program to fit out the house as they wanted it. Alice directed this work since Laurence was frequently away in the early days trying to get support and approval for his plans to introduce a railroad to connect Haifa with nearby centers to improve trade and development. Just as the house was ready, three more Broctonites arrived to join them: the Reverend Alfred R. Buckner, whose relocation to the Holy Land was the fulfillment of a "lifelong dream," together with Mrs. Fowler and her son James, originally from Scotland, who had joined Harris's brotherhood "with considerable means."[4] Later Reverend Buckner's son Pitt, who was the Oliphants' property manager at Brocton, would come out to stay for a year, and Dr. and Mrs. Martin would also come for a time.

Alice organized the household, giving everyone their separate responsibilities, and made it a beehive of activity, just as they had established for their routine in the last months in Turkey:

> They rose at 6:30, by which time Buckner was already hard at work among the rows of corn and potatoes. Emily [Cuthbert] was delegated to the laundry and the chickens, young Mr. Fowler took care of cleaning the house, and Alice was responsible for the food: by ten o'clock she had selected the menu, made the bread, and prepared the soup for cooking. At midday they ate their meal, after which they rested from their labours, and the afternoons were occupied with various activities.[5]

In the evenings, Laurence would read everyone excerpts from his writing and by 10 o'clock they had all retired. Alice and Laurence's green-painted room on the second storey looked onto Mount Carmel, and, as we know from one painting, had bright blue curtains on the windows.

Their secretary, Naphtali Imber, in particular, was becoming smitten with Alice and the loving way she led the household. Later he wrote very fondly, remembering Alice:

> My hostess, Mrs.Oliphant, was a highly educated lady, who combined the elastic vigour and polished manners of a French beauty with the grace and kindness of an English lady. She wrote and spoke fluently English, French, German and Italian. Moreover she was a good singer and dancer and a splendid pianoforte player. And as she was a queen in the salon, so she knew how to reign in the kitchen. There she was an incarnate cookery-book.[6]

Imber also remembered how kind Alice was to others, and how she was happiest when making other people more comfortable. At her express wish, Imber called Alice "dear Mother" and she addressed him as "Herzel." Faithful to the end, he would be one of the few friends who traveled to attend Laurence's funeral years later in London.

Laurence was continually writing to support his brood. There was his voluminous correspondence, written up and translated as necessary by secretary Imber, and dispatched off in the daily mails to London, New York and the many emigration committees and sympathizers across Europe. He wrote his columns for the *New York Sun*, whose editor was his close friend, Charles Dana, and later packaged those pieces up into a book called *Haifa: or Life in Modern Palestine*. Meanwhile Blackwood published *The Land of Gilead*, *The Land of Khemi*, and *Traits and Travesties* during 1882.

They also all continued to help the Jews, in any way they could. Many emigrants were destitute and detained in Haifa until new colonies under construction were ready. Imber recorded one typical event:

> Once in the middle of the night a German brought nearly a score of Jewish colonists, men, women and children, famished, parched, wet

and weary from their journey and Mr. and Mrs. Oliphant and myself got up and prepared coffee and warm dry clothes for them. "Herzel," Mrs. Oliphant said to me, "you are a noble Samaritan; run to the Hotel Carmel, and carry off all the bread they have, for your brethren are starving." She herself waited upon them, handing round the coffee and the food to these poor sufferers.[7]

Winter was eased by the warm and breezy climate at the shore, but when the hot weather arrived in summer, the Oliphants retreated for camping trips high up on Mount Carmel, living in a Bedouin tent, just as Laurence's parents had escaped Colombo for their idyllic cottage in the high hills of Ceylon. Initially, Alice and Laurence had no luck looking for land to buy from the wary Arabs and Druze villagers in the high country, but as the local people became familiar with their kind and exotic new neighbors, that reluctance softened and they were received "with a warmth apparently reserved for such dreamers and visionaries." Then one day a headman from a local village turned to Laurence for help paying the cash fees that would allow his son and other village lads to legally avoid Ottoman army conscription. When Laurence gave the money, the chief returned the favor with the gift of an orchard and vineyard where the Oliphants went on to build their mountain retreat at the village of Dalieh. With the help of his German neighbors down below, they engineered and erected a sturdy turreted two-storey stone house, somewhat reminiscent of ancestral Condie. It still stands there today, with verandas looking down across the fields and hills to the mountain ranges to the west.

Fortunately, one of the pastimes of the commune was sketching and painting. Alice honed her artistic talents during years teaching students in California while she proved her capacity for self-supported independent living outside of the Fountaingrove estate. By the time she was in Palestine, Alice also added photography to the mix. In addition, Emily Fawcett Cuthbert was a talented artist. One of her paintings gives a remarkable real-world glimpse into the surroundings in which the Oliphants and their friends lived and entertained. From the artist's vantage point, the painting looks across the living and dining rooms at Dalieh, showing Laurence writing, Alice seated at the dining-room table, and a Druze servant cooking in the adjoining kitchen. These public rooms were as large as could be made, with a high-beamed ceiling. When the house was overflowing with guests, which happened all the time, they would hang textile covers off the building, to make tent-like extra rooms furnished with oriental carpets and beds. Prime places were on the roof and in the gardens. Another of my favorite paintings is a watercolor of the veranda at Dalieh, looking out across a field in front, with horse-pulled plough and farmer standing against a background panorama of miles and miles of rolling hills below and mountains in the distance. The Oliphants' dog is holding his head up to look out across the scene while stretched out on a matt next to Laurence's red bedroom slippers and binoculars on a hand-made end table next to his sling chair.

All told, the interlude in Palestine lasted from 1882 to 1886, and was the period of happiest fulfillment in their two lives. Laurence published a well-received comic novel, *Altiora Peto*, in 1883. The title is actually the family motto of the Oliphants of Condie, as carved on their village church at Forgandenny, Scotland. It translates ambitiously as "I seek something higher." But in the novel, Altiora Peto is the name of an overly thoughtful young lady, whose name always forces her "to soar," making her aim as high as her late father had hoped. Laurence also wrote another work of fiction, based on their all too real experiences with Harris in America, called *Masollam*, published in 1886. It tells the story of a sinister wild-eyed prophet who enslaves unwary followers in an oppressive cult. Laurence then collected seventeen essays about incidents in his earlier life into a partial autobiography called *Episodes in a Life of Adventure, Or Moss from a Rolling Stone* (1887). These were anecdotes from childhood through his war correspondent days, and did not go into any spiritual territory, although in the final chapter entitled "The Moral of it All" he promised such a discussion would be forthcoming in the future. But Laurence and Alice must have thought the most significant achievement of those times was the remarkable book *Sympneumata*, which was primarily dictated by Alice to Laurence, "under the influence of a higher mind," and which sets forth the principles of their own sexual and mystical creed.

Although, the Oliphants shared with Harris and Swedenborg the belief that the original nature of God was a balanced combination of male and female halves, their emphasis on couples and the demonstrated equality of the male and female halves was somewhat different. Whereas Harris, as "the pivotal man," planned to use a terrestrial female – either Mrs. Requa (Golden Rose) or Alice – as a mere tool to get himself in the mood to find his celestial counterpart Queen Lily, the Oliphants believed a loving terrestrial couple were needed for a true marriage of counterparts in heaven. Sympneumata was a word coined by the Oliphants from Greek, and broadly means "souls coming together." The realized unity would be a more balanced fulfillment, with a terrestrial woman finding her celestial male, and a terrestrial male finding his celestial female. The path to this unity would begin on earth with a male and female lying together in bed, in "tempting proximity" in each other's arms, and practicing deep breathing. That suppressed sexual passion would ultimately transport the breathers to the celestial realm where they could re-unite with their counterparts and experience the equivalent of a spiritual orgasm. Normal copulation was to be avoided, so the vile lust currents could be constrained, and the true female and male halves could unite, mimicking the true nature of the Deity before the fall.

Meanwhile the chosen trying to find and unite with their counterparts should live together in celibate communities run by a female and a male of equal status, like the Oliphants in Palestine. And the theory of the bi-une nature of mankind should be taught to those willing to receive the message, along with the techniques of lying and breathing together to achieve Sympneumata, even if that means Laurence and Alice might have to strip down, hug and breathe deeply with potential converts of the opposite sex, to show the way. Indeed that enthusiasm would get them into trouble later.

When they finished the declaration of this mysterious creed in their joint book, the manuscript was then dispatched to their mainstream publisher back in Scotland, where Mr. Blackwood had absolutely no idea what to make of it. But Laurence was one of his most popular and successful contributors both to the magazine and the Blackwoods catalogue of books. That track record, together with Laurence's offer to pay the cost of production, led to *Sympneumata* appearing in a very reputable looking clothbound edition of 1,000 copies. Laurence was only too proud to help with its distribution and at one point presented Queen Victoria with her own copy. The Queen was then to write in her journal a note reminding herself how clever Mr. Oliphant was and what strange ideas he had about religion.[8]

The popular reception of the work was essentially a baffled silence, but this did not seem to bother Laurence or Alice. They delighted in continuing their lively commune in Palestine, welcoming a swelling stream of visitors to the Holy Land, who were only too happy to include a highly entertaining visit to the refreshingly odd Oliphants on their itineraries. One fellow spiritualist, however, who seemed to understand and accept both the bi-une Deity and the regimen of breathing together in search of counterpartal union was General George Gordon, who spent a few days at Dalieh before continuing on to Khartoum in the Sudan and his untimely death at the hands of the Mahdi. Imber recorded long conversations between himself and Gordon, discussing Palestine's history.[9]

Alice also apparently became popular visiting local villagers to share cooking tips and nurse the sick. And, if anyone in Dalieh needed help or money, the Oliphants were always likely to help. On the mystical side, Alice always had the courage of her convictions, and sometimes demonstrated for Druze and Arab neighbors the practical application of lying together and breathing, offering herself as the female proxy for the male to seek his counterpart. How she communicated what all this was supposed to mean with her limited command of the local language is an interesting question to ponder.

Instruction in seeking counterparts also probably inflamed the volcanic sexual desires of secretary Imber, who wrote the most ardent love poetry about Alice—and later virtual pornography about his wife—but probably never was able to achieve the down-to-earth intercourse he longed to have with Mrs. Oliphant. His advances, however, no doubt led to him being asked to leave the household and escape the temptation he felt whenever he was near Alice. He did leave, but remained in correspondence over the years with the Oliphants who many times helped him with financial aid and modest investments in business ventures, such as a store selling watches in Jerusalem, to keep him busy and solvent in spite of his bohemian nature and voracious love of alcohol.

Laurence meanwhile stayed true to his original mission of facilitating Jewish emigration to Palestine. In one column for the *New York Sun*, he gives a humorous commentary on the efforts of the Romanian Jewish Committee as they bought significant acreage south of Haifa, and then tried to negotiate with local Arab workers to get them to work on the agricultural necessities as the Jews observed and learnt how to become farmers. On one occasion, he accompanied the Romanians and their interpreter to a business meeting with the Arabs:

> The meeting took place in the storehouse, where Jews and Arabs squatted promiscuously amid the heaps of grain, and chaffered over the terms of their mutual copartnership. It would be difficult to imagine anything more utterly incongruous than the spectacle thus

presented—the stalwart fellahin, with their wild, shaggy, black beards, the brass hilts of their pistols projecting from their waistbands, their tassled kufeihahs drawn tightly over their heads and girdled with coarse black cords, their loose, flowing abbas, and sturdy bare legs and feet; and the ringleted, effeminate-looking Jews, in caftans reaching almost to their ankles, as oily as their red or sandy locks, or the expression of their countenances—the former inured to hard labour on the burning hillsides of Palestine, the latter fresh from the Ghetto of some Roumanian town, unaccustomed to any other description of exercise than that of their wits, but already quite convinced they knew more about agriculture than the people of the country, full of suspicion of all advice tendered to them, and animated by a pleasing self-confidence which I fear the first practical experience will rudely belie.[10]

Things did not go particularly well at first, with each side dug into their own positions, certain that the other side was trying to swindle them. The conversation went late, with the natives screaming in Arabic, and the visitors in German, with an overwrought interpreter in between. After everyone shouted until exhaustion, the group quieted down for the night. Laurence concluded "sleep brought better counsel to both sides, and an arrangement was finally arrived at next morning."[11] That particular settlement did start off and then flirt with ruin, but was saved by the efforts of Rabbi Mohilever back in Europe who won the support of Baron Edmond de Rothschild.[12] The baron stepped in with architects and city planners to transform the venture into an attractive seaside community called Zikron Ya'akov (Jacob's Memorial), named as a memorial for his late father. It flourished with crops, the first winery in Israel, schools and a beautiful synagogue.

The agreeable pattern of daily life at the Oliphant commune—entertaining visitors, writing continuously, and launching a succession of enjoyable projects connected with the emigration mission—continued through the years of 1883 to 1885 in total happiness. Alice's brother Guy le Strange was a noted Arabian scholar, and he virtually moved in to the German Colony's hotel, which Laurence had invested in building a second storey for their continuous stream of visitors. Guy and Laurence became the best of friends and collaborators. Because of their long absence in Palestine, Laurence and Alice planned to spend time in London during the 1886 fall and winter "season" to catch up with family, friends and publishers. However, care was first taken to not disappoint Alice's older sister, Jamesina, and her husband Adolphus Waller, the vicar of Hunstanton, Norfolk. They had been planning a visit to the Oliphants in the Holy Land for a very long time, and they finally arrived in the fall of 1885.

Professional art critics looking over the work of the Oliphant circle note that Jamesina "was the only professional artist in the group."[13] Her plan for the visit was to produce a portfolio of paintings illustrating famous sites of the Holy Land. In addition, we can tell from the paintings which remain that Alice and some of the others already with the Oliphants painted with Jamesina, obviously on easels that must have stood side by side with hers in front of sights such as the ancient monastery on Mount Carmel. To accommodate Jamesina's ambitious mission, Laurence and Alice had carefully planned out a seventeen-day camping trip around the north of the country, including Nazareth, Cana and the Sea of Galilee, also known as Lake Tiberias. As documented in the Gospels, this area was the setting for most of Jesus Christ's ministry on earth. He recruited four of his apostles from among the fishermen on the Sea of Galilee, walked upon the water there, and calmed the storm. He multiplied a few fishes from those waters to feed a crowd of thousands, and gave the Sermon on the Mount on a hillside overlooking its shores.

They set out November 26, 1885, accompanied by an Egyptian cook and his young son, who had to come along because his mother could not control him alone at home. While traveling by wagon and camels around the thirty-five mile coastline of the Sea, they sometimes would take shelter in the guest rooms of ancient monasteries or convents. But, more often, they would erect Laurence and Alice's Bedouin tent, in which they had summered before building their vacation home at Dalieh. Alice was troubled by headaches, but did not want to spoil the fun. One evening they returned, wet and tired to their campsite, but found the tent had been blown down by the "hurricane" wind. They could not fasten the tent poles in the blowing sand, so they had to seek make-shift shelter in a nearby "wheat-vault" or small shed. The Sea of Galilee is also below sea level, much like the Dead Sea, and at certain times insects and "bad air" combined to threaten unwary visitors with "malaria." In the 1860's, an entire colony of American emigrants from Maine and New Hampshire was wiped out by that dread disease, and it was always in the background as a possible scourge for western visitors in the Nineteenth Century. On the tenth and eleventh days of the journey Alice wrote:[14]

> *10th* – L. O. excursed, A. O. headache and fever; still in the wheat-vault; marshes all around.

> *11th* – Better after quinine; rode off early to get away from the marshes (buffaloes in them); pitched tent in heart of a great Bedouin camp, at the entrance of Wady Semack, east side of the lake.

They completed their itinerary by December 20, 1885, when Alice wrote a letter from Haifa home to her oldest brother Hamon, lord of the estate at Hunstanton, reporting on the adventure:

> We have just returned from a trip which frightened us a little in the prospect on account of my headaches, but which I managed, with only one and a half, and so little loss of strength, and on the whole enjoyed very much. The important particulars you will see, three or four months doubtless in the "English Illustrated Magazine" where Laurence will have three articles on it, so I will give you the more intimate story rapidly...[15]

There wasn't much time for Alice to rest and recover, because the plan was to spend Christmas up at the mountain retreat in Dalieh. So even though the weather was wet and miserable just at that time, Alice and Laurence made the difficult muddy journey to the high country to make sure everything was ready for the festivities. Those exertions proved a recipe for disaster. When Jamesina arrived a few days later, she found both Laurence and Alice delirious with fever. Hurriedly, word was sent down to the German Colony in Haifa to summon the doctor, who came immediately. Unfortunately, he decided to administer only natural homeopathic medicines. Alice was soon in the worst shape, and Jamesina gave her a "mustard bath" to break the fever, even though it caused the top layer of Alice's skin to come off. The patient seemed to revive briefly, and became lucid for a while, sitting up in a chair, talking, and then walking. But then her condition turned, and on January 2, 1886, Alice tragically died.

Word went out around the village and the neighboring communities that the beautiful lady all revered as an angel of mercy was dead and crowds surrounded the house, even in the driving rain. A handmade coffin was sent up from the German colony below and arguments broke out among the crowd as to who would have the honor of carrying Alice in her coffin down to the German cemetery. Eventually a group of about 50 villagers set off and shared that honor, carrying Alice shoulder high, and reportedly dropping her once or twice on the muddy track along the way. When the parade arrived at Haifa, they found the full leadership of the town, including the Moslem Governor of Haifa, all the German colonists and all the diplomatic consuls, assembled in and around Laurence's house, where the group from Dalieh dried out a while after their five-hour procession down the mountain. Alice's coffin was laid out in a front room, draped with a purple cloth and red rose cross made by the German neighbors, which mourners filed past solemnly. Jamesina wrote to their mother:

Had she been a queen she could not have been received with more respectful homage, and it was all spontaneous expression of love—personal love for her. Laurence felt it very much, for we had expected nothing of the kind; and I think the sympathy really helped him to go through the hard task.[16]

John Walker, who had accompanied Jamesina on many of her painting excursions, later drew two beautiful views of Alice's grave for her family and Laurence: one with the floral wreath from the funeral still in place and another of a later view. With the raised memorial stone around her plot, she seems almost alone with the scenery.

Laurence was obviously shattered—but not as shattered as you might think. For most of us today, a loss like this would be an abrupt and total separation from our dearest daily companion and love mate, as well as a reminder that we also will be transitioning soon into nothingness ourselves. This was not the case for Laurence who had a vivid life in the celestial realm that he had developed since his days with Harris. In a letter home to her mother about one week after Alice's death, he wrote:

Suddenly one night the light seemed to burst through, and she came to me so radiant, and at the same time so sad, at seeing me so unhappy, that my own grief seemed to be lifted by the effort she made to dispel it. She seemed literally to be rolling some great burden off my soul, and I felt my first duty to her was to be cheerful, and to fight against the morbid condition that was creeping over me. From that time I have continued to feel her more and more, and to be regaining my own health and spirits. She seems sensationally to invade my frame, thrilling my nerves when the sad fit is coming on, and shaking me out of it, flooding my brain occasionally with her thoughts, so that I can feel her thinking in me and inspiring me.[17]

And it wasn't just Laurence who was experiencing the return of Alice. Laurence continued that the current house guest, and former Harris member, Mrs. Cuthbert:

> is in some respects more conscious of her than I am, for she is more sensitive organically to such influences: and we are thus continually able to have the consolation of her presence, which has really robbed death of all its bitterest sting.[18]

The religious beliefs he shared so strenuously with Alice, told him that her soul had simply migrated to the celestial realm on the other side. And he became convinced that Harris had been wrong about Alice not being his true counterpart. Now he knew that Alice was the divine female part of his own god-like androgynous soul, and, through the practice of deep breathing and spirit travel he had mastered back in Brocton, he could unite with Alice as his counterpart, and experience the true bliss of "the two-in-one."

> Henceforward I live in her, as she will, if I am faithful to my own highest aspirations, in me: we are indissolubly bound to all eternity— more firmly wedded now than we could ever be below; and my great desire will be to let her love flow through me in the channel in which she wills it to flow, and which will assuredly be to those she loved so dearly on earth.[19]

Thus alone in earthly life, but accompanied by his Alice on the other side, Laurence embarked on the rather bizarre final chapter in his life.

He kept to the plans he and Alice had made to go back to England – and, why not? As Margaret Oliphant wrote, "She was with him," as far as he was concerned. One of his first calls in May was at Cumberland Lodge in Windsor Great Park, home of his childhood friend Princess Helena-Christian, daughter of Queen Victoria, and married to Prince

Christian of Schleswig-Holstein. She had earlier supported his mission for Jewish emigration to Palestine with the Prime Minister, helping Laurence build a strong base of support. Now, Laurence took ill there, with fever, had had to stay several nights. He recovered and went south to visit his old friends, the Cowpers, even demonstrating to Georgiana Cowper how lying together and deeply breathing can impart the Sympneumata, in spite of protests from her friend who thought Laurence just wanted to get into bed with her. Soldiering on, Laurence then visited a Mrs. Hankin, an intimate correspondent of Alice, although they had never met in person. When he first had written her, she wrote back to explain she had recently been rather ill, but that she would still welcome his coming. Laurence then did and go visit the lady. Afterward, Mrs Hankin wrote that, on arrival, he did not look as she had expected:

> I saw before me not the cheerful, brisk, hopeful man of the world, but a sad, weary-looking mystic, who looked larger than his height and older than his years, with thin, scattered iron-grey hair, a worn, sensitive face, and tired eyes.[20]

But everything changed when the evening got underway, with dinner and the inevitable dining-table conversation:

> then it was that I recognized the Laurence Oliphant of my photograph as, to a certain degree, still living in the tired, pale mystic of the afternoon. He told us anecdote after anecdote, as only he could tell, of his past life at home and abroad, or of his literary contemporaries and their modes of thought and action; and throughout proved himself the very perfection of a *raconteur*, absolutely free from egotism, vanity or ill-nature.[21]

After the success of the dinner, the following day's events took a somewhat stranger course, as before breakfast, Mrs. Hankin came into the bedroom of a lady friend also staying with her and told her that Mr. Oliphant wanted to see her immediately in the drawing room. The friend rose and readied herself accordingly, believing the "Alice" she had heard so much about the night before possibly wanted to help her from heaven in some way. She recorded the following testimony:

> I sat by his [Laurence's] side and held his hand for some time, finding that a strong current poured through him, shaking my hand and arm with a powerful vibration—a motion liked that produced by the current from a galvanic battery, though the sensation was not similar; indeed I only felt at first a warm and pleasant tingling in my arm and shoulder, and afterwards a great exhilaration and exaltation of spirits... The mental and spiritual exaltation was upon me for two days, and for a considerable time the faintness and other discomforts connected with my ailments were greatly ameliorated.[22]

Oliphant holiday house on Mount Carmel.

Laurence continued his ongoing activities, working on his writing while also visiting with the Prince of Wales and dining at Balmoral, and traveling up to see family and publishers in Scotland.

Then, by January 1887, Laurence fled the winter in England and visited Alice's mother in Paris. Soon after, by the end of February, he was home in Haifa, welcomed back by his friends and his neighbors at the German Colony. He stayed busy with miscellaneous writing projects, but a great enterprise began to weigh on his mind. As the customary summer time came in 1887, Laurence made the usual migration up to the mountain house in Dalieh. There he opened the floodgates of what he felt were influences from Alice to put down on paper more clarifications of the thinking that had begun with their remarkable volume *Sympneumata*. He worked all of the days and into the evenings in the living room at the Dalieh house, with a picture of Alice on the table in front of him. He also adopted a regimen of eating only rice to be a pure and simple vessel for receiving her messages from beyond. When the volume was finally published as *Scientific Religion* by the long-suffering Blackwood, Laurence inserted a one-page "Postscript to the Preface" to explain the singular circumstances around its publication.

> I had no sooner taken my pen in hand... than the thoughts which find expression in the following pages were projected into my mind with the greatest rapidity, and irrespective of any mental study or prearrangement on my part, often overpowering my own preconceptions, and still more often presenting the subject treated of in an entirely new light to myself.[23]

In writing this remarkable book (or taking it down in dictation from the deceased Alice) Laurence was able to clear up several points. First the confusion about counterparts caused by both he and Alice being together on the terrestial side could now be removed: Alice now in heaven was indeed Laurence's true counterpart, the missing female half of his own soul. Next, the changes about to take place as the spirits returned to earth would not be "catastrophic." Familiarity with celestial beings would inform more seekers after wisdom, and the enlightenment would spread gradually. Next, the whole notion of "a pivotal man" is only "the cruel lash of a slave-driver" (like Harris) and is absolute rubbish. Finally, the path to discovering the new intimacy is not a solitary one, but something that comes from putting oneself in close intimate proximity with other seekers "by which electromagnetic forces can be generated, sufficiently powerful to resist the invasion of the infernal lust currents." Now, after this intense collaboration with the deceased Alice, the remainder of the story becomes rather strange.

With *Scientific Religion* published by Blackwood in 1888, Laurence returned to Paris. Alice's mother was shocked by his haggard appearance, but at least he was lively in conversation as he regaled her with the story of the parties he hosted in Haifa for the Queen's jubilee, which involved erecting two huge tents and entertaining a very diverse group of international and multi-cultural people as guests. He particularly enjoyed describing the Arab women guests, not usually invited or present at such mixed gatherings, who spent the party corralled together in a tight circle giggling with each other in the exotic presence of all the music, drinking and dancing. He also visited a young Scottish acquaintance named Murray Templeton who was studying painting in Paris. Templeton showed Laurence some letters he had received from one Rosamond Dale Owen in America. She was the granddaughter of Robert Owen who founded the successful utopian community of New Harmony, Indiana, where Rosamond was then living. Her father, Robert Dale Owen, is also credited with convincing Abraham Lincoln to issue the Emancipation Proclamation, freeing the slaves during the American Civil War, by making a very carefully framed argument for its merits, which President Lincoln said "thrilled him like a trumpet call." Rosamond's letters to Templeton were full of her thoughts about spirituality, and apparently that was enough for Laurence to declare that he must go see their author immediately. He wrote an introduction for himself to Rosamond, and started to prepare to travel.

Meanwhile, at the other end, Rosamond was working on writing a philosophical book, *The Mediators*, which was to follow another work of hers named *Duality: Male and Female He Created Them*. In her autobiographical work much later, *My Perilous Life in Palestine*, she describes stretching out in a hammock at the end of a cloudless July day, and having a premonition her life was going to change. The next day, she "awoke with the word 'Prepare' on my lips" and told her friend, after breakfast, "I wish to buy a traveling outfit" and "I must get some nice under clothing." A day or two later, she received Laurence's letter of introduction, together with a copy of *Scientific Religion*. She replied that he should, indeed, come visit her.

In very short order, they soon met, got on well together, and departed for Palestine. On board ship, Laurence proposed. Even though she answered that she believed Alice, on the other side, had been Laurence's true soul mate, Rosamond accepted, believing she could help him (and Alice) accomplish their new mission in Palestine. Laurence also confided to her that he had previously had a celibate marriage with Alice, "sleeping with my beloved and beautiful Alice in my arms for twelve years without claiming the rights of a husband," in order to teach himself self-control. He also shared that lately, while in Paris, he had been trying to spread similar self-control by "placing two or three young couples, who were not married, in a tempting proximity." His doctors told him his "continence" might have caused his health problems. Although this was quite a lot of information about her potential new husband for Rosamond to take on board, she told Laurence there would be no need for any further self-control during sex with her, and they should just get on with it and behave normally. She did, however, advise him to stop coaching young people in hugging, breathing and self-control, telling him the Lord should deliver that instruction.

Shortly after the boat landed, a simple marriage ceremony was arranged for these two oddballs, but sadly it was only a few days later that Laurence started to show signs of his final illness. The newlyweds had been planning only a short visit, staying at the small house of a friend who started sending signals they were becoming an imposition there. Fortunately they were scooped up by Laurence's rich old friend, Sir Grant Duff, who had visited Alice and Laurence in Palestine, and was happy to give them quarters at his roomy and magnificent residence, a mansion built on the site of a former palace of Queen Anne in Twickenham. There, after a few weeks of highs and lows, Laurence died. Just earlier, he had said "I have no doubt the Harris devils are at me." His former secretary Napthali Imber visited him there immediately after the event:

> I have just been to take the last look at my dear friend and benefactor. He lies, as peacefully asleep, in his bed at the house of Sir Mountstuart Grant Duff, at Twickenham, in a bright and lofty room. As I gazed, in deep emotion, upon his noble features, there flitted through my mind all that he had been, and all that he had done for me; and I murmured the Hebrew saying: "The pious of all nations have a share in the world to come." Near his bed lie his books and manuscripts. He must have been working up to the last moment. His funeral (which Mrs. Oliphant has kindly invited me to attend, and which will be strictly private) will take place at Twickenham Cemetery at mid-day on Thursday, the 27th inst. Peace to his ashes![24]

Two weeks later, Rosamond reported Laurence's spirit returned, appearing to her and giving her the message "Death is delicious."[25]

CHAPTER 12

PASSING THE TORCH

Despite her marriage of only a few months, the death of her husband, and the uncertainties of her future, Rosamond Dale Owen Oliphant was determined to soldier on with Laurence's mission to Palestine. She gathered up Murray Templeton from Paris and set out for Haifa to check on the current state of the colony Laurence and Alice had started. Templeton confided that he and a young American widow named Mrs. Tuttle had been two of the young people Laurence had put in "tempting proximity" in Paris and that widow Tuttle was now busily spreading lurid stories about the experience around London, even as they traveled. In Haifa, word of this had also reached the little community, putting doubts in the minds of Laurence's friends and leaving most of Laurence's projects in complete disarray. Letters from England and America told her about the fast-growing reports that Laurence had been spreading unsavory practices. And newly christened champions of decency at London's new National Vigilance Association were rumored to be taking notice.

That association had been formed after a sensational series of articles about child prostitution appeared in the *Pall Mall Gazette* in 1885, authored by its editor, William T. Stead. The articles were provocatively entitled "The Maiden Tribute of Modern Babylon" and documented how traffic in young virgins called "fresh girls" had become common business for some wealthy British customers. The top retail rate was most usually £20 (over £1000 in today's money) and buyers had no interference from the authorities. Stead was a practitioner of the sensational "new journalism," and, for the articles, he actually bought a young virgin to prove his point and, although he had in no way harmed her, he was prosecuted and sent to jail for three months by those same authorities, in retaliation for the bad publicity. At the time of Laurence's death, however, Stead was back at work as head of the executive committee of the National Vigilance Association. This organization's purpose was to draw attention to the trafficking in women and children and to advocate new laws against vice. A new law was passed in 1885 called the Criminal Law Amendment Act specifying steep penalties for acts such as male homosexuality and any other form of "gross indecency." This was in fact the same law invoked to imprison Oscar Wilde for gay activity, but it also included punishment for anyone who was a party to the commission of any form of gross indecency, which was not well-defined in the statute. Stead would go on to be a lifelong reporter and reformer, honored by commemorative statues in both London and New York's Central Park, which also mention his heroic behavior before his death during the sinking of the Titanic in 1912. And now, in 1886, his agents were on the lookout for any dubious moral behavior to pounce on.

After a few weeks of trying to settle down in Haifa and Dalieh, Rosamond received hysterical letters from Mrs. Tuttle verifying the interest of the National Vigilance Association in pursuing both Rosamond herself and Laurence's estate. Rather heroically, Rosamond immediately traveled back to London to face the music and fight for their good names. As soon as she arrived back in England, new correspondence from Mrs. Tuttle trumpeted authorities were coming to arrest her. The new Mrs. Oliphant was very cool, and did not panic. Then, within a few days, a representative of the National

Vigilance Association did indeed call on her, not to make an arrest, but to attempt a "sting" operation. The gentleman said he wanted to experience the new esoteric practices she and her husband had advocated, but instead all he got was an indignant diatribe from Rosamond defending Laurence, putting the investigator in his place. He carried on, however, asking if he might hold her hand to experience the out flowing of energy he had heard about, but again he was fiercely re-buffed, and he left. Finally, Rosamond found Mrs. Tuttle, who had been up to Scotland where she caused a threatening letter to be sent by Murray Templeton's father to Laurence's close cousin, Arthur Oliphant, alleging all sorts of lurid acts and promising imminent legal action. The two ladies agreed to a face-to-face meeting, which was arranged in the office of a neutral physician, where Mrs. Tuttle repeated all her claims. These were so extreme that the doctor stopped her declarations, and said it was now time to show proof. When none was forthcoming, the doctor pronounced the interview over, and that was that.

Unfortunately, in the absence of exonerating evidence and legal rulings, stories would continue to circulate. Because indeed Laurence had been so odd—and Alice was dead and defenseless—he two were easy marks for whispered rumors. In the face of the Templeton's letter to Arthur, the Oliphant family solicitors forbade any formal response, and as a result, over time, a shadow fell over Laurence and Alice's reputations.

Meanwhile, Rosamond was determined to set the record straight by writing a biography of the couple, and started contacting Laurence's publishers and circle of friends for contributions and copies of correspondence so she could begin the task herself. Frankly, Rosamond did not have the winning interpersonal and social skills that made Laurence so many staunch friends for life. In fact, she was not at all liked by the Oliphant family in Scotland nor by the former members of the happy Oliphant household in Palestine. As a result, just about everyone in Laurence and Alice's circles were nervous about Rosamond trying to tell the remarkable tale, especially since she hardly knew the couple. Publisher John Blackwood was therefore particularly happy when Laurence's distant cousin Margaret Oliphant, perhaps the most prolific of all the Blackwood writers, with over one hundred books to her credit, decided to expand the single article on the Oliphants she had promised *Blackwood's Magazine*, and stepped forward to write a definitive two volume biography. The publisher, the Oliphant family and friends all heaved sighs of relief and gave Margaret access to all their archives for the work to get underway.

With Margaret Oliphant taking on the burden of the biography, Rosamond felt she could simply put the lies behind her and move on. In Paris, she swept up Murray Templeton again, now disowned by his wealthy Scottish family, and together with her two nieces moved back to Palestine to continue her own, rather different, fulfillment of Laurence's mission. Unfortunately, Rosamond was not Alice, and her neighbors in Haifa and Dalieh thought her both very plain and very annoying. She did marry Murray Templeton, who she felt had suffered because of his involvement with Laurence and the risqué techniques of Sympneumata, but he was never happy. In fact, finally he heard voices telling him to jump overboard at the end of a sea crossing from Beirut to Haifa—which he did, and was assumed drowned.

Rosamond persevered, even invoking Laurence's name to advocate the conversion of the Jews to Christianity, although Laurence certainly would have disagreed with her. She worked hard to clear up the loose ends of Laurence's estate, and eventually won clear title to many properties in Palestine, the sale of which allowed her to move back to a retirement in comfort near Brighton in Britain. To ease her loneliness, and in spite of the appearance of scandal, she even adopted a twenty year-old young man from the diplomatic community in Haifa named Carlos Ronzeville. She focused on teaching him the need for purity in sex, and lived with him throughout the remainder of her long life. Along the way, Rosamond wrote her own story, including her memories of Laurence, in her memoir *My Perilous Life in Palestine*, published in 1928.

Meanwhile, at the news of Laurence's passing, there were celebrations in California, where Harris loudly claimed he himself caused both Laurence and Alice's deaths[1] by attacking them from the celestial realm and smothering the life out of them. He wrote a poem at the time of Alice's death describing how he killed her:

By a doom-stroke, swift and tragic,
Died the siren of the snake.

He then took pains to spread stories and rumors about his former disciples. But he was not to get off very easily himself.

The practical business affairs of Fountaingrove were in great shape. From the time of the break with the Oliphants, Harris and Kanaye Nagasawa had groomed the California property into an earthly paradise for the spirits expected from the celestial realm. The building program included Harris's central mansion, called Aestivossa, then the amber redwood Commndery for the men, and then the white clapboard Familistry for the women. The vast winery itself was complete by 1882, with outside dimensions of 132 by 112 feet and had steam heat throughout. One floor alone, full of the latest and finest vats, barrels and machinery, was capable of storing 600,000 gallons of wine and brandies. There were many outbuildings as well as two large barns, including the famous Round Barn which still stands today as a popular tourist attraction. Besides the vineyards, there were large fields of wheat and orchards of fruits. While few of the spiritually burdensome brothers in Brocton were invited to migrate to the new campus, local newcomers joined as the community became more widely known. And Father Harris recovered from the shock of his separation from the Oliphants, and continued his important celestial work. Sometime in 1890 that the prophet finished the sixth and entered his seventh and final "round of the occult," and, with that, dark clouds began to appear.

Although Harris believed his followers all knew he had progressed to a lofty state where he could be trusted to continue the front-line fight against evil, critics outside the Brotherhood were gathering. First, the press picked up rumors that families at Fountaingrove were being broken up, with wives, husbands and children separated and re-assigned to new living arrangements. This was most certainly true, as it had been since the days in Brocton. Other more suggestive allegations were made that men and women members were washing each other daily in a completely nude state—also true. Suggestive documents such as the Experiences of a Sister had certainly been leaked beyond the membership to eager outside readers. Such materials and stories could easily lead on to more lurid suspicions.

Then Laurence and Alice's very warm and sympathetic biography by Margaret Oliphant hit the bookstores in 1891, going a long way towards restoring their good reputations. While British readers loved it, at Fountaingrove the work was seen as an attack on Harris, whom the book portrayed as a controlling and cash-motivated charlatan. A review was published in the popular magazine *The Illustrated American*, along with excellent pictures of the prophet, some members, and the grounds at Fountaingrove. It was not a good sign that the subtitle of the review began with two quotes from the Bible:

Woe to the inhabitants of the earth and the sea! for the Devil is come down unto you, having great wrath, because he knoweth that he hath but a short time.—*Revelation xii, 12.*

For there shall arise false prophets, and shall show great signs and wonders; insomuch that, if it were possible, they shall deceive the very elect…—*Matthew xxiv, 24*[2]

Describing the setting, the review begins by making a favorable introduction of the setting of Fountaingrove to the largely Eastern American readership:

> Splendidly fertile fields, thoroughly cultivated, and a magnificent grapery furnish the financial part of the organization; and elegant buildings, handsomely adorned and furnished, and supplied with a large and comprehensive library, complete a settlement which is certainly most creditable, in all particulars, to its founders and sustainers.

But now the review provides a recap of Laurence Oliphant, who at this point has been dead almost five years and was remembered largely by unflattering insinuations and allegations, many of which were piled on top of his reputation by the Harrisites:

> Oliphant was in many respects a very remarkable man. He was a traveller of wide experience and a writer of admitted ability. Further, he was judged as a man of more than ordinary mental solidity and force, and when it became known he had succumbed to the fascinations of Thomas Lake Harris, it is not surprising that a great deal of astonishment should have been experienced by his acquaintances and friends. Oliphant was possibly a mystic; certainly, he had a tendency and a leaning quite beyond his fellows. As much as in this thing is emotional, especially in the cases of characters not perfectly balanced, it is, perhaps, not surprising that Oliphant should have become deeply interested, and even enthusiastic, in the direction of the theories and views advanced by Thomas Lake Harris. For it is to be conceded, and has been admitted by all who have had relations with Mr, Harris that he possesses and has always possessed extraordinarily attractive powers: what is commonly called personal magnetism. Combining with such powers remarkable fluency of language and exuberance of imagination,

there is nothing strange in the fact that a man of Oliphant's peculiar nature should have been drawn to acceptance of his tenets.[3]

Next, with Laurence now before the reader as a basically positive, yet gullible character, subject to manipulation and exploitation, the reviewer moves on to Harris:

The biographer of Laurence Oliphant, who has certainly had ample opportunity for judging, has discerned, what any reader should perceive, the vague and incoherent character of Mr. Harris's output in the shape of a belief. Those who read between the lines, and those who read outside the lines, can readily perceive… there is neither clearness nor positiveness in the enunciations of Mr. Harris.[4]

The rest of the article consists of responding commentary by Harrisites, but leaves the impression of a confused and garrulous prophet, producing voluminous pronouncements about a not-very-clear view of the cosmos. It ends with Harris's own sad words about himself, now growing older in his mountain retreat some miles away from Fountaingrove, trying to figure out exactly how he is supposed to lead mankind through the final stages of rejuvenation, resurrection and redemption. In short, the reviewer probably hit the nail on the head describing both Oliphant and Harris to the readership of *The Illustrated American.*

The Oliphant memoir and its reviews were bad enough for Harris, but there's no doubt the most ominous threat of all against him began in 1891 when a lady from Boston named Miss Alzire A. Chevaillier arrived with her mother for a long stay in California, allegedly seeking instruction in Harris's beliefs. New York mutual friends of Harris and Miss Chevaillier had written ahead to Harris, asking if he could provide a restful retreat for her. Harris already had a rustic haven called Linn Lilla where he retired from the tiresome states of the members at nearby Fountaingrove from time to time. And since he was at that moment staying at the main house in a more social state of mind, he installed Miss Chevaillier and her mother at Linn Lilla.

The visiting ladies seemed seeming to get on well with Harris, after almost six months of his hospitality. But then, one fateful day, after a spirited argument about Harris's new book *The New Republic: A Discourse of the Prospects, Dangers, Duties and Safeties of the Times*, in which he critiqued the society of the day, Miss Chevaillier and her mother were shunned by the inner circle and exiled to eat alone in a corner of the dining room, set off from the rest with a screen. They had dared to disagree with the great man – to his face! Another day of shunning and enough was enough for the Chevailliers. The guests decided to leave Fountaingrove, fuming. Harris suddenly saw that that might mean trouble, and he turned on the charm, trying his best to convince them to stay. Dovie sent flowers to them at the hotel in Santa Rosa where they had de-camped. But to no avail, because as soon as she was safely away from the ranch, Miss Chevaillier as a kind of one-woman National Vigilance Association took pen in hand to skewer them all.

Miss Chevaillier's true intentions came out with daggers in the form of an exposé series of articles in the *San Francisco Chronicle* beginning 13 December 1891. Describing the first days of her stay, she wrote that she and her mother had been met on arrival by "Prince Kanaye Nagasawa" in an ostentatious and elaborate carriage and shown the fine libraries and furnishings of the main house, which she called a "lavish display of wealth." Next day she was taken to Harris's cottage retreat at Linn Lilla where the prophet, with Dovie, greeted her with a kiss. He then startled her by suddenly putting his hand on her solar plexus and grunting loudly, as he assessed the strength of her respiration. The prophet may have been comfortable fondling her frame at that point, but Miss Chevaillier was not.

Another morning soon after at his cottage, Harris made a disturbing performance she was happy to draw out and linger over for the *Chronicle* readers:

> He was sitting on a sofa. Of a sudden, he straightened out, threw back his arms, kicked up his legs, and began some queer, convulsive movements. His face wore a horrible look and in a few minutes he muttered something about being in Hell. Miss Waring explained that the jumping-jack actions were the result of father going into an infernal state. He had gone down into Hades to redeem a lost soul. Mr. Harris kept up his contortions and raved about what he was seeing in Hell. Then he took on the state of the person he was trying to redeem, and used the coarsest kind of language, in which profanity and vulgarisms abounded.. This shocked me and I arose to leave the room, when Mr. Harris suddenly assumed the state of the "Lily Mother" and in a high piping voice, which was, of course, assumed, he said: "We want the dear child to stay—let her stay." "Yes," said Miss Waring, "stay and see what he suffers."

"A fine piece of acting," wrote Chevaillier. Mission accomplished apparently, Harris recovered and called for Communion wine. He was handed a large glass of port instead. Finally, Dovie stroked him until he seemed to come around and recover more completely. Generally, Miss Chevaillier said Dovie pranced around like "the light of the harem," in fine white clothes with red trimming, lording it over the other attendant ladies. At another point, Chevaillier observed Harris sitting rather intimately with his toes in Dovie's lap. Together with some more saucy observations of the California routine, Chevaillier went on to accuse Harris of founding " a new sexology" which was "worse than anything revealed to the Utah and Oneida practices."

After the lurid newspaper articles, Harris pretty much kept to a plan of not dignifying the allegations with a formal response. In a letter of the time, he wrote of Miss Chevaillier "there is not enough good in her character to give the evil any subtlety of power – not enough for gilding, behind which the evil can hide itself." In defense of Harris, letters from supporters accused Miss Chevaillier of "selling sensational articles to newspapers." Firing back in February, an editorial in the *San Francisco Wave* wrote, "the place is an idealized house of sin, whose only religion is the satisfaction of the passions, and where both sexes are of one family bed like dogs in a kennel."

The denouement occurred at a well-advertised event in Santa Rosa where Miss Chevaillier delivered a lecture in late February, at 50 cents per head attending, calling for Harris's expulsion from the county. She said if she was lying, then she should be put in prison, but if she was not, then Harris should. But, odd as he was, Harris had an almost twenty-year track record as a good citizen and landowner, supporting the Santa Rosa economy with his substantial and successful wine business. He had made friends lecturing at the local Masonic Lodge and by doing business with local merchants. The last shot in the exchange seems to have been an advertisement placed in the 27 February 1892 edition of the *Sonoma Democrat* newspaper signed by 31 "business and professional men" of the community endorsing Harris and the Brotherhood.

The fight had been ugly, but probably resulted in at least a draw, and possibly a pyrrhic victory for Harris. But, all the commotion soured Harris on California as the labors of the seventh stage of the occult needed his full attention. He acted decisively. Since his second wife had died in a lunatic asylum in 1885, Harris was free to marry his closest companion, Dovie (Jane Lee Waring) in March 1892, allowing them to be together in a traditionally acceptable relationship and not a sexual cult. Trying to continue the titillation of recent events, one newspaper headlined this news as "Celibate No More." Not distracted, however, Harris then placed operational control of Fountaingrove in the hands of Kanaye Nagasawa, now about 40 years old and an accomplished wine expert and businessman.

Cuthbert described these steps with finality. By choosing Dovie, Harris essentially severed his direct ties with the general membership and in future would only communicate with Nagasawa and his partners. And separating himself from Fountaingrove relieved him of any ownership worries. So he was now free of his former temporal obligations and was now going to "go it alone" through the daunting challenges of the final stage seven of his occult work. For their new, lonely beginning Harris and Dovie bought a townhouse on the Upper West Side of New York City, not too far from the Fountaingrove winery's east coast office downtown, where Harris would frequently appear to have a few glasses of wine and hold court. Harris never wavered in his belief in his celestial connections, and spent the remainder of his years until his death in 1906 with most of his time in the other world and writing more voluminous volumes of pronouncements which are rarely read today.

Fountaingrove itself continued to operate in the safest hands possible under the leadership of Kanaye Nagasawa. He went on to return from Harris's spring 1906 funeral to help with the reconstruction of San Francisco after the famous April 1906 earthquake. He represented both Japan and the California wine industry at the San Francisco Panama-Pacific Exhibition world's fair of 1915, which was an extravaganza to mark San Francisco's full recovery from the earthquake and return to the world stage as a major city. He received honors from the Emperor of Japan for his work assisting Japanese immigrants to America, and, most amazingly, stewarded the Fountaingrove winery through Prohibition so that, on the legislation's repeal in 1936, it was ready with fine grapes to re-assume its leadership role in restoring the fine wine industry to California before others with vision allowed that industry to reach the full potential it has achieved today.

Rosamond Dale Owen Oliphant continued on to be the last principal player in the story until her peaceful death was reported by her adopted son Carlos in 1937 at age 92. Perhaps the final curiosity in her story was captured in a December 1, 1930, story in the *New York Times*, a copy of which is filed among the Harris-Oliphant papers at Columbia University. Apparently, under a subsidy from John D. Rockefeller Jr., the University of Chicago had been digging for years at archaeological work on Mount Carmel and the nearby site of the biblical Battle of Armageddon. Arab villagers had been charging very high rates for the necessary leases, which led the University to investigate more closely. The *New York Times* wrote:

> When the time came for the renewal of the high-priced leases... an investigation of the titles to the land by P. L. O. Guy, field director of the Palestine expedition, revealed that the ownership of Armageddon and the desired thirteen acres atop Mount Carmel really rested with the 90-year old widow of Laurence Oliphant, an American woman living in the South of England. Visiting Mrs. Oliphant, Mr. Guy found her surprised at learning she was the owner of the famous Armageddon battlefield, but willing to sell it.[5]

$3,500 richer for the sale of Armageddon, Rosamond finished her days in comfort on the Southern English sea coast.

Both Laurence and Alice left legacies. Alice was much loved by many friends in Palestine, and, together with Laurence, is remembered in Israel today because of their early Zionist efforts and philanthropy. Both of their houses, the one down in Haifa and the other up on Mount Carmel, have been restored by the Israeli government and are maintained as public buildings and visitor attractions. Streets in Haifa and Jerusalem are named for them. Museums at Haifa have had successful exhibitions of paintings by Alice and her circle—including her friend Emily Fawcett Cuthbert and her sister Jamesina—documenting their years in Palestine. The last exhibition was as recently as 2000. And Laurence is fondly remembered as a pioneer Zionist who was both visionary and practical in his help for distressed refugees. He is also one of the most colorful and much-loved characters in his Scottish ancestral clan Oliphant. So I think they came through the storm of their lives with Harris all right, and made a great success together before their ends.

The only negative assessments of Laurence came from Harris and those closest to the prophet in his inner circle. James Freeman, who was dragged into the Brotherhood by his parents about 1865, sent the following scathing indictment of Laurence to American poet and former Harris believer Edwin Markham in 1923:

> The truth and facts about Oliphant have not been advertised like the excuses for his half insane causes. I will state from knowledge of both that Laurence Oliphant, diseased morally, mentally and physically sought healing at the hands of Thomas Lake Harris whose words promised healing. The promise involved heroic personal persistent effort of the individual... Oliphant like many others after a time grew weary of the discipline that he personally should subject himself in order that he might cleanse his tainted body and mind; and became possessed with the idea that he was superior to the hand that was helping him; and base ingrate that he was, with the spirit of an adventurer set out on a course of his own... Some apparently serious people in the world today still consider the insignificant character of Laurence Oliphant. A traitor to his friends, a renegade, an adventurer, and lastly an apostate of the deepest dies; as one worth a word, whereas he was only a terrible example of what treachery and ambition will do for a diseased mind.[6]

That is a stunning assessment, and I believe it was written by a very bitter man, angry about the loss of his parents' money at the depressed time Brocton properties were sold to make settlements with the dissenting members. Remarkably, James Freeman does not lay any blame at the feet of Harris, the prophet, who actually took all the Brotherhood members' funds into his own custody, to support his extremely opulent lifestyle. Freeman remained a Harrisite believer for life.

On a contrasting note, Robert Martin gives a more positive view. Martin was another child of members who joined Harris immediately after the Civil War. His family had, in fact, been neighbors of the Freemans in pre-Civil War Georgia. He would have grown up side by side at the commune with James Freeman. He wrote the following in his 1930 letter to Professor George Lawton in response for a request for recollections and information about Laurence:

> As to Laurence Oliphant, he was naturally a good fellow, and would pass muster in the very best of company anywhere. A World traveler, he had been everywhere, seen a great deal—with a wonderfully retentive memory; he had the faculty possessed of so many well-bred Englishmen, of being able to relate wonderful experiences and thrilling escapades with no attempt to show off, or be "spotlighted." A trifle "touchy" on matters around 1776-1812—and July 4th, but a man who stood well and was dependable. I am speaking you will understand, of Oliphant the MAN, and not the Puppet who succeeding Harris went forth unarmoured and unshod, to give battle to the foe.[7]

And, just as a final word on Laurence, I'd like to include the ending of a memoir written just after Laurence's death by his lifelong acquaintance and friend, Oswald Smith, who had been Laurence's surprised but willing companion on the adventure that became Oliphant's second book, *The Russian Shores of the Black Sea in the Autumn of 1852*. Smith concluded:

> Oliphant was never known, as far as my experience goes, to speak unkindly of any one, and so it is, now that he has been taken from us in the prime of his power and influence that there appears to be but one feeling and one language in reference to him. We all grieve that we shall not see that pleasant presence again, that we shall never hear that

delightful laugh no more, and that the companionship, of which the memory is so sweet, is now a memory only, and nothing more.[8]

Looking back on Laurence's story, it does seem sad that such a pleasant, accomplished and gregarious man could not find full satisfaction and happiness in a more traditional path, which could have left him surrounded by children and close friends at the end, instead of in a lonely friend's house tended by the quirky Rosamond, with his reputation unraveling in disarray. It may have been that the real or imagined specter of venereal disease from his playboy lifestyle before submitting to Harris made it impossible for him to enjoy a normal sexual relationship—either from shame or perceived risk of spreading infection—and that drove him to discover a more fantastic path for explaining the longings of his spiritual side for a true religious alternative to the empty dogmas more accepted in his time. However, no matter how convoluted his rationalizations and theories became, there can be no doubt of the serene happiness he found in marriage to the beautiful Alice le Strange and the harmonious years they spent together in the Holy Land. He certainly would be amazed today at the state of Israel built in the middle of the lands he found for his recommended colony.

Perhaps it might have been easier for Laurence to have gone over to "the other side" at the same time Alice did, instead of carrying on through his manic closing years with Rosamond and the rumors of scandal? But such is the untidiness of the human condition. And, in conclusion, it seems best to celebrate Laurence, Alice and even Rosamond as lives lived to the fullest, all refreshingly free of the customary restraints put on themselves by more timid souls, and to remember their own attempts at solving the human puzzle with affection and a wry smile.

ACKNOWLEDGMENTS

I would first like to express my thanks to Professor Jerome Buckley of Harvard whose course in the 1960s called Literature of Travel first introduced me to the travel writing of eccentric Victorians such as Sir Richard Burton, Sir Samuel White Baker, C. M. Doughty and Laurence Oliphant. Next, I would like to thank the library at the University of Vermont in Burlington, where in 1973 I first discovered a volume of trance-poetry dictated by Thomas Lake Harris in partnership with the deceased spirits of Dante, Shelley, Bryon, Keats and Poe. It would still be a few years until I connected the lives of Oliphant and Harris, but Harvard and UVM together helped me make a start.

After that, I spent decades collecting works by Oliphant and Harris in the used bookshops of former British Empire countries, before deciding to actually get serious enough to write this book. Then, I would like to thank the following resource centers for help making that possible: The Butler Library of Columbia University, home to more than twenty archival boxes containing the Harris-Oliphant Papers; the main branch of the New York Public Library at Fifth Avenue and 42nd Street in New York City; the Charles Shultz Information Center at Sonoma State University in California, home of the Gaye LeBaron archive containing a treasure trove of information about Thomas Lake Harris and his community at Fountaingrove; and the incomparable British Library nestled between King's Cross and St. Pancras stations in London.

I am personally indebted to Rod and Richard Oliphant for speaking with me about their colorful ancestor Laurence—and also to Gregory Ross, historian of Forgandenny, Scotland, who joined Rod Oliphant and me for a rainy afternoon stomping around the ruins of the Oliphant ancestral estate of Condie, just north of Edinburgh. I also thank Amy Mori, niece of Harris's deputy Kanaye Nagasawa, who spent an entire Sunday afternoon sharing her memories of her uncle and her early life at Fountaingrove, where she was born. Thanks also to Amy's niece Mary Ijichi who escorted me on that interview, kindly driving us back and forth to San Francisco on the day. I also appreciate the time spent by the Byck family who own the magnificent Paradise Ridge Winery on land immediately adjacent to the site of the old Fountaingrove estate. They educated me on why their local conditions for wine-growing are so extraordinary, and also let me tour their exhibits of memorabilia about Fountaingrove, Kanaye Nagasawa and Thomas Lake Harris. Thanks also to Betsy Strauss of the Amenia New York Historical Society who drove around with me one early spring day in search of Harris's first breath-house and his early community sites in Amenia and Wassaic. I am also very thankful for the feedback from Professor Yossi Ben-Artzi of Haifa University who gave me excellent advice on the chapters specifically detailing the Oliphants' work in Palestine.

For actually helping me with writing the book, I am extremely grateful for the opinions of my wife, Marilyn, and our adult children Matthew, Lauren and Michael who constantly gave me candid feedback on the curious story. Thanks also to Ann and Jack Pascal who helped me with photographs and ideas for the cover. I also appreciate the hours spent reading the early drafts of the story by

Laird Stiefvater, my erudite colleague and office-mate at Ogilvy & Mather Advertising, my former employer in New York. Finally, I want to express my special thanks to my editor, Paul De Angelis, who delivered on his promise to make my manuscript into a book—thank you, Paul. And I also want to thank my enthusiastic agent Lynne Rabinoff, who simply thought it all a very good story and promised to sell it—which she did—putting the final phase of the project into the capable hands of the pleasant and thoroughly professional team at Post Hill Press who then made the book a reality.

ABOUT THE AUTHOR

Bart Casey is a writer living in Brattleboro, Vermont, where he also trades as an internet rare book dealer. Bart moved to Vermont recently after a 40-year career in international advertising and direct marketing, where his work allowed him to travel the world and gather background for *The Double Life of Laurence Oliphant*.

FURTHER READING

I. Previously published biographies of Laurence Oliphant, in chronological order

1. 1887 autobiography. *Episodes in a Life of Adventure, or Moss from a Rolling Stone* by Laurence Oliphant. Edinburgh and London, William Blackwood and Sons, 1887. 420 pages.

Laurence did not write a traditional autobiography. This is a collection of 18 personal essays on incidents in his earlier and more traditional career, largely before his commitment to Harris and other spiritual adventures. There is also a concluding short summary piece called "The Moral of it All" which mentions a planned future work, never realized, to include his spiritual quest.

My favorite pieces are the first, about his sixty-day journey as a twelve-year-old from London to Ceylon with his tutor and two others on the Indian Mutiny and the assassination attempt he suffered in Japan. All are written in his best, light and highly readable style.

2. 1891 biography. *Memoir of the Life of Laurence Oliphant and of Alice Oliphant, His Wife* by Margaret Oliphant W. Oliphant (sic). Edinburgh and London, William Blackwood and Sons, 1891. Two volumes: I, 314 pages; II, 386 pages.

A warm and sympathetic biography, charmingly written by Laurence's distant cousin and fellow Oliphant clan member Margaret, who herself was a prolific author. She contributed more than 100 articles to *Blackwoods Magazine* and wrote more than 100 novels and histories as well.

Margaret knew Laurence and Alice personally and, after writing a short *Blackwoods Magazine* article about Laurence immediately after his death, stepped forward as an apologist for friends, family and publisher to record the lives of the Oliphants from the point of view of those who knew and loved them. It is a calm and insightful biography, appearing in 1891, at a time when Laurence and Alice's reputations were clouded by rumors, innuendo and scandal. She was not too interested in their peculiar religious beliefs or their involvement with Harris, to whom she was dismissive and hostile.

3. 1942 Dual biography of Thomas Lake Harris and Laurence Oliphant. *A Prophet and A Pilgrim: Being the Incredible History of Thomas Lake Harris and Laurence Oliphant; Their Sexual Mysticisms and Utopian Communities Amply Documented to Confound the Skeptic* (Number 11 of the Columbia Studies in American Culture) by Herbert W. Schneider and George Lawton. New York, Columbia University Press, 1942. 589 pages.

This is the essential, and voluminous, work for anyone wanting to know more about the intertwining of Thomas Lake Harris and Laurence

Oliphant. Since many of the sources collected by its professional academic authors are "exceedingly rare," they have included long, fascinating excerpts and transcripts in the text and appendices. The book can be hard to find, but it was also reprinted by the AMS Press in New York in 1970.

Schneider was Professor of Religion and Philosophy on the Columbia faculty from 1918 to 1957 (he died in 1984 aged 92). George Lawton was also a Columbia faculty member and practicing psychologist who published papers on spiritualism, such as "The Drama of Life After Death" (1932) and later many publications on the psychology of old age (e.g. "retire *to* something" not *from* something… old age should be a time of productivity and personal realization, etc.)

Writing this book "we did not want to write" occupied Schneider and Lawton for more than ten years, "rummaging in a mass of moulding (sic) materials, deciphering wearisome manuscripts, and reading books our curiosity alone could not have induced us to read." Indeed the Harris-Oliphant Papers in the Butler Library rare book department at Columbia University fill more than two dozen archival boxes, stuffed with folders, onion skin paper carbon copies and handwritten notes. One newspaper clipping there from the *Santa Rosa Democrat* of November 21, 1931—eleven years before the book's publication—shows Professor and Mrs. Schneider preparing on the eve of visiting Kanaye Nagasawa at Fountaingrove for an interview and a tour. (I read his notes from the interview, and Nagasawa didn't say much!)

The reason for their perseverance was "something elemental and genuine beneath all the make-believe, something earnest beneath the adventures" that captivated their attention. They didn't know what to make of it all, but wanted readers to know enough to judge for themselves. They wrote the "themes" of the story were the belief in a Divine God who made man in his image, and the dual male-female nature of that God as shown in the theory of the counterparts. Those themes then came to life with Harris playing God while Oliphant emptied himself through "humiliation" to experience the adventure of a real religion.

A Prophet and A Pilgrim is a classic, intriguing and exhausting work.

4. 1956 biography. *The Life of Laurence Oliphant: Traveller, Diplomat and Mystic* by Philip Henderson. London, Robert Hale Limited, 1956. 281 pages.

This is a more "realistic" and close-up biography of Laurence, compared to the idealistic and detached one by Margaret Oliphant. Henderson digs into details and associations between Laurence and his fellow travelers in the Victorian age. On the spiritual–sexual side, the author is not very interested in the deluded dogmas and practices of Harris, Laurence and Alice.

This is an excellent companion piece to Margaret Oliphant's book, filling in some of the gritty details she glosses over.

5. 1982 biography. *Laurence Oliphant 1829-1888* by Anne Taylor. Oxford, Oxford University Press, 1982. 306 pages.

This is a well-researched, studious and judicious biography of Laurence, with illumination of his relationships with the British elite and the more mainstream social, political and diplomatic society.

Taylor makes extensive use of letters in private, university and government archives in the U.K., such as the Royal Archives, the

Palmerston Papers and the Blackwoods archives in Scotland. She collected information also from Alice's side of the story from the Le Strange family. She also waded through the Harris-Oliphant papers at Columbia as well as the Library of Congress in the U.S.A. All her findings are meticulously footnoted and her conclusions judiciously balanced.

Like Henderson, Taylor does not pay too much attention to Harris's occult journey or the Oliphant's own modified version of the same.

II. Shorter Reminiscences about Laurence Oliphant

1. 1889. *Memoir on Laurence Oliphant* by Oswald Smith. London, *Time, Second Series,* January-June, 1889.

Smith was Laurence's travel companion for their 1852 adventure across Russia from St. Petersburg to the Crimea. He remained a lifelong friend and fellow London club member. Smith told several stories about Laurence, such as the skating party I mention in Chapter One. He said his friend was "essentially an excitable man, fond of amusement, very impulsive, and averse to any restraint" and most memorable for "that delightful laugh."

2. 1892. *Personal Reminiscences of Laurence Oliphant: A Note of Warning* by Louis Liesching. London, Marshall Brothers, undated. 40 pages.

There is no date on this pamphlet, but since it opens mentioning Margaret Oliphant's new biography of Laurence, it is likely from 1891 or 1892. Liesching grew up with Laurence in Ceylon and even lived with the Oliphants for a few years. He shares his memories but also issues a "warning" about "how far astray the keenest intellects… may be led when once they abandon their reason and moral sense to the guidance of another."

3. 1928. *My Perilous Life in Palestine* by Rosamond Dale Owen (Mrs. Laurence Olphant, the owner of Armageddon). London, George Allen & Unwin, Ltd.

Although only married to Laurence for less than six months, Rosamond carried the torch for him for the next fifty years, fighting to clear his name and sort out all the legal entanglements surrounding the diverse property he owned, including the field of Armageddon in the Holy Land. This book is mostly about her own somewhat wacky adventure, but also has unique personal reminiscences about Laurence and the stories he told her about himself.

III. Selected Books by Laurence Oliphant

A Journey to Katmandu (The Capital of Nepaul) with the Camp of Jung Bahadoor; Including a Sketch of the Nepaulese Ambassador at Home. London, John Murray, 1852.
This is the book about elephant hunting in Nepal that started Laurence's writing career.

The Russian Shores of the Black Sea. Edinburgh and London, Blackwood, 1853. An adventure traveling 1,400 miles by land and boat from St. Petersburg to report on the fortifications of the closed military city of Sebastopol on the eve of the Crimean War.

Minnesota and the Far West. Edinburgh and London, Blackwood, 1855. As temporary Superintendent of Indian Affairs in Canada, Laurence travels as the Great White Father to settle disputes, sign treaties, open schools and buy more land from the natives.

Narrative of the Earl of Elgin's Mission to China and Japan in 1857, '58, '59. Edinburgh and London, Blackwood, 1860. Laurence's report on two years' work to open China and Japan to the west, with a surprise side trip to help put down the Indian Mutiny.

Piccadilly, A Fragment of Contemporary Biography. Edinburgh and London, Blackwood, 1870. Laurence's farewell satire as he sheds his vapid life in society for a path of celestial exploration with Thomas Lake Harris.

The Land of Gilead. Edinburgh and London, Blackwood, 1882. Laurence's report on the suitability of Palestine for a colony of persecuted Jews from Eastern Europe.

The Land of Khmei: Up and Down the Middle Nile. Edinburgh and London, Blackwood, 1882. Laurence and his wife Alice le Strange convalescing in obscure parts of Egypt.

Altiora Peto: a Novel. Edinburgh and London, Blackwood, 1883. A refreshing American girl takes the hearts of English aristocrats by storm.

Masollam: a Problem of the Period. Edinburgh and London, Blackwood, 1886. A novel about a strange prophet remarkably similar to Thomas Lake Harris.

Sympneumata: or, Evolutionary Forces Now Active in Man. Edinburgh and London, Blackwood, 1885. The mystical-sexual manifesto of Laurence and Alice's beliefs once they have broken with the despotic Thomas Lake Harris.

Scientific Religion: or, Higher Possibilities of Life and Practice through the Operation of Natural Forces. Edinburgh and London, Blackwood, 1888. Mostly dictated to Laurence by the spirit of Alice, his dead wife, to clear up a few misconceptions from her point of view in heaven.

IV. Related biographies of the Oliphant Circle

6. Harris biography. *Life and World View of Thomas Lake Harris, Written from Direct Personal Experience by Arthur A. Cuthbert, An Almost Life-long Associate.* Glasgow, C. W. Pearce & Co, 1908. 413 pages plus Appendices.

Cuthbert met Harris in Scotland just as Harris was delivering his first lectures in Britain, and became, as he wrote, an "almost life-long associate" of the prophet. Indeed, when he joined the Brotherhood of the New Life, he took his fiancée, Emily Fawcett (a friend of Lady Oliphant) to the community's first home north of New York City, and was married there by Harris in one of the great man's few approved terrestrial marriages. Cuthbert remained true to Harris after the break with the Oliphants, even though his wife Emily left him to go to Palestine with Laurence and Alice.

Later Cuthbert returned to Britain with the title "Departmental Secretary, Brotherhood of the New Life, Department of Great Britain, Moseley, Worcestershire." This formal title no doubt was to help establish his supremacy over Great Britain after the rapture surrounding the eminent Second Coming of Christ and Queen Lily to Earth, when most people would simply disappear while the chosen would remain to administrate the affairs of remaining spirits and human counterparts.

Cuthbert wrote his book as a scribe serving in the shadow of the great man. He recounts a few actual events, but more often simply reprints long passages of Harris's own writings, about which he did not believe himself worthy of commenting.

7. Kanaye Nagasawa biography. "Samurai of the Wine Country: A Biography of Kanaye Nagasawa" by Terry Jones. Unpublished Master's Thesis, Department of History, Sonoma State College, Rohnert Park, California, 1970.

This thesis is on the shelf at the Sonoma County History & Genealogy Library, Santa Rosa, California (and also, most likely, at the Gaye Le Baron Archive at the Sonoma State College Library in Rohnert Park, California).

Jones wrote a well-researched and highly readable history of Kanaye Nagasawa's time at the Fountaingrove estate in Santa Rosa, from 1876 when he accompanied Harris on the trip to buy the land, to his own death there in 1936. The author even records who Harris bought the lumber from to build the main house on the estate.

8. Kanaye Nagasawa biography. *Kanaye Nagasawa: A Biography of a Satsuma Student* (Regional Studies Series No. 4) by Paul Akira Kadota and Terry Earl Jones. Kagoshima, Japan, Kagoshima Prefectural Junior College, 1970.

This book completes the work started by Jones's thesis immediately above. Japanese professor Paul Kadota wrote the first section, detailing Nagasawa's ancestry and early education and upbringing in Japan, and Jones updated his thesis to finish the story with Nagasawa's almost seventy-year membership in the Brotherhood of the New Life.

Nagasawa was a true samurai and gentleman. He adopted Harris as his *de facto* father and gave him complete filial loyalty. He did not care too much about the religious goings-on around Harris, but he was totally dedicated to the grape-growing and wine making that came to bankroll the whole venture. After Harris died in 1906, Nagasawa became the master of the estate and fulfilled his promise to keep Fountaingrove as the heaven-on-earth meant to serve as headquarters for the new world order after the Second Coming was fully completed. The estate was maintained at its full level of opulence throughout the Great Depression, and even Prohibition, thanks to Nagasawa's unflappable discipline and dedication to quality.

V. *Some Selected Other Works*

1. Rosa Emerson, *Among the Chosen*, New York, Henry Holt and Company, 1884.

This is a novel about growing up in the Harris community by the beautiful daughter of early members of the Brotherhood. The family left after Harris made unwelcome advances to Rosa and amid other disputes about how Harris was running things. Mr. Emerson then bought the Brotherhood winery in New York State from its founding family and ran it as a competitor to Harris. The Brotherhood winery is still in business today.

2. Shalom Goldman, *Zeal for Zion: Christians, Jews & the Idea of the Promised Land*, Chapel Hill, The University of North Carolina Press, 2009.

The 46-page first chapter of this book on the early Zionists tells the story of Laurence and Alice Oliphant, as well as their secretary, Napthali Imber, who wrote the poem *Hativah (Our Hope)*, dedicated to the Oliphants, which is now set to music as the Israeli national anthem. The song is about the longing of the Jewish people for a home in Palestine.

3. Emma Hardinge, *Modern American Spiritualism: A Twenty Years' Record of the Communion Between Earth and the World of Spirits from 1848 to 1868*, New York, 1870 (reprinted by University Books, New Hyde Park NY, 1970).

In more than 500 pages, Hardinge was a medium herself and in this book she catalogs the many marvels of the mediums and seers of America during the spiritual awakening of the mid-nineteenth century. It includes chapters on Thomas Lake Harris and also his early mentor Andrew Jackson Davies. One miracle after another.

4. Thomas Lake Harris, a few of his many volumes:

— The trance poetry, which is somewhat gifted versifying (in a sing-song sort of way). It fills his first three books: *An Epic of the Starry Heaven* (1854), *A Lyric of the Morning Land* (1854) and *A Lyric of the Golden Age* (1856)

— *The Breath of God with Man; An Essay on the Grounds and Evidences of Universal Religion*, New York, Brotherhood of the New Life, 1867. This is Harris's work on divine breathing — the key foundation for his celestial visions

— *The Lord: the Two-in-One, Declared, Manifested and Glorified*, Santa Rosa, Fountain Grove, 1876. This was to be the key volume for the history of mankind, detailing how Jesus Christ appeared to Harris and advised him, after which the actual Second Coming of Christ took place, with God occupying Harris's earthly body right there at the winery in Sonoma County. Unfortunately, no one believed him.

ARTWORK

Frontispiece: Laurence Oliphant at 25 years old.
Pascal, Jack.1854 daguerreotype. Reproduced with permission from the Oliphant family private collection.

Chapter 1: Condie, the Oliphant ancestral home outside Edinburgh.
Oliphant, Catherine Maria. 1839 sketch. Reproduced with permission from the Oliphant family private collection.

Chapter 4: Thomas Lake Harris at 63 years old.
Unknown photographer. 1886 photograph. Found in *A Prophet and a Pilgrim*. Oliphant, Laurence. New York: Columbia University Press, 1942. Columbia Rare Book and Manuscript Library, New York.

Chapter 4: Outrage at the British Legation at Yeddo: Attack on Mssrs. Oliphant and Morrison.
Unknown artist. London: *Illustrated London News*, October 12, 1861.

Chapter 4: Author Laurence Oliphant as Lord Frank Vanecourt, embossed on the cover of 'Picadilly,' 1870.

Doyle, Richard. Embossed cover illustration. Found in *Piccadilly: A Fragment of Contemporary Biography*. 2nd ed. Oliphant, Laurence. Edinburgh and London: William Blackwood and Sons, 1870. Courtesy of author's private collection.

Chapter 5: Vine Cliff, Harris's waterfront house in Brocton, New York, sketched by Laurence Oliphant.

Oliphant, Laurence. 1881 sketch. Reproduced with permission from the Oliphant family private collection.

Chapter 6: Alice Oliphant in her twenties.

Pascal, Jack. Circa 1870 photograph. Courtesy of author's private collection.

Chapter 7: Thomas Lake Harris surrounded by some of his female devotees, with Alice Oliphant at his side.

Unknown photographer. Circa 1877 photograph. Sonoma County Museum, California.

Chapter 8: Alice after reuniting with Laurence.

Unknown photographer. Circa 1881 photograph, albumen print. Reproduced with permission from the National Maritime Museum, Haifa.

Chapter 11: Oliphant house in Haifa.

Walker, John. 1884 watercolor. Reproduced with permission from the National Maritime Museum, Haifa.

Chapter 11: Oliphant holiday house on Mount Carmel.

Cuthbert, Emily. 1883 ink drawing. Reproduced with permission from the National Maritime Museum, Haifa.

ENDNOTES

Chapter 1. Son of Empire

[1] Details of Laurence's family are drawn from several sources, especially Margaret Oliphant's book *Memoir of the Life of Laurence Oliphant and of Alice Oliphant* (1891), and Gregory R. M Ross' book *Forgandenny: A Place in History* (2007). In Laurence's father's generation, Sir Anthony was the third son, born after his brother Laurence, the 8th Laird of Condie (b. 1791) and William (b. 1792). The other brothers were James (b. 1796), Thomas (b. 1799), Robert (b. 1802) and a sister Christian (b. 1795).

[2] For details on the early days of Britain's Cape Colony, I have used Gordon-Brown's classic *Yearbook and Guide to Southern Africa* (1953), especially pages 19-23.

[3] Louis Liesching, *Personal Reminiscences of Laurence Oliphant* (c. 1891).

[4] Margaret Oliphant, *Memoir*, volume I, page 8.

[5] Shalom L. Goldman, *Zeal for Zion* (2009), pages 46-7.

[6] Margaret Oliphant, *Memoir*, volume I, page 13.

7   Ibid., page 15.

8   Ibid., pages 7-9.

9   The story of Laurence's overland journey from England to Ceylon with his tutor is described in Laurence's book of autobiographical sketches, *Episodes in a Life of Adventure or Moss from a Rolling Stone* (1887), pages 1-13.

10 Sir Samuel White Baker, *Eight Years Wandering in Ceylon* (1842), page 4.

11 Laurence Oliphant, *Episodes*, page 141.

12 Baker, *Wanderings*, page 6.

13 You can, in fact, still buy "Sir Anthony Oliphant's Ceylon Tea" today at his plantation or by mail order from the East India Company's e-commerce pages at Amazon.co.uk.

14 Laurence Oliphant, *Episodes*, pages 17-18.

15 Laurence tells the story of his family's European adventures on his Grand Tour in *Episodes*, pages 23-31.

16 Laurence's remarks on seeing the exhibit on venereal disease in Paris were recorded by his second wife, Rosamond, in her memoir *My Perilous Life in Palestine* (1928), page 23.

17 Margaret Oliphant, *Memoir*, volume I, pages 81-2.

18 Oswald Smith, *Memoir on Laurence Oliphant* (1889).

19 Margaret Oliphant, *Memoir*, volume I, page 57.

20 Ibid., page 60.

Chapter Two. The Writing Trade

1   Laurence Oliphant, *Episodes*, page 40.

2   Oswald Smith's comments on their Russian expedition are in his 1889 *Memoir on Laurence Oliphant*.

[3]   Laurence Oliphant, *The Russian Shores of the Black Sea* (1853), page 252.

[4]   Margaret Oliphant, *Memoir*, volume I, page 108.

[5]   Ibid., page 111.

[6]   Laurence Oliphant, *Episodes*, page 45.

[7]   Ibid., page 47.

[8]   Ibid., pages 55-6.

[9]   Margaret Oliphant, *Memoir*, volume I, page 139.

[10] Laurence Oliphant, *Episodes*, page 67.

[11] Margaret Oliphant, *Memoir*, volume I, page 154.

[12] Ibid., pages 142-3.

[13] Ibid., pages 153-4.

[14] Ibid., page 167.

[15] Ibid., pages 177-9 describe Laurence's battlefield adventures as a war correspondent in the Crimea.

[16] Ibid., page 189.

[17] Laurence Oliphant, *Patriots and Filibusters* (1860), page 173.

[18] Margaret Oliphant, *Memoir*, volume I, page 193.

[19] Philip Henderson, *The Life of Laurence Oliphant* (1956), page 60.

[20] Article on Swedenborg, Emanuel in *Encyclopaedia Britannica* (1964), volume 21, pages 653-4.

[21] John Stoughton, *Religion in England from 1800 to 1850* (1884), volume II, page 85.

[22] These are the concluding lines in a speech by Ralph Waldo Emerson, *An Oration delivered before the Phi Beta Kappa Society*, at Cambridge, August 31, 1837.

[23] The story of the Fox family rappings I adapted from Emma Hardinge's work, *Modern American Spiritualism* (1870), pages 31-71.

[24] Oswald Smith, *Memoir on Laurence Oliphant* (1889).

Chapter 3. Diplomacy and Loss

1   Allingham, Philip V. "England and China: The Opium Wars 1839-60." Victorian Web (with internet citation following): http://www.victorianweb.org/history/empire/opiumwars/opiumwar1.html

2   Article in *Encyclopaedia Britannica* (1964), volume 5, page 584. "China: 19ᵗʰ Century and Revolution, First War with Great Britain and First Group of Foreign Treaties (1839-44).

3   Laurence Oliphant, *Narrative of the Earl of Elgin's Mission to China and Japan in the Years 1857, 1858, 1859* (1860), page 24.

4   Ibid., pages 29-30.

5   Ibid., page 33.

6   Laurence Oliphant, *Episodes*, page 102.

7   John Harris, *The Indian Mutiny* (2001), page 95.

8   Harold E Raugh, *The Victorians at War, 1815-1914* (2004), page 89.

9   Margaret Oliphant, *Memoir*, volume I, page 203.

10 Ibid., page 211.

11 Laurence Oliphant, *Episodes*, page 109.

12 Laurence Oliphant, *Narrative of the Earl of Elgin's Mission*, page 120.

13 Laurence Oliphant, *Episodes*, page 136.

14 Laurence Oliphant, *Narrative*, page 306.

15 Ibid., page 311.

16 Laurence Oliphant, *Episodes*, page 233.

17 Laurence Oliphant, *Narrative*, page 391.

18 Arthur Cuthbert, *Life and World-View of Thomas Lake Harris* (1908), page 87.

19 Schneider and Lawton, *A Prophet and a Pilgrim* (1942), page 4.

20 For his surprising story, see John DeSalvo's book *Andrew Jackson Davis, The First American Prophet and Clairvoyant* (2005).

21 *The West Virginia Encyclopedia*, web address www. wvencyclopedia.org, "Mountain Cove Spiritualist Community."

22 Emma Hardinge, *Modern American Spiritualism*, page 85.

23 Thomas Lake Harris, *Epic of a Starry Night*, page vi.

24 Thomas Lake Harris, *Song of Satan*, page lxxxiii.

Chapter 4. Uneasy in London

1 Richard Lines, *James John Garth Wilkinson 1812-1899: Author, Physician, Swedenborgian.*

2 Richard Lines, *Swedenborgianism and Pugilism: the William White Affair.*

3 Laurence Oliphant, *Masollam*, pages 29-34.

4 *British Spiritual Telegraph*, Number 1, volume IV, June 1, 1859, page 11.

5 *British Spiritual Telegraph*, Number 2, volume IV, June 15, 1859, page 15.

6 Clement John Wilkinson, *James John Garth Wilkinson: A Memoir of his Life, with a Selection from his Letters*, page 103.

7 The story of the fighting over the Swedenborgian bookshop is detailed in Richard Lines' article referenced above, *Swedenborgianism and Pugilism.*

8 Arthur Cuthbert, *Life and World View of Thomas Lake Harris* (1908), page 12.

9 Schneider and Lawton, *A Prophet and a Pilgrim* (1942), page 44.

10 Cuthbert, page 185.

11 Schneider and Lawton, page 55.

12 Ibid., page 56.

13 Laurence Oliphant, *Episodes*, page 148.

14 Ibid., page 198.

15 Ibid., page 197.

16   Ibid., page 204.

17   There was an exhibition in 2013 at The Queen's Gallery, Palace of Holyroodhouse in Edinburgh of "The Journal of Albert Edward, Prince of Wales (later King Edward VII) from his 1862 tour to the Middle East." The Prince was with Laurence Oliphant as a travel companion from February 14 through a day of wild boar hunting in Albania on February 22nd.

18   Laurence Oliphant, *Episodes*, page 234.

19   Margaret Oliphant, *Memoir*, page 139.

20   Laurence Oliphant, *Piccadilly* (1870), page 78.

21   Ibid., page 20.

22   Ibid., page 256.

23   Ibid., page 266.

24   Laurence Oliphant installment, "Piccadilly: an Episode of Contemporaneous Autobiography – Part VI," *Blackwoods Magazine*, August 1865, page 229.

25   Laurence Oliphant, *Piccadilly* (1870), page 248.

26   Laurence Oliphant, "Conclusion—Piccadilly," *Blackwoods Magazine*, September 1865, page 322.

27   Schneider and Lawton, page 115, footnote 27.

28   Ibid., page 113, footnote 21.

29   Ibid., pages 113-14, footnote 22.

30   Margaret Oliphant, Memoir, volume II, page 14.

31   Laurence Oliphant, *Letters to Cowpers*, autumn 1867, *Harris-Oliphant Papers*, Columbia.

Chapter 5. The Brotherhood of the New Life

1   Letter of Robert Martin to George Lawton, February 27, 1930, *Harris-Oliphant Papers*, Columbia, page 3.

[2] Arthur Cuthbert, *Life and World View of Thomas Lake Harris* (1908), page 17.

[3] Schneider and Lawton, page 169.

[4] Ibid., page 175.

[5] Thomas Lake Harris, *The Breath of God with Man* (1867), pages 43-4.

[6] Ibid. page 49.

[7] Ibid., page 176.

[8] Cuthbert, page 13.

[9] Ibid., page 187.

[10] Ibid., page 190.

[11] Joseph Slade, editor. *The Markham Review*, Published by the Hormann Library of Wagner College, Number 4, February 1969.

[12] John E. Van Sant, *Pacific Pioneers: Japanese Journeys to America and Hawaii, 1850-80* (2000), page 2.

[13] Laurence Oliphant (Woodbine), letter to Jane Waring (Dovie), on departing Liverpool for the Harris community in America, July 27, 1867, *Harris-Oliphant Papers*, Columbia.

[14] Laurence Oliphant, Letter to Georgiana Cowper, October 26, 1867, *Harris-Oliphant Papers*, Columbia.

[15] Schneider and Lawton, page 125, Letter of Laurence Oliphant to Georgiana Cowper on first settling in to Amenia, August-September 1867, *Harris-Oliphant Papers*, Columbia.

[16] Schneider and Lawton, pages 147-8.

[17] Kadota and Jones, *Kanaye Nagasawa: A Biography of a Satsuma Student* (1970), page 193.

[18] Schneider and Lawton, page 141, Letter of Laurence and Maria Oliphant to Louis Liesching.

[19] Rosa Emerson, *Among the Chosen* (1884), pages 147-8.

[20] Schneider and Lawton, page 156.

[21] Margaret Oliphant, *Memoir*, pages 24-5.

22   Laurence Oliphant, Letter to Georgiana Cowper, April 1868, section dated April 12 Transcript in the collection of the Oliphant family. Also quoted by Schneider and Lawton, page 210.

23   Thomas Lake Harris, *Lyra Triumphalis* (1891), page 19.

24   Schneider and Lawton, page 181.

25   Ibid., page 149.

26   Laurence Oliphant, *Masollam*, volume I, pages 56-7.

27   Schneider and Lawton, pages 510-11.

Chapter 6. From a Farm at Brocton to a War in Paris

1   Rosa Emerson, *Among the Chosen*, page 2.

2   Ibid., page 32.

3   Ibid., page 7.

4   Ibid., page 9.

5   Laurence Oliphant, Letter to Georgiana Cowper, May 28, 1869, Oliphant family transcript.

6   Laurence Oliphant, Letter to Georgina Cowper, April 5, 1868, Oliphant family transcript.

7   Laurence Oliphant, Letter to Georgiana Cowper (Lowly), November 6, 1868, *Harris-Oliphant Papers*, Columbia.

8   Kanaye Nagasawa, transcript of 1871 diary at Gaye LeBaron archive, courtesy Sonoma State University.

9   Margaret Oliphant, *Memoir*, volume II, pages 66-7.

10   Edward Crankshaw, *Bismarck*, page 268.

11   David McCullough, *The Greater Journey*, pages 257-8.

12   Anne Taylor, *Laurence Oliphant*, page 150.

13   Laurence Oliphant, writing as a correspondent for *The Times of London*, November 26, 1870.

14 Laurence Oliphant, *Traits and Travesties* (1882), "Adventures of a War Correspondent," pages 325-6.

15 David McCullough, page 290.

16 Ibid., page 296.

17 Ibid., page 294, and caption to illustration 55.

18 Ibid., pages 305-7.

19 Kanaye Nagasawa, transcript of 1871 diary, Sonoma State University, page 1.

20 Jane Waring, Letter and transcript of poem by Thomas Lake Harris sent to Broctonites from Paris in May 1871, *Harris-Oliphant Papers*, Columbia.

21 David McCullough, page 324.

22 Laurence Oliphant, as quoted by Rosamond Dale Owen Oliphant in *My Perilous Life in Palestine* (1928), page 23.

23 Laurence Oliphant, Letter to the Cowpers at Broadlands, August 23, 1872, *Harris-Oliphat Papers*, Columbia.

24 Anne Taylor, *Laurence Oliphant*, page 173.

25 Schneider and Lawton, pages 269-70.

Chapter 7. Living Apart

1 Schneider and Lawton, page 271.

2 Ibid., page 273.

3 Cuthbert, page 211.

4 Ibid., page 218.

5 Kanaye Nagasawa, Interview notes, *Harris-Oliphant Papers*, Columbia.

6 Robert Louis Stevenson, *Across the Plains: Leaves from the Notebook of an Emigrant between New York and San Francisco*, chapter 2, "The Emigrant Train."

7 Berger, page 144.

8   Jules Verne, *Around the World in Eighty Days* (1872), chapter XXV, page 78.

9   M. F. K. Fisher, *Musings on Wine and Other Libations* (2012), editor Anne Zimmerman, page 196.

10   Cuthbert, pages 220-1.

11   Ibid., page 222.

12   Louis Liesching, Personal Reminiscences of Laurence Oliphant (1892).

13   Cuthbert, page 292.

Chapter 8. Embracing a New Quest

1   Laurence Oliphant, Letter to William Cowper, January 10, 1877, transcript belonging to Oliphant family.

2   Anne Taylor, *Laurence Oliphant* (1982), page 186.

3   Laurence Oliphant, Letter to William Cowper, June 30, 1877, transcript belonging to Oliphant family.

4   Ibid.

5   Palestine was a loose geographic term used by English-speakers in the 1880s synonymous with the Holy Land or the Promised Land. It was not a precise area nor a hot-seat of the world's attention until the 20th century and today.

6   Anne Taylor, page 192.

7   Ibid., page 193.

8   Shalom Goldman, Zeal for Zion (2009), page 44.

9   Laurence Oliphant, *The Land of Gilead* (1882), page 246.

10   Ibid., page 256.

11   Margaret Oliphant, Memoir, volume II, pages 180-1.

12   Anne Taylor, page 198.

13   *Jewish Chronicle*, June 11, 1880, page 4.

14   *Jewish Chronicle*, September 24, 1880, page 5.

15 *Jewish Chronicle*, October 22, 1880, page 12.

16 Schneider and Lawton, page 336.

17 Margaret Oliphant, *Memoir*, volume II, page 166.

18 Ibid., page 194.

19 Ibid., page 191.

20 Ibid., page 192.

21 Laurence Oliphant, *The Land of Khemi* (1882), page vi.

22 Ibid., page 55.

23 Ibid., page 156.

24 Ibid., page 179.

25 Margaret Oliphant, *Memoir*, volume II, page 197.

26 Ibid., page 198.

Chapter 9. Breaking with Harris

1   Schneider and Lawton, pages 510-11.

2   Ibid., page 515.

3   Ibid., page 519.

4   Ibid., page 523.

5   Ibid., page 525.

6   Ibid., page 533.

7   Robert Martin, Letter to George Lawton, February 27, 1930. Page four details the dissolution of the Brocton community. *Harris-Oliphant Papers*, Columbia.

8   Schneider and Lawton, page 346.

9   James Freeman, Letter to Markham or Schneider, April 16, 1923, *Harris-Oliphant Papers*, Columbia.

10 Thomas Lake Harris, Letter to S. Swan, M.D., December 22, 1881, quoted in Schneider and Lawton, page 321.

11 Schneider and Lawton, page 338.

12 Schneider and Lawton, page 355.

13   Samuel Clark, Letter to a Friend in England, February 17, 1882. Quoted in Schneider and Lawton, page 359.

14   Ibid., page 353.

15   Robert Martin, Letter to George Lawton, February 27, 1930. *Harris-Oliphant Papers*, Columbia.

Chapter 10. Migrating East

1   Details of the atrocities against the Jews appeared in the *Jewish Chronicle*, January 6, 1882, page 7; January 13, page 7; and, at greatest length, January 20, page 9.

2   *Times of London*, January 11, 1882.

3   *Times of London*, January 13, 1882.

4   *Jewish Chronicle*, January 20, 1882, page 8.

5   *Jewish Chronicle*, January 13, 1882, page 11.

6   Geoffrey Alderman, *Modern British Jewry* (1998), page 110.

7   *Jewish Chronicle*, January 6, 1882, page 5.

8   Anne Taylor, page 206.

9   *Jewish Chronicle*, March 10, 1882, page 14.

10 *Jewish Chronicle*, February 24, 1882, page 14.

11 *Jewish Chronicle*, March 17, 1882, pages 11-12.

12 Margaret Oliphant, *Memoir*, volume II, page 215.

13 Ibid., page 218.

14 *Jewish Chronicle*, June 2, 1882, page 11.

15 Sadagora is the spelling of this town used by Laurence. It is also spelled today as Sadagura, Sadigora and Sadhora.

16 *Blackwoods Magazine*, November 1882, page 642.

17 Ibid., page 644.

18 *Jewish Chronicle*, June 2, 1882, page 11.

19 Ibid.

20 Margaret Oliphant, *Memoir*, pages 226-230.

21 Ibid., page 222.

22 Ibid., page 232.

23 Anne Taylor, page 213.

24 Naphtali Herz Imber, *Leaves from My Palestine and Other Diaries*, page 455.

25 Imber wrote his poem in 1878 and it was adopted as an anthem by the First Zionist Conferencce in 1897. It was officially made the Israeli national anthem in 2004.

26 Margaret Oliphant, *Memoir*, volume II, page 234.

Chapter 11. The Promised Land

1 Laurence Oliphant, *Haifa: Life in Modern Palestine*, page 22.

2 Ibid., page 24.

3 Yossi Ben-Artzi, "Alice Oliphant—A Personality in Her Own Right," Exhibition Brochure, *In Lady Oliphant's Drawing Room*, The National Maritime Museum, Haifa (2000), page 50.

4 Schneider and Lawton, page 149.

5 Yossi Ben-Artzi, pages 49-50.

6 Naphtali Herz Imber, *Leaves from My Palestine and Other Diaries*, pages 418-9.

7 Ibid., page 454.

8 Anne Taylor, page 233.

9 Imber, page 410.

10 Laurence Oliphant, *Haifa*, pages 11-12.

11 Ibid., pages 12-13.

12 In 1883, the Baron also cooperated with Rabbi Mohilever to establish a community at Ekron called Mazkeret Batya as an example for future settlements.

13 Lida Sharet-Massad, "Alice Oliphant and Her Friends: Living and Painting in Haifa," Exhibition Brochure, *In Lady Oliphant's*

Drawing Room, The National Maritime Museum, Haifa (2000), page 37.

14   Margaret Oliphant, *Memoir*, volume II, page 303.

15   Ibid., page 300.

16   Ibid., pages 311-12.

17   Ibid., pages 316-17.

18   Ibid., page 317.

19   Ibid., page 318.

20   Ibid., page 323.

21   Ibid., pages 324-25.

22   Ibid., pages 325-26.

23   Laurence Oliphant, *Scientific Religion* (1888), pages vii-viii.

24   Imber, page 453.

25   Rosamond Dale Owen Oliphant, *My Perilous Life in Palestine* (1928), page 66.

Chapter 12. Passing the Torch

1   Schneider and Lawton, page 412, footnote 19.

2   *The Illustrated American*, April 16, 1892, page 400.

3   Ibid., page 401.

4   Ibid.

5   *New York Times*, December 1, 1930.

6   James Freeman, Letter to Edwin Markham or Herbert Schneider, April 16, 1923, *Harris-Oliphant Papers*, Columbia.

7   Robert Martin, Letter to Herbert Schneider, February 27, 1930, *Harris-Oliphant Papers*, Columbia.

8   Oswald Smith, *Memoir on Laurence Oliphant* (1889), typed transcript, page 11, *Harris-Oliphant Papers*, Columbia.